THE OPPOSITION TO SLAVERY IN GEORGIA PRIOR TO 1860

BY

RUTH SCARBOROUGH, Ph.D.

NEGRO UNIVERSITIES PRESS

NEW YORK

Reprinted in 1968
by Negro Universities Press
A DIVISION OF GREENWOOD PUBLISHING CORP.
New York

Library of Congress Catalogue Card Number: 68-55914

Reprinted from a copy in the collections of
The New York Public Library,
Astor, Lenox and Tilden Foundations

Printed in the United States of America

"HAS ANY MAN LIVING A RIGHT TO USE ANOTHER AS
A SLAVE? IT CANNOT BE . . . . LIBERTY IS THE
RIGHT OF EVERY HUMAN CREATURE . . . AND NO
HUMAN LAW CAN DEPRIVE HIM OF THAT RIGHT
WHICH HE DERIVES FROM THE LAW OF NATURE."

—*John Wesley.*

ACKNOWLEDGMENT

The following study was undertaken at the suggestion of Doctor Fremont P. Wirth of George Peabody College for Teachers. It is a genuine pleasure for me to acknowledge and express my thanks for the interest he has shown at every stage of the work. As a result of his instruction I have come to appreciate the importance of historical research and a critical evaluation of historical evidence. I wish to thank Doctor Charles S. Pendleton of Peabody College who read and criticised the entire monograph. I wish to thank Colonel John M. Graham of Atlanta for his criticisms and suggestions. My thanks are also due to: Miss Ruth Blair, state historian of Georgia; Miss Ella May Thornton, Georgia State Librarian; Mr. William Harden, librarian of the Georgia Historical Society; Miss Sally Akin, librarian of the Washington Memorial Library, Macon, Georgia; Mrs. Floyd of Hodgson Hall in Savannah; Miss Ola M. Wyeth of the Savannah Public Library, and other librarians in whose libraries I have worked. I am very grateful to the County Historians who contributed directly to this work. Mr. Warren Grice of Macon gave very helpful suggestions and information. Mr. Wymberley W. De Renne, of Savannah, permitted the use of the De Renne Library of Georgia History. Acknowledgment must also be made of the constant faith and encouragement of a few friends here unnamed.

RUTH SCARBOROUGH.

PREFACE

The purpose of this study is to show the opposition to slavery which existed in Georgia prior to 1860, to discover the anti-slavery sentiment which was expressed during that period, to trace the growth of this sentiment, and to indicate the extent to which it was influenced by the spirit of the time. The chief sources of information have been the Colonial Records of Georgia, the Collections of the Georgia Historical Society, Digests and Compilations of the laws of Georgia, the Journals of the House and Senate, magazine and newspaper files, and a selected number of letters, diaries, journals, and biographies.

The period covered is treated chronologically. The introduction and use of slavery in Georgia was opposed by the Trustees and some of the earliest settlers, but this objection was overcome in 1750 when slaves were finally allowed. All during the slavery period rigid rules were in force regarding negro slaves, and many laws were passed to prevent the slave-trade and the further introduction of negroes. Many wills were made in which slaves were emancipated, laws were passed to prevent such manumission, and many attempts were made on the part of the masters to free the slaves. Sometimes these attempts were thwarted by the state legislature or by the Supreme Court of Georgia, but in most cases the wishes of the masters were carried out and the slaves were given their freedom. Considerable attention is given to the efforts of the American Colonization Society in Georgia and the accomplishments of the many local societies there.

A study of this subject and period has revealed the fact that opposition to slavery was based upon a variety of grounds. The opposition of the Trustees was based on expediency. They refused to allow slavery chiefly because they wanted the whites to feel their responsibility to work.

Although the rulers sought to make the colony free they were thwarted by the dictates of geography. While there were manifestations of the humanitarian spirit, there was little moral or religious opposition to slavery in Georgia. The chief objection was from the economic standpoint. These various reasons for objection to slavery—moral, religious, sentimental, social, economic, and political—are shown in this study.

CONTENTS

I

Slavery Prohibited in Georgia—England and the slave-trade—Reasons for the founding of the colony of Georgia—A refuge for the poor debtors—A military colony—A refuge for distressed Protestants—A base for the Western fur trade—A place for the production of silk and wine—Economic argument—Reasons in the preamble of the charter—Summary of motives—Passage of the act fobidding the importation of negroes—The act recorded—Praise uttered in London—Purpose of the act—Terms of the act—Reasons of the Trustees for prohibiting slavery—Georgia was founded for the poor—Every negro sent would prevent the sending of a white man—Slavery would cause shiftlessness—Fear of a negro insurrection—The military purpose of the colony—Danger from the Spaniards—Negroes unnecessary in producing silk and wine—Cause discouragement to the poor farmers; destroy democracy—Absentee landlordism; planters would become debtors—Facilitate desertion of Carolina negroes—Summary of reasons—Opposition to slavery—White servants allowed—Attitude of the early settlers—Conclusion.

II

Introduction—First attempt to import negroes—Negroes in Augusta—Imported from South Carolina—Indifference of Augusta to the prohibition—Reasons why negroes were desired—Adaptability to the climate and heavy work—Denied by the Germans and by John Wesley—Inefficiency of the white servants—Failure of the silk and wine industry—Failure to prevent the desertion of Carolina negroes—The low condition of the colony—The Scotch Club; their representation—Stephens versus the malcontents; the two papers—Richard Lawley's description—Depopulation of the province—Petitions and Counter-petitions to the Trustees—Petition of 1735—Petition of 1737—Petition of 1738—Defeated in Darien, Ebenezer and Frederica—Counter-petitions to the petition of 1738—Counter-petition of Darien, January 3, 1739—Counter-petition of Ebenezer, March 13, 1739—Petition sent to Oglethorpe—Refusal of the Trustees—Rules rigidly enforced—Favorable acceptance of the

Contents

of slaves—Negroes during the revolution—Case of Austin Dabney—Conclusion.

VI

VII

VIII

IX

X

Contents

street—Lewis W. Paine—Free negroes—Law of 1807—Law of 1818—
Laws of 1824 and 1826—Acts of 1835 and 1837—Attempt to remove
the free negro—Laws of 1859—Sentiment of the people regarding
slavery—Sentiment of Georgia leaders—Slavery considered an evil—
Slavery considered a burden—Judge Bowen's charge to the Grand
Jury of Chatham County—Opinion of Congressman Reid—Opinion
of Alexander H. Stephens—Decline of the Anti-slavery sentiment—
Progress of opinion elsewhere—The abolition agitation—William
Lloyd Garrison—Attitude of Georgia toward abolitionists—Price
placed on Garrison's head—Southern sensitiveness—Voluntary
emancipation prevented—The defense of slavery—The persecution
of Southern slaveholders—Opinion of William H. Crawford—Defended by the Georgia legislature, 1835—Conclusion.

XI

The American Colonization Society—The Problem of the free negro
—The organization of the American Colonization Society—The
colony of Liberia—New Georgia—Objects of the Society—Influ-
ence of the Colonization Society in Georgia—Branches in Georgia—
The Jackson County Auxiliary Society—The Augusta Societies—
The Augusta Colonization Society—The Augusta Female Society—
Letter from Robert Finley—Other branches of the society—Negroes
sent to Africa—Law of 1817—Negroes saved from slavery in 1819—
Negroes liberated from 1819–1830—Negroes liberated from 1830–1835
—Conclusion.

XII

Negroes sent to Africa—Negroes liberated from 1835–1860—Cases
before the Court—Court decisions—Departure of the Hercules, 1833—
Expedition of eighty-three negroes, November, 1833—Contributions to the Society—Contributions from Augusta—Contributions
from Columbus, Athens, etc.—Miscellaneous contributions—Sentiment regarding the colonization society—From a clergyman in Georgia—From a Gentleman in Georgia—Opinion of the negroes from
letters—Supported by newspapers—Progress of the Society—Resolutions of the Board of Managers—Address of the Reverend Robert
Finley—Proposal to colonize the negroes in Hayti—Failure of the
Society—Resolutions of the Georgia Legislature—Adoption of
abolition propoganda—Conclusion.

XIII

THE OPPOSITION TO SLAVERY IN GEORGIA PRIOR TO 1860

CHAPTER I

THE FREE COLONY OF GEORGIA

Georgia was the only one of the original thirteen colonies which prohibited the introduction of negroes. One of the earliest rules of the trustees was that negroes should not be introduced into the colony. This restriction was not removed until 1749. Meanwhile every one of the other colonies was receiving slaves from Africa within its borders. All the other colonies, from the time that Virginia received the first cargo in 1619, sooner or later had patronized the African slave trade.[1] The other colonies not only were slaveholding but were deriving great profits from the importation and sale of native Africans. Conceived in the spirit of reform, Georgia was the first of all the colonies to put a ban upon African slavery.[2]

The time of the settlement of Georgia was a period especially favorable to the slave trade. The prosperity of England was involved in maintaining it. The king, the parliament, and the merchants of England not only favored the importation of negroes but were participants in the slave traffic. The Royal African Company, chartered by Charles II, was organized for the purpose of exploiting the slave trade. By the treaty of Utrecht of 1713 England secured from Spain the Asiento, a contract by which England was to supply the Spanish colonies with African slaves

---

[1] Alexander Hamilton Stephens, *History of the United States* (New York, 1872), 134.
[2] Lucian Lamar Knight, *A Standard History of Georgia and Georgians* (New York, 1917), I, 5.

for thirty years; and England engaged to supply the colonies within that time with at least 144,000 slaves, at the rate of 4,800 per year.[3] This lucrative monopoly made England the great slave trading power of the world. Any excess of supply was "dumped" on the American colonies. England was gaining money from it and therefore strongly supported and upheld the slave trade. The imperial government defeated the efforts of the colonial assemblies to check the trade. When the act of 1735 which prohibited the introduction of negroes into Georgia was being discussed in the Parliament of England, the Earl of Dartmouth said: "We can not allow the colonies to check or discourage in any degree a traffic so beneficial to the nation."[4] Under these circumstances the establishment of a free colony seems the more extraordinary.

The original charter of Georgia, granted by George II to the Trustees in 1732, neither permitted nor prohibited the introduction of negroes into the province. The rules that were made by the Trustees for the government of the province prohibited slavery. A copy of these rules, drawn up by Benjamin Martyn, Secretary of the Trustees, and dated July 1735, contains the rule prohibiting the introduction of negroes into the colony.[5] The reasons for the founding of the colony, which the preamble of the charter set forth, were evidently construed by the Trustees to virtually prohibit negro slavery, or at least to be incompatible with it. Since these reasons for the founding the colony were inconsistent with the institution of slavery, it will be necessary here to state them.

The immediate cause of the founding of Georgia was the desire to relieve unfortunate prisoners for debt. There were multitudes of the poor in eighteenth century England. If these poor were unable to pay their debts they were

---

[3] W. E. B. DuBois, *The Suppression of the African Slave Trade to the United States of America, 1638–1870* (Cambridge, 1896), 3.
[4] Harriet C. Cooper, *James Oglethorpe, The Founder of Georgia* (New York, 1904), 54.
[5] "Rules for the year 1735," *Colonial Records of Georgia,* (Atlanta, 1905), III, 410. Hereafter referred to as *Colonial Records.*

thrown in prison for an unlimited time. According to the writers of the time, four thousand per year were committed to prison for debts in the city of London alone.[6] James Edward Oglethorpe, a member of Parliament, was very much interested in these conditions. He criticized these social conditions on the floor of the House of Commons; he was therefore made chairman of a committee to investigate the prison conditions and to make a report to Parliament.[7] The members of this committee, in their report, proposed the colonizing of these unfortunate people in America. They proposed to send these luckless captives to the New World and there to found a colony where they might have a chance to get ahead in the world; they proposed to erect for them a refuge in America where they could start life afresh. Thus the new colony was to be a kind of an asylum for the distressed poor of Britain. Oglethorpe enlisted the sympathy of many prominent noblemen and clergymen. They appealed to King George II and received, on June 9, 1732, a charter incorporating them as "The Trustees for establishing the Colony of Georgia in America." The twenty-one trustees were vested with almost complete power over the colony for a period of twenty-one years; at the end of the proprietary period the colony was to revert to the crown. They were granted a strip of territory lying between the Savannah and Altamaha rivers, and extending from their headwaters westward to the South Sea.

But this philanthropic feature was only one side of the scheme. Georgia was also to be a military colony for the protection of South Carolina against the Indians and the Spaniards. The policy of planting a colony South of the Savannah which would be essentially different in principles and government from that of South Carolina was an object of great importance. Spain held Florida, and claimed the

---

[6] "Reasons for Establishing the Colony of Georgia in America" (London, 1733), *Collections of the Georgia Historical Society* (Savannah, 1840), I, 216. Hereafter referred to as *Georgia Historical Collections*.
[7] Charles C. Jones Jr., *History of Georgia* (Boston, 1883), I, 85.

land far to the North of her actual possessions.   For sixty
years after the settlement of South Carolina there was no
settlement South of the Savannah; during this time this
territory was claimed by both England and Spain.   Oglethorpe saw the desirability of founding a settlement South
of the Carolinas and holding it for England.   The Spaniards
in Florida were a constant menace to the English; they
were continually threatening South Carolina, encouraging
slave insurrections, and harboring runaway slaves.   South
Carolina was weak in a military way because there were
so many slaves in the province and so few white persons.
In 1734 there were three times as many negroes in South
Carolina as whites. [8]   In the year 1737 there were twenty-
two thousand negroes and only five thousand white fighting
men. [9]   The Trustees planned to make Georgia strong
enough to protect South Carolina.

Georgia was also to be an asylum for the persecuted
Protestants of other lands.   At this time there was much
sympathy for the German Protestants who were persecuted
in the ecclesiastical principality of Salzburg, and who now
sought refuge under the British flag.   The Trustees encouraged the immigration of these Salzburgers and many
came over to Georgia during the first few years. [10]   Ebenezer,
in Effingham County, about twenty-five miles above Savannah, was settled by these German Protestants.   Later
these Salzburgers were very persistent in their opposition
to slavery.   These Germans came to Georgia for religious
liberty.   They settled in groups or congregations with the
church as the religious, social, and civic center of their
community life.   Their pastors shaped the public opinion
of the group and controlled their political life.   We shall
see later how the Reverend Martin Bolzius, pastor of the

---

[8] "Memorial and Representation of the State and Condition of South Carolina," *Colonial Records*, III, Appendix V, 418.
[9] "Journal of the Earl of Egmont," *Colonial Records*, V, 475.
[10] "An Impartial Inquiry into the State and the Utility of the Province of
  Georgia" (London, 1741), *Georgia Historical Collections*, I, 178–179.
  For further information on the Salzburgers see P. A. Strobel, *The Salzburgers* (Baltimore 1855).   This book, published in 1855, and now out of
  print, gives the main facts about the Salzburger settlement.

Salzburgers at Ebenezer, upheld the policy of Oglethorpe and of the Trustees. They were determined to keep negroes out of the colony of Georgia.

Imperialistic motives were also at work. England, France, and Spain, were particularly interested in the fur trade. There was a triangular competition between these countries for trade with the Indians and for political influence as a means of extending that trade.[11] English fur traders had long been pushing through the mountains around the Southern end of the Appalachian chain. The fate of the whole Southwestern region hung in the balance. England was interested in securing this trade for herself to the exclusion of the French and Spanish.

England was also interested in the production of silk and wine. The Trustees had heard that mulberry trees and grapes grew along the Savannah river. It was thought that silk and wine would be the chief products of the colony. It was even hoped that Georgia might enable England to export silk, since both land and mulberry leaves would be free in the new colony, and since the cost of production would thus be cheaper than in competing countries.[12] Great Britain, who was anxious to become independent of Southern European countries in this regard, did everything possible to encourage silk production in Georgia and even offered a bounty to the colonists for the production of the raw material. The government bought the raw silk and bore the expense of preparing it for market and of shipping it to England, besides paying a high price for it.

Arguments from an economic point of view were urged in favor of the project. The population of England had increased faster than the means of sustenance, especially among the poorer classes. Figures were brought forth to show that it took two thousand pounds to support one hundred families in London, while families of the class

---

[11] Everts Boutell Greene, *The Foundations of American Nationality* (New York, 1922), 315.
[12] "Reasons for Establishing the Colony of Georgia" (London, 1733), *Georgia Historical Collections*, I, 210.

that would be sent to Georgia could earn only one thousand pounds. Thus, in order to support these families in London, there would be a loss to the public of one thousand pounds per year per hundred families. It was estimated that in Georgia these hundred families ought to earn six thousand pounds. Allowing two thousand pounds per hundred families for the sustenance, there would still be a surplus of four thousand pounds with which to buy English merchandise.[13] Thus these families, if they were sent to Georgia, would cease to be a financial drain on the mother country and would add to the producing power and economic stability of the realm.

The preamble of the charter of Georgia states the principal objects of the province.

> Whereas we are credibly informed, that many of our poor subjects are, through misfortune and want of employment, reduced to great necessity, insomuch as by their labor they are not able to provide a maintenance for themselves and families; and if they had means to defray their charges of passage, and other expenses incident to new settlements, they would be glad to settle in any of our provinces in America, where, by cultivating the lands at present waste and desolate, they might not only gain a comfortable subsistence for themselves and families, but also strengthen our colonies and increase the trade, navigation, and wealth of these our realms. And whereas our provinces in North America have been frequently ravaged by Indian enemies; more especially that of South Carolina, which in the late war, by the neighboring savages, was laid waste by fire and sword, and great numbers of the English inhabitants miserably massacred; and our loving subjects who now inhabit there, by reason of the smallness of their numbers, will, in case of a new war, be exposed to the like calamities; inasmuch as their whole southern frontier continueth unsettled, and lieth open to the said savages; and whereas we think it highly becoming our crown and royal dignity to protect

---

[13] "A New And Accurate Account of the Provinces of South Carolina and Georgia," *Georgia Historical Collections,* I, 62.

all our loving subjects, be they never so distant from us; to extend our fatherly compassion even to the meanest and most infatuate of our people, and to relieve the wants of our above mentioned poor subjects; and that it will be highly conducive for accomplishing those ends, that a regular colony of the said poor people be settled and established in the southern territories of Carolina; and whereas we have been well assured, that if we would be graciously pleased to erect and settle a corporation, for the receiving, managing and disposing of the contributions of our loving subjects, divers persons would be induced to contribute to the purposes aforesaid.[14]

Georgia was thus expected to combine the advantages or a philanthropic establishment, a military garrison against the Spaniards and Indians, a refuge for distressed Protestants of Europe, a base for the Western fur trade, a suitable place for the production of silk and wine, and an opportunity to build up the economic resources of the realm. From these fundamental principles and aims the Trustees naturally concluded that the admission of negroes would prevent the carrying out the purposes of the charter. They evidently considered slavery to be incompatible with the purposes for which the colony was founded. We shall see later that each of these reasons for founding the colony of Georgia was interpreted by the Trustees to be a reason for excluding slavery from the province. For such an unusual colony something different from the ordinary type of plantation settlements was needed. Regulations were made to prevent the growth of large landed estates; land was to be distributed among small proprietors capable of defending themselves against hostile neighbors; rum was excluded, and slavery was prohibited.

On January 9, 1735, the committee on laws and regulations for the colony of Georgia recommended the passage of an act forbidding the importation of negroes into Georgia. Before its passage there was some opposition to the bill, but it was ardently supported by Oglethorpe.[15] There was

---

[14] "Charter of the Colony of Georgia," *Colonial Records*, I, 11.
[15] Harriet C. Cooper, *James Oglethorpe, the Founder of Georgia*, 54.

no precedent for such a regulation in any of the other colonies. The act was endorsed by the imperial Board of Trade and received the assent of the Privy Council of England; it was presented to the king in council in the month of January, 1735, and thereby ratified.

Of a meeting of the Common Council of the Trustees in the Palace Court, January 9, 1735, at which Oglethorpe was present, we find the following minute: "An Act for rendering the Colony of Georgia more Defensible [sic] by prohibiting the Importation and Use of Black Slaves or Negroes into the same. Which Act being read and an Amendment made thereto, Order'd: That the said Act with the said Amendment be engross'd."[16] This act was officially recorded on May 21, 1735.[17] The act was prepared in harmony with the avowed objects of the Trust which have been stated above. The negro free or slave was henceforth to be a stranger on Georgia soil. Oglethorpe was chairman of the committee which prepared this law and was chiefly instrumental in having it passed.[18] Thus it was that, according to the law of 1735, slavery was excluded from the colony of Georgia. When Oglethorpe on his return from Georgia resumed his seat in the House of Commons he caused this measure to be introduced and passed for the purpose of re-enforcing the regulation already made by the trust.[19]

The praise of Georgia was uttered in London in a pamphlet published in 1734. This pamphlet gives us a glimpse of the moral sentiment in support of the prohibition of negro slavery in Georgia. The author expresses the idea that no settlement was ever before established on so humane a plan. He says: "Slavery, the misfortune, if not the dishonour, of other plantations, is absolutely proscribed. Let avarice defend it as it will, there is an honest reluctance in humanity against buying and selling, and regarding those of our own

---

[16] "Journal of the Trustees," *Colonial Records*, I, 197–198.
[17] *Ibid*, I, 216.
[18] *Ibid*, I, 70.
[19] Lucian Lamar Knight, *Standard History of Georgia and Georgians*, I, 103.

species as our wealth and possessions . . . . The name of slavery is here unheard, and every inhabitant is free from unchosen masters and oppression."[20]

The preamble to this act of 1735 which excluded slavery in Georgia states the purpose of the Act. It cited the sad experiences of other colonies and plantations where there was a large number of blacks. It was passed because experience had shown that the settling of colonies with slaves had prevented the increase of whites, and that such colonies proved weak either for suppressing internal tumults or for carrying on external warfare.[21]

Then followed the law prohibiting the importation of negroes. It provided that after June 24, 1735, no negro should be brought within the province or sold or bought therein. If any person should be found guilty of importing, or causing to be imported, any negro, such person should forfeit fifty pounds for every negro imported into the colony. Half of this fine was to go to the colony, the other half to the prosecutor. It was also provided that all negroes found in the colony after June 24, 1735, should be seized and taken as the property of the Trustees, to be sold or exported as the common council might direct.[22] This act also contained a law against fugitive slaves. If any negroes should run away from Carolina into Georgia, and if they should be claimed within three months by the owner, and if the owner should pay the costs of apprehending the slave and should make satisfaction for all damages that the negro might have committed—then the court of Savannah would restore to the owner such black or negro.[23] In case of fines and penalties under this act, the common council of the Trustees was to have the power of mitigating forfeitures and penalties if it desired to do so.[24] This act was officially ratified April 3, 1735.[25]

[20] George Bancroft, *History of the United States* (New York, 1888), II, 287; Henry Bruce, *Life of General Oglethorpe* (New York, 1890), 99.
[21] "By-Laws and Laws," *Colonial Records*, I, 50.
[22] *Ibid*, I, 50–51.
[23] *Ibid*, I, 51.
[24] *Ibid*, I, 52.
[25] *Ibid*, I, 53–54.

Thus we find that negroes were excluded from the province of Georgia from the beginning. Georgia was the first of the thirteen original colonies to rule slavery from the colony; we shall find later that the state of Georgia prohibited the slave trade ten years before it was prohibited by the federal constitution. In January, 1741, the Trustees of Georgia ordered their secretary to draw up an account showing the progress of the colony.[26] Thus Benjamin Martyn, secretary of the Trustees, published in 1741 "An Account Showing the Progress of the Colony of Georgia in America from its First Establishment."[27] This article was later read to and approved by the Trustees.[28] In this article Secretary Martyn states the reasons of the Trustees for excluding negroes from the colony. A comparison of this article with other articles giving the reasons of the Trustees for establishing the colony of Georgia shows that the Trustees considered slavery to be antagonistic to the purposes of the colony. A variety of motives actuated the Trustees in excluding negroes from the colony. These motives for excluding negroes closely parallel the reasons for establishing the colony of Georgia and show the inconsistency between the purposes of the founders and the institution of slavery.

The original intention of the founders of the colony was to provide for the poor but honest people incapable of supporting themselves at home. It was thought impossible that these poor settlers and the foreign persecuted Protestants would be able to purchase or subsist negroes if they had them.[29] It was inconceivable to the Trustees that the poor people to be colonized in Georgia, however worthy in mind or heart, would be able to buy, own, and support slaves. It was considered that they would have their hands full supporting themselves and families, with the

---

[26] "Journal of the Trustees," *Colonial Records*, I, 377.
[27] *Colonial Records*, III, 369–403; also *Georgia Historical Collections*, II, 267–325.
[28] "Journal of the Trustees," *Colonial Records*, I, 378, 379, 380, 381.
[29] Benjamin Martyn, "An Account Showing the Progress of the Colony of Georgia in America" (London, 1742), *Georgia Historical Collections*, II, 279.

fullest of opportunities offered. These poverty-stricken people, having failed once in life, were to be given a new opportunity in Georgia to succeed. Therefore temptation to own slaves was not placed before the colonist.

The Trustees sought to win the colonists over to their belief by telling them that money could be better expended in transporting white men than negroes, and that slaves would be a source of weakness to the colony. The first cost of a negro was about thirty pounds. This thirty pounds would pay the passage over, provide tools and other necessaries, and defray the expenses of a white man for a year.[30] Consequently the purchase money of every negro, by being applied that way, would prevent the sending over a white man who would be a security to the province, whereas a negro would render that security dangerous. It was a charge too great for the Trustees to undertake as they would thereby be disabled from sending white people. To permit slaves would lessen the ability of the Trustees to maintain white settlers. Also, it was thought that if the settler should spend thirty pounds for a negro, he would exhaust so much of his capital as to cripple his means at the very outset of his career.

The Trustees also feared that slavery would cause shift-lessness. It was thought that the white man, if he had a negro slave, would be less disposed to labor himself, and that a large portion of his time would be employed in keeping the negro at work.[31] The philanthropists wisely figured that it would be poor business and abused charity on their part to convey a colonist over free of charge, to give him tools, arms, and tenure of land, and enable him to spend his own time fishing or pleasure-seeking while his work was being carried on by a negro. Such was not in harmony with the spirit of the Georgia undertaking. There was a feeling that the labor of slaves was really less profitable than that of whites, and that the whites would

---

[30] *Ibid*, II, 279–280.
[31] Benjamin Martyn, "An Account Showing the Progress . . . . *Georgia Historical Collections,* II, 280.

be unwilling to work in a country where slave labor existed.[32] It was also thought that shiftlessness was, to a great extent, the cause of the failure of these people in England; after their removal to Georgia every effort was made to prevent this recurrence rather than to encourage it by an introduction of negroes.

There was also the fear of a negro insurrection and the consequent danger to the planter and his family. Much of the planter's time would be occupied in guarding against danger which he or his family might apprehend from the slaves. The planter's wife and children would, by the death or even the absence of the planter, be at the mercy of the negro. The province of South Carolina was frequently alarmed for fear of insurrections there. Colonel William Stephens, in his journal, makes frequent references to these insurrections.[33] The Trustees of Georgia intended to profit by the experience of South Carolina. A colony so near the frontier could not run the risk of slave insurrections. An insurrection of negroes in Jamaica was used as an argument against the introduction of them into Georgia.[34] We shall see in a later chapter how this fear was justified. After the removal of the restriction against negroes in 1750, the settlers in Georgia lived in continual fear of a slave insurrection, and harsh rules for governing the negroes were passed accordingly.

Another reason for the prohibition of negroes in Georgia was found in the military purpose of the colony, to protect South Carolina. The defenseless condition of South Carolina was due to the large number of negroes in proportion to the whites. These negroes had been brought over from Africa by British merchants and sold to the planters whose wealth was estimated almost exclusively by the number of their slaves. In 1739, there were about thirty-five thousand

---

[32] "An Impartial Inquiry into the State and Utility of the Province of Georgia," *Georgia Historical Collections,* I, 168–169, 172.
[33] "Stephen's Journal," *Colonial Records,* IV, 275–276, 277, 412–413, 592.
[34] "An Impartial Inquiry into the State and Utility of the Province of Georgia" (London, 1741), *Georgia Historical Collections,* I, 171.

negroes in Carolina and only about nine thousand whites.[35]
The black population continued to increase so that in 1740
there were about forty thousand negroes and only about
five thousand whites.[36] The whites, considerably outnum-
bered, were powerless to protect themselves against the
Spaniards or to subdue domestic insurrections. South
Carolina, weakened by excessively large slave population,
was, in a most critical sense, at the mercy of the foe. South
of the Savannah lurked the Indians who had no love for
the white intruders; in Florida was the Spaniard; in Louisiana and along the Gulf coast were the French—all enemies
of England. With such enemies within and without the
very existence of Carolina was in danger. It was clear
that (as the Earl of Egmont expressed it in his Journal)
"Had we permitted the use of Negroes, both South Carolina and Georgia might have been undone by this time."[37]
It was justly reasoned that only a colony settled by a white
population capable of bearing arms would be an efficient
protection to South Carolina, and one of the most cogent
reasons for establishing the new colony South of the Savannah was that expressed in the charter—to give a frontier
to South Carolina. Every slave sent over would mean a
white man displaced or a soldier withdrawn from the garrison. Thus to allow slaves would subtract from the fighting
strength of the province. If Georgia should allow negroes
she would not only fail to give protection to South Carolina
but she would endanger her own security.

It was also apprehended that the Spaniards of St. Augustine would be continually enticing away the negroes or
encouraging them to insurrection.[38] It would be to the
advantage of Spain to place every impediment in the way
of English colonization. And none could be more effective
than that of inveigling the negroes from the service of their

[35] "Stephens' Journal," *Colonial Records*, IV, 276.
[36] Benjamin Martyn, "An Account Showing the Progress of the Colony of
Georgia in America," *Georgia Historical Collections*, II, 302.
[37] "Journal of the Earl of Egmont," *Colonial Records*, V, 342.
[38] Benjamin Martyn, *Op. cit.*, II, 280; H. A. Scomp, "Georgia, The Only
Free Colony," *The Magazine of American History*, October 1889, 283.

owners. The governor of St. Augustine proclaimed freedom and protection to all negroes who should join his standard.[39] Many Carolina negroes took advantage of the governor's proclamation and went to St. Augustine. The governor of St. Augustine refused to return the negroes. A black regiment was actually formed consisting entirely of runaway slaves from Carolina.[40] This had become a serious problem of difference between the Carolina English and the Florida Spanish. In a letter of Oglethorpe, dated May 28, 1742, he speaks of the activity of the Spaniards in stirring up discontent. The Spaniards incited the malcontents of Georgia to demand slaves because they felt that, in case of war, the negroes would join the Spanish or become plunder for them.[41] The Trustees reasoned that nothing but a free white colony could arrest the incursions of the savages and Spaniards; that plantations of great extent, widely separated, with a large negro population, and but few whites, would be no effectual obstacle, because the blacks could be easily seduced from their masters who were too feeble and scattered to resist. They argued that if negroes should be introduced into Georgia, that which had taken place in Carolina would occur in Georgia; that it would be no protection to Carolina on the North, and would only imperil the existence of the new colony by throwing it into the very arms of the Spaniards.[42] The Trustees intended to profit by the experience of South Carolina which had scarcely enough white people to secure her against her own slaves. Some of the Carolina negroes had escaped to Florida; others had been incited to insurrection which endangered the loss of that province.

Oglethorpe wrote to the Duke of Newcastle in 1739 that many negroes were escaping by sea to St. Augustine, and that the planters feared that most of their slaves

[39] Benjamin Martyn, *Op. cit.*, II, 301–302.
[40] Hugh McCall, *History of Georgia* (Atlanta, 1909), I, 4.
[41] "General Oglethorpe to the Trustees," *Georgia Historical Collections*, III, 120–122.
[42] William Bacon Stevens, *History of Georgia*, I, 288–289.

would leave them.[43] A Spanish prisoner who was brought to Frederica in 1741 told the authorities there that twenty or twenty-five runaway negroes had been armed by the Spaniards. In the same year Kenneth Baillie testified at Frederica that the attacking force at Fort Moosa consisted of Spaniards, Indians, and negroes; that the negroes afterward told him that they had been promised freedom if they would help to expel the English.[44] Oglethorpe charged that Spanish emissaries were responsible for inciting the white settlers to demand negroes.[45]

It was also calculated that the produce designed to be raised in Georgia would not require such labor as to make the assistance of negroes necessary. The Trustees had proposed that silk and wine should be the chief products of Georgia. It was thought that women and children would be just as useful in the cultivation of these products as negroes would be.[46] The silk and wine industries demanded skilled labor and for such the whites were better fitted than the slaves. The province of South Carolina produced chiefly rice which necessitated negro labor; the products designed to be raised in Georgia did not require such labor as to render negroes necessary. The inhabitants of Georgia were expected to turn their attention elsewhere than to the raising of such heavy commodities as required black labor. It was found also that rice and other productions of Georgia could be raised without negroes, and the importation of white servants from Germany for a term of years was considered preferable.[47] The Salzburg emigrants wrote to General Oglethorpe in 1739 and protested that negro labor was not necessary in the production of rice.[48] These Germans preferred white servants. They opposed negro slaves from the beginning and, when the other colonists

---

[43] H. A. Scomp, "Georgia—The Only Free Colony," *Magazine of American History*, October, 1889, 286.
[44] *Ibid*, 286–287.
[45] "Journal of the Earl of Egmont," *Colonial Records*, V, 522.
[46] Benjamin Martyn, *Op. cit.*, II, 280.
[47] "An Impartial Inquiry Into the State and Utility of the Province of Georgia," *Georgia Historical Collections*, I, 169.
[48] "The Salzburgers to General Oglethorpe," *Colonial Records*, III, 430.

clamored for negroes, they became more persistent in their opposition. Whatever justification there may have been for permitting slaves in South Carolina, no such pretext could be urged in Georgia where the culture of grapes and the production of silk imposed lighter burdens upon the laborer.

It was also apprehended that if the persons who should go over to Georgia at their own expense should be permitted the use of negroes, it would dispirit and ruin the poor people who could not get them and who, by their numbers, were intended to give strength to the province. It would lead to a class consciousness between those who could afford negroes and those who could not afford them. The latter class would become dissatisfied; they would insist that negroes be allowed them and, if refused, they would leave the province or they would neglect their land. They would disdain to work like negroes and would rather let themselves out to the wealthy planters as overseers of their negroes.[49]   Thus it was feared that if negro slaves were permitted, those of the colony who were able to own negroes would necessarily inculcate a spirit of jealousy among those who would not be able to own them. Slave labor worked a hardship upon the poorer whites who would be forced to work side by side with the negroes. This would destroy the high ideals and assuredly the democracy of the undertaking.[50]   Slavery would cause class distinctions to appear and would place an undue emphasis upon existing inequalities. It was feared that white men would not work where there were negroes unless they had negroes of their own.[51]   They feared that to do the work commonly assigned to slaves would make them look like slaves. The concentration of slaves in the hands of a few wealthy persons and the necessity of working alongside the blacks would discourage the poor whites.

It was further thought that if negroes were admitted, the wealthy planters would, as in all the other colonies,

---

[49] Benjamin Martyn, *Op. cit.*, II, 280.
[50] "An Impartial Inquiry into the State and Utility of the Province of Georgia," *Georgia Historical Collections*, I, 172.
[51] "Journal of the Earl of Egmont," *Colonial Records*, V, 476.

be more induced to absent themselves to more pleasant places of residence, leaving the care of the plantations and of their negroes to overseers.[52] This would give rise to the problem of absentee landlordism and its attendant evils. It was also thought that the poor planter sent on charity, as well as the planter who should settle at his own expense, would, because of his desire for negroes, mortgage his land to the slave trader for them, or at least become a debtor for the purchase of such negroes.[53] Under these discouragements the planter would be induced to sell his slaves again upon any necessity and would leave the province and his lot to his creditors. In this way the slave trader would soon swallow up the small holdings and the slaves of the planters.

It was feared that the admission of negroes into Georgia would facilitate the desertion of the Carolina negroes through the province of Georgia. It would furnish a place of shelter for fugitive negroes with the connivance of Georgia allies. Therefore Georgia, instead of proving a frontier and adding to the strength of South Carolina, would be a means of drawing off slaves of Carolina and adding to the strength of St. Augustine.[54] As long as negroes were prohibited in Georgia, it was easy to apprehend runaways because "Every Negro at his first Appearance [sic] in Georgia must be immediately known to be a Runaway, since there are no Negroes in Georgia."[55] Every negro found in Georgia was sold back into Carolina if not claimed by some owner.[56] It was feared that the admission of negroes into Georgia would prevent the arrest and return of fugitive slaves from Carolina and would lead to the failure of Georgia as a military province. To show how the military province of Georgia did prevent the desertion of Carolina negroes, the following is quoted from Stephens' Journal of August 31, 1738.

---

[52] Benjamin Martyn, *Op. cit.*, II, 281.
[53] *Ibid.*
[54] *Ibid.*
[55] "Journal of the Trustees," *Colonial Records*, I, 363.
[56] W. B. Stevens, *History of Georgia*, I, 288.

Mr. Causton calling upon me, showed me a Letter he received from Capt. Gascoigne, importing his having stopt a Canoe going by, wherein were three runaway Negroes from Carolina, whereupon it was thought advisable to send, and let publick Advertisements be made of it at Charles-Town, that the Proprietors might make a legal Claim of them in the Court of Savannah, pursuant to the Rules laid down in the Act made for prohibiting the Use of Negroes in the Province of Georgia.[57]

The most important arguments which influenced the Trustees in prohibiting slavery may be summarized as follows:

1.   Slavery might be a detriment to the poor and unfortunate for whom Georgia was founded;

2.   The sending of negroes would prevent the sending of whites;

3.   The fear that the use of slaves might cause shiftlessness among the whites;

4.   The fear of insurrections;

5.   It would defeat the military purpose of the colony;

6.   It would invite danger from the Spaniards;

7.   The products to be raised in the colony did not make slaves necessary;

8.   It might produce jealousy, cause discouragement to the poor planters who could not own slaves, and destroy the democracy of the undertaking;

9.   It might lead to absentee landlordism and its attendant evils;

10.   Planters might become financially involved by becoming debtors to the negro merchants;

11.   It might facilitate the desertion of Carolina negroes.

Cobb gives a good summary of the reasons for prohibiting the introduction of negroes in his historical sketch. He says that negroes were excluded, not from any principles of humanity to the negro, but "as a matter purely of policy;

---

[57] "Stephens' Journal," *Colonial Records*, IV, 191–192.

to stimulate the colonists to personal exertions, to provide a home for the poor and starving population of the
mother country; to create a colony densely populated with
whites, to serve as a barrier against incursions from the
Spanish settlements in Florida, and also to promote the
cultivation of silk and wine, to which the negro was by
no means adapted."[58] The prohibition of negroes was in
harmony with the purposes of the Trustees in founding
the colony and with their labor policy in governing the
colony. "The development of individual initiative among
small landholders, the utilization of white indentured
servants, and the exclusion of negroes and slaves: These
were the foundation stones of the labor policy fashioned
by the managers of proprietary Georgia."[59]

Substantially the same reasons against the admission
of negroes were given in their defense of the province a
few years later from the aspersions of the discontented
element in and around Savannah.[60] In this pamphlet the
Trustees say also that they had taken warning from South
Carolina where the number of negroes greatly exceeded
that of the whites and the plantations were large. But
they had made an agrarian law for Georgia which allowed
to no settlers more than five hundred acres, and to no
charity immigrant more than fifty acres, which allotments
would not allow the purchase of negroes. A limit of fifty
acres was set for each man who came to Georgia at the
expense of the Trust; anyone who came at his own expense
and brought as many as ten white servants was allowed
five hundred acres. This arrangement would place one
white fighting man on each fifty acres of land and thus aid
in protecting South Carolina. In no case were negroes
to be allowed. The settlers were even prohibited from

[58] Thomas R. R. Cobb, *An Historical Sketch of Slavery from the Earliest Periods* (Philadelphia, 1858), 150–151.
[59] H. B. Fant, "The Labor Policy of the Trustees for Establishing the Colony of Georgia in America," *Georgia Historical Quarterly*, XVI, 3.
[60] "An Impartial Inquiry into the State and Utility of the Province of Georgia (London, 1741)," *Georgia Historical Collections*, I, 153–201.

selling, mortgaging or giving away their land.   By denying entire control over the land it was designed to create a permanent class of small landholders, to prevent the growth of large plantations, to prevent the less industrous from sinking into the condition of tenants, servants, and day laborers, and to make the use of negro labor unnecessary. Most of the opposition to slavery was based on economic considerations.   The philanthropic trustees of Georgia, although they were far ahead of their age in their humanitarian views and efforts, considered the economic phase of the question more than the humanitarian.   They discussed slavery from the white man's standpoint.   How the system might affect the white man was the question; they gave little consideration to the effect it might have on the negro.[61]

Although slaves were prohibited, white servants were allowed.   These servants were people whose expenses in coming from Europe to America had been paid on condition that they bind themselves to serve for a certain term of years the men who advanced the money.   The Trustees offered grants of twenty acres and later of fifty acres to those indented servants who faithfully worked out their time and desired to remain.   Many of the servants brought over under this arrangement gave very satisfactory service and took advantage of the Trustees' offer.[62]   However, a large number of them refused to work after a short time, became idle, and ran away to South Carolina where every obstacle was put in the way of their recapture.[63]   The Trustees thought that these white servants would supply the demand, and that negro labor would be unnecessary. The inefficiency of these white servants was used later as an argument for the introduction of negroes.

The first settlement in Georgia was made at Savannah in 1733 under the personal supervision of Oglethorpe.

---

[61] H. A. Scomp, "Georgia—The Only Free Colony," *Magazine of American History*, October, 1889, 280–281.
[62] "Journal of the Earl of Egmont," *Colonial Records*, V, 202, 241.
[63] "Stephens' Journal," *Ibid*, IV, 192.

In 1734 Ebenezer, twenty-five miles above Savannah, was settled by a band of persecuted Salzburgers who had been driven out of Bavaria in Germany because of their religious beliefs.[64]   In 1735 Augusta was founded still further up the Savannah river as a center for Indian trade.   In 1736 New Inverness, later known as Darien, on the Altamaha, was settled by a band of Scotch Highlanders.   In the same year Frederica, a military fort, was founded on St. Simons island.   For many years the population of Georgia belonged almost entirely to these towns.   The classes of people in these five towns differed widely from one another. Savannah, largely a charity colony, was the least thrifty; the colonists there, as will be shown later, blamed their failure to the lack of efficient labor and clamored for negroes. The Salzburgers, a very thrifty people who were accustomed to hard manual toil, were almost unanimous in their opposition to slavery.[65]   They never complained of their condition or treatment and appeared to be duly impressed with a sense of their obligation to the Trustees.   Augusta, settled largely by Carolina Indian traders, hardly deigned to recognize the colonial authorities of Georgia and imported negroes regardless of the prohibition.[66]   The Scotch Highlanders of Darien were a thrifty people and they too were opposed to the introduction of negroes.[67]   Frederica, where the military fort was situated, was occupied chiefly by a garrison under the leadership of Oglethorpe who was determined to keep negroes out.

Thus we see that Georgia was founded as a free colony, that negroes were excluded from the province from the beginning, and that there was a decided opposition to their importation.   The majority of the Trustees seem not to

---

[64] For full account see: P. A. Strobel, *The Salzburgers.*
[65] Inhabitants of Ebenezer to Oglethorpe, *Colonial Records,* III, Appendix X, 428–431.
[66] Patrick Tailfer, Hugh Anderson, David Douglas and Others, "A True and Historical Narrative of the Colony of Georgia in America, from the First Settlement thereof until This Present Period" (Charleston, 1741), *Georgia Historical Collections,* II, 260.
[67] "Letter of the Inhabitants of New Inverness to Oglethorpe," *Colonial Records,* III, Appendix IX, 427–428.

have been actuated by moral objections in making this prohibition. The opposition was based on expediency. Georgia refused to have slaves, not because she thought that slavery was sinful or inhuman, but because she wanted the whites to feel their responsibility to work. The official publications of the Trustees base the inhibition more on political and prudential, rather than on humane and liberal grounds. That the Trustees prohibited negro slavery upon grounds of expediency, rather than upon moral or humane grounds, is indicated by the caption of the act, which was entitled "An Act for rendering the Colony of Georgia more defencible, by prohibiting the importation and use of black slaves or Negroes in the same." As the colony grew agriculturally and commercially, the interests and ambitions of the inhabitants changed likewise, and it was found necessary to abrogate this original inhibition. We shall see and study this as the story of Georgia develops.

CHAPTER II

THE DESIRE OF THE COLONISTS FOR NEGROES

In the first chapter it was shown that the plan of the founders of Georgia was that negroes should be excluded. From 1732–1750 Georgia had the distinction of being a free colony. In this chapter and the succeeding one we shall see how the colonists continually petitioned for negroes until the restriction was finally removed in 1750. The standards for the colony, as set up by the trustees, were too high to fit the circumstances; consequently they had to be lowered to suit the demands of the discontented colonists. In inquiring into the causes which led to the introduction of slavery into Georgia, I shall endeavor to show: (1) the early attempts to import negroes into the province; (2) the dissatisfaction of the colonists which led to their desire for slaves; and (3) the numerous petitions and counter-petitions for and against slavery.

It is probable that negroes were used in laying out the town of Savannah in 1733. The malcontents, in their article written in 1741,[1] say: "They worked hard indeed, in building some houses in town; but then they laboured in common and were likewise assisted by negroes from Carolina, who did the heaviest work."[2] But these were Carolina negroes used temporarily by Oglethorpe. The first account of an attempt to introduce negroes into Georgia appears in 1736. In that year some Carolinians, in defiance of the law, swam large herds of cattle over the Savannah. The cattle destroyed the corn of the friendly Uchee Indians

[1] Patrick Tailfer, Hugh Anderson, David Douglas and Others, "A True and Historical Narrative of the Colony of Georgia in America, from the First Settlement thereof until This Present Period" (Charleston, 1741), *Georgia Historical Collections*, II, 163–263.
[2] *Ibid*, II, 199.

above Ebenezer.   Not content with this outrage, they brought over negroes and opened up a plantation near the Indian town.   When the Uchees complained to Oglethorpe, he promptly sent back both negroes and cattle.   The Indians assured Oglethorpe of their love and confidence, and, in an attempt to show their appreciation, they offered him the aid of four score warriors against the Spaniards. Oglethorpe, in a letter to the Trustees May 18, 1746, says: "But what vext [sic] the Uchees more was that some of the Carolina people swam a great Herd of Cattle over Savannah and sent up Negroes and began a Plantation on the Georgia side not far from the Uchees Town.   The Uchees instead of taking Green's advice and beginning Hostilities with us sent up their King and 20 Warriors with a Message of Thanks to me for having ordered back the cattle and sent away the Negroes which I did as soon as ever I arrived."[3]

Augusta, Carolinian in all respects, had introduced negroes as early as 1738.   The prosperity of Augusta was attributed to the use of negro labor.   Other towns envied Augusta because of the ease with which she hoodwinked the officials and smuggled in negroes.   In March, 1740, a complaint was lodged with the authorities in Savannah that in consequence of the introduction of negro slaves from South Carolina, who performed all the manual labor, an ordinary workman could find but little employment in Augusta.[4] In the bitter attack made by the Savannah malcontents upon Oglethorpe in 1741, we are informed that the production of a considerable quantity of corn about Augusta was due chiefly to two circumstances: first, the goodness of the land, and second and chiefly, because "the settlers there are indulged in and connived at the use of negroes, by whom they execute all the laborious parts of culture; and the fact is undoubted and certain, that upwards of eighty negroes are

---

[3] "Letter of Oglethorpe to the Trustees," *Georgia Historical Collections*, III, 36; *Colonial Records*, XXI, 161–162.
[4] C. C. Jones Jr. and Salem Dutcher, *Memorial History of Augusta, Georgia* (Syracuse, 1890), 34, hereafter referred to as, Jones and Dutcher, *History of Augusta.*

now in the settlements belonging to that place."[5] Some
Georgia planters also held plantations on the Carolina
shore of the Savannah where they were allowed the use of
negroes. It was an easy matter to transfer these negroes
to the Georgia side of the river. Sir William Stephens,
President of the colony, in his journal for October 21, 1741,
makes the following entry:

> Some of the People of Augusta having Plantations on the
> Carolina Side of the River, as well as in Georgia, where they
> find it more advantageous to settle, and carry on the Trade
> with the Indians, together with making great Improvements
> on their Lands; by such Means they have an Opportunity of
> sliding two or three Negroes now and then at a Pinch into
> their Plantations, where during their skulking a while (which
> is not hard to conceive, considering the great Extent of the
> township of Augusta, by reason of large Tracts of Land)
> they are not presently to be discovered.[6]

Thus we find that Augusta, located just across the Savannah river from South Carolina where slaves were plentiful,
paid little heed to the Trustees' prohibition. The people
there declared that if not allowed the use of negroes on the
Georgia side of the river, they would go across to the Carolina shore where they could have as many negroes as they
wanted.[7] In spite of restrictive measures negroes were
continually imported and the rules of the officials evaded.
In case the negroes were discovered by the officials, it was
claimed that they belonged to the Carolina plantations
on the other side of the river. Under such circumstances
it was difficult to enforce the prohibition.

Almost immediately after the act prohibiting slavery
had been passed, the English element among the settlers—
that is to say, those living in Savannah and its neighborhood—became dissatisfied and begged to be allowed to
bring in negroes.[8] When the colonists saw their Carolina
neighbors growing rich with unhampered commerce, and

---

[5] Patrick Tailfer, Hugh Anderson, David Douglas and Others, *Op. cit.,* II, 260.
[6] "Stephens' Journal," *Colonial Records,* Supplement to Volume IV, 272.
[7] "Letter from the President and Assistants to Mr. Martyn," *Ibid,* XXV, 237.
[8] "Stephens' Journal," *Colonial Records,* Supplement to Volume IV, 200–201.

broad fields cultivated by negro labor, their discontent
was so great that they repeatedly demanded that slaves
should be allowed. Many reasons were advanced in support of this demand.

It was urged that the negro could easily adapt himself
to the heat and to the heavy work; that the climate was
such that a white man could not work in it. It was argued
that white men could not clear the immense tracts of dense
forests; that negro labor was necessary for such heavy
work. The Trustees were accused of having ruined Georgia
by their persistent denial of negroes.[9]   Patrick Tailfer,
leader of the discontents, and his colleagues said: "The
falling of timber was a task very unequal to the strength
and constitution of white servants; and the hoeing the
ground, they being exposed to the sultry heat of the sun,
insupportable; and it is well known that this labor is one
of the hardest upon the negroes, even though their constitutions are much stronger than white people, and the
heat no way disagreeable nor hurtful to them; but in
us it created inflamatory fevers of various kinds . . . ."[10]
Thomas Stephens said in one of his pamphlets: "In spite
of all endeavors to disguise this point, it is as clear as light
itself, that negroes are as essentially necessary to the cultivation of Georgia, as axes, hoes, or any other utensil of agriculture."[11]

However, the German settlers, who were opposed to
slavery, denied these assertions. They were accustomed
to labor with their own hands and they denied that such
manual labor worked a hardship upon the white people.
They insisted that negroes were not necessary. These
Salzburgers did not find the climate too hot nor too disagreeable for heavy work. The following extract is from
the memorial of the Germans to his Excellency James
Oglethorpe:

---

[9] Patrick Tailfer, Hugh Anderson, David Douglas and Others, *Op. cit.*, II,
   262–263.
[10] *Ibid*, II, 200.
[11] "A Brief Account of the Causes that have Retarded the Colony of Georgia
   in America," *Georgia Historical Collections*, II, 93.

Though it is here a hotter climate than our native country is, yet not so extremely hot as we were told on the first time of our arrival; but since we have now been used to the country, we find it tolerable, and for working people convenient, setting themselves to work early in the morning till ten o'clock, and in the afternoon from three to sunset; and having business at home, we do it in our huts and houses in the middle of the day, till the greatest heat is over. People in Germany are hindered by frost and snow, in the winter, from doing any work in the fields and vineyards; but we have this preference, to do the most and heaviest work at such a time, preparing the ground sufficiently for planting in the spring.[12]

These sentiments were reiterated by Wesley in his pamphlet "Thoughts on Slavery." He said: "It is not true . . . that white men are not able to labor, even in hot climates, full as well as black. But, if they were not, it would be better that none should labor there, that the work should be left undone, than that myriads of innocent men should be murdered, and myriads more dragged into the basest slavery."[13]

The white servants had failed to answer the expectations of the trustees. The limited number of these servants, their unwillingness to continue in a servile condition, and the high cost of maintaining them left the land without the means of efficient cultivation. The white servant class gained a reputation for low morality and unsatisfactory industry. William Stephens describes them as a "vile crew," utterly worthless, lazy, and some being handicapped by illness.[14] The expense of keeping white servants was greater than the value of the produce; they were a liability to the province rather than an asset. The malcontents insisted that white people could not gain a livelihood in the province without negroes. They gave as the chief cause of

---

[12] Found in *Colonial Records*, III, 430.
[13] John Wesley, "Thoughts Upon Slavery," Anthony Benezet and John Wesley, *Views of American Slavery Taken a Century Ago* (Philadelphia, 1858), 90–91.
[14] "William Stephens to Mr. Harman Verelst," *Colonial Records*, XXII, Part I, 173–174.

the distress: "The denying the use of negroes, and the persisting in such denial after, by repeated applications, we had humbly remonstrated the impossibility of making improvements to any advantage with white servants."[15] Many of the white servants, dissatisfied with their present conditions, deserted their masters and fled to South Carolina where they could be protected.[16]

It was also urged that the cultivation of silk and wine, which were to have been the staple products of Georgia and which required the skilled labor of the whites, was a failure. Governor James Wright, in a report in 1768,[17] gave serveral reasons why the silk industry was unprofitable: the variableness of the climate which caused the silkworms to die, the greater profit to be made from other lines of agriculture for which conditions were more favorable, the sparsity of the population, and the scarcity of efficient labor. It was necessary, in order to adapt their agriculture to existing physical conditions, to abandon the wine and silk industries. The colonists turned their attention to heavier forms of work such as rice and corn production. They claimed that the cultivation of these heavier crops necessitated negro labor. The Germans, staunch opponents of slavery, denied that negro labor was necessary in the production of corn and rice. In their representation to Oglethorpe of March, 1739, they said: "We were told by several People [sic] after our Arrival, that it proves quite impossible and dangerous, for White People to plant and manufacture Rice, being a Work for Negroes, not for European People; but having experience to the contrary, we laugh at such a Talking, seeing that several People of us had, in last Harvest, a greater Crop of Rice than they wanted for their own Consumption."[18]

---

[15] Patrick Tailfer, Hugh Anderson, David Douglas and Others, *Op. cit.*, II, 262–263.
[16] "Stephens' Journal," *Colonial Records*, IV, 192.
[17] Charles C. Jones, *History of Georgia*, II, 75–78.
[18] "Inhabitants of Ebenezer to General Oglethorpe," *Colonial Records*, III, 429.

It was also urged that the refusal to import negroes into Georgia did not prevent the desertion of the Carolina negroes and their escape through the province into Florida. It was useless to try to prevent the escape of the negroes to the Spaniards and equally useless to attempt the recovery of the fugitives. In January, 1738, the Council and Assembly of South Carolina sent a solemn deputation to the governor of St. Augustine to demand some runaway slaves. However, he promptly refused to deliver them up, declaring that his orders from the king of Spain were to receive and to protect such fugitives.[19] Carolina negroes continued to come through Georgia on their way to promised freedom in Florida.[20] Therefore, according to the reasoning of the malcontents, it was no longer necessary to prohibit the introduction of slavery in Georgia in order to prevent the escape of Carolina negroes.

As a consequence of the inability to procure adequate help, the lands granted to them remained uncleared; the silk and wine failed through want of encouragement; the planting of indigo was mostly abandoned; and the preparing of lumber for export became impossible. Every profitable employment which would have strengthened the colony was neglected. Discontent supplied the place of labor. For these reasons there accumulated on the Trustees' hands a body of idle, clamorous, mischief making men. The indulgences granted to the Carolinians increased their discontent. They had been a burden to the mother country at home, and it seemed that they were determined to be equally so abroad; and "as they generally had nothing to lose, they were resolved obstinately to persist in their demands, until their wishes were satisfied or the colony ruined."[21] Their idleness and dissipation prevailed to such a degree that the people were on the verge of starvation. The purpose of the severe rules of the Trustees

---

[19] "An Account Showing The Progress of the Colony of Georgia," *Georgia Historical Collections,* II, 301–302.
[20] "Stephens' Journal," *Colonial Records,* IV, 192.
[21] Daniel R. Goodloe, *The Southern Platform* (Boston, 1858), 84.

was to compel the colonists to labor; the object of this idle and discontented class was to live without labor. The industrious Salzburgers, who had been compelled to labor at home, had no grievance because of the prohibition of negroes. These Germans were brought up in habits of industry. They labored for the public good and with the full confidence that the Trustees would in due time extend to them such privileges as would eventually lead to their interest and happiness.

A club of malcontents (called the Scotch Club or the St. Andrews Club) was organized at Savannah. It was composed of such members as Patrick Tailfer, Thomas Stephens (son of the president), Graham, David Douglas, Hugh Anderson, and others, who occupied their time in declaiming against the government. This clique gave Oglethorpe and the Trustees a great deal of trouble. Robert Williams, a negro merchant who was plying a profitable trade in his illicit importation and sale of negroes, was open and violent in his denunciation of the Trustees' policy. He and Patrick Tailfer, an apothecary of Savannah, were the chief instigators in fomenting strife among the colonists and they kept the public mind in a constant ferment. Colonel William Stephens was continually complaining of Tailfer.[22] He was the leader of the malcontents whose conduct became so notorious that he was forced, in September, 1740, to leave the province and to take refuge in South Carolina. While he was beyond the jurisdiction of the Georgia authorities, he, in association with Hugh Anderson, David Douglas, and others wrote and published the defamatory pamphlet entitled "A True and Historical Narrative of the Colony of Georgia in America,"[23] which was ironically dedicated to General Oglethorpe. The General was charged with cowardice, despotism, cruelty, and bribery. Every act of the Trustees was severely criticised, especially the prohibition of the importation of negroes.

---

[22] "Stephens' Journal," *Colonial Records*, IV, 447–448, 449, 517, 576, 579, 604, 628.
[23] Found in *Georgia Historical Collections*, II, 163–263.

The pamphlet was filled with insults and veiled insinuations without any regard for good manners or common civility.

The Trustees were blamed for the lack of prosperity of the colony. In 1740 Colonel William Stephens, then secretary of the colony, drew up a paper which was to be read in open court in Savannah and which would vindicate the Trustees from the criticism of their administration. The paper was entitled "A State of the Province of Georgia, Attested upon Oath in the Court of Savannah."[24] When the malcontents heard of this another formal paper was drawn up entitled "A Brief Account of the Causes that have retarded the progress of the Colony of Georgia in America "[25] This pamphlet was a counter representation of the former one and contradicted the statements made therein.

Richard Lawley, February 6, 1741, gave a gloomy picture of the colony. He stated: that all of the Jews were gone; that only forty-two freeholders were left in Savannah; that only thirty-four freeholders were left in Frederica; that the people who had gone away were really industrious; that the industrious went away because they found that they could not subsist without negroes; that there were only forty freeholders and eighty souls left in Darien; that the people in general were reduced to great poverty; and that the Purysburgers (who had negroes) were very flourishing.[26] He suggested, as a remedy, that negroes should be allowed; that negroes could be kept for six pence a week; "that if Negroes were allow'd the Colony [sic] would people apace, for tis very healthy & pays no taxes, so that Planters would bring their Negroes from all quarters, & take up land & cultivate."[27]

The depressing conditions did not seem to improve. Many people left the colony. Those who remained were dispirited and heart-broken over the depressing prospects.

---

[24] *Ibid*, II, 67–85.
[25] *Ibid*, II, 89–161.
[26] "Journal of the Earl of Egmont," *Colonial Records*, V, 451–452.
[27] *Ibid*, V, 453.

In a communication made to the Trustees on August 10, 1740, by Grant, Douglas, Stirling, and Baillie, they stated that the colony was reduced to one-sixth of its former number and that the few who remained were in a starving and despicable condition.[28] The colonists who came with Oglethorpe in 1733 were chiefly poor and unfortunate people who were sent on charity. These thought little of attaining to mastery and ownership of slaves. Probably, had they not been brought into contact with slavery just across the river, the desire for negroes would not have prevailed to the extent of introducing them into the colony. As it was, two years had not elapsed since the landing of Oglethorpe before many complaints originated from the lack of negroes in the colony, and many petitions were sent to the Trustees for their importation.

In the summer of 1735 a petition for negroes, signed by seventeen freeholders of Savannah, was carried by Hugh Stirling to the Trustees.[29] This petition set forth the unprofitableness of white servants and the necessity for negroes in the province. However, the Trustees resented the appeal as an insult to their honor. ". . . No regard was had to it, or to what he [Mr. Hugh Sterling] could say, and great resentment was even shown to Mr. Thompson, the master of the vessel in which it went."[30] Nothing was done by the government and the people continued to clamor for the repeal of the restriction.

Another representation was made to the Trustees on September 1, 1737, by the grand jury of Savannah. They declared: "That the great want of servants in this town and county doth render the freeholders thereof incapable of proceeding with proper vigor in the cultivating their lands . . . . We do, with all humility, lay before your honors the great and general want of servants in this town

---

[28] "Grant, Douglas, Stirling and Baillie to the Trustees," *Ibid*, XXII, Part II, 413.
[29] Patrick Tailfer, Hugh Anderson, David Douglas and Others, *Op. cit.*, II, 200.
[30] *Ibid*, II, 200.

and country; not doubting your timely assistance therein."[31]
This petition was duly signed by the forty-four members
of the grand jury and sent to the Trustees who took no
notice of it.[32] Oglethorpe, in spite of contrary opinion,
continued to uphold the law which forbade the importation of negroes. Shortly after this representation had been
sent he declared openly in the courthouse of Savannah that
he would have nothing more to do with the colony of Georgia if negroes were admitted.[33]

On December 9, 1738, another petition, signed by one
hundred and seventeen freeholders of the county of Savannah, the names of several magistrates leading the list, was
sent to the Trustees setting forth the need for negroes.
The petition was directed to the Trustees in the hope that
they might see fit to change their governing regulations.
These freeholders recalled the fact that the former petitions
had been ignored. "We must beg Leave [sic] to observe
That it has afforded us a great deal of Concern and Uneasiness, that former Representations made to you of the
same Nature, have not been thought worthy of due Consideration, nor even of an Answer."[34] This memorial asserted that their best efforts in tilling the soil had failed
to secure sufficient provisions and the means requisite
for purchasing clothing and medicine; that in the absence
of cheap labor they were unable to compete successfully
with their neighbors in South Carolina; that the cultivation of silk and wine could never be made remunerative
so long as white servants only were employed; that commerce languished because they were incapable of offering
their lands as security to merchants for goods; that numbers
had left the province because of the many restrictions; and
many other causes which retarded the progress of the colony
of Georgia. They prayed that negroes might be admitted

---

[31] *Ibid,* II, 212–213.
[32] *Ibid,* II, 214.
[33] *Ibid,* II, 215.
[34] "Petition of The Inhabitants of Savannah to the Trustees," *Georgia Historical Collections,* II, 217; *Colonial Records,* III, 422.

with certain limitations. They gave as one of the chief causes of their misfortune:

> The Want [sic] of the Use of Negroes with proper Limitations; which if granted, would both induce great Numbers of White People to come here, and also render us capable to subsist ourselves by raising Provisions upon our Lands, until we could make some Produce fit for Export, and in some measure to balance our importation. We are very sensible of the Inconveniences and Mischiefs that have already, and do daily arise, from an unlimited Use of Negroes; but we are as sensible, that these may be prevented by a due Limitation, such as so many to each White Man, or so many to such a Quantity of Land; or in any other manner which your Honours shall think most proper.[35]

The petitioners then assured the Trustees that the granting of this petition would prevent impending ruin, would make the colony prosperous, and would perpetuate the memory of the Trustees to posterity as the founders, patrons, and guardians of the colony. On the other hand they assured the Trustees that if the request was refused the memory of the Trustees would be perpetuated to posterity as the cause and authors of all the misfortunes and calamities of the colony.

This petition of 1738 gave rise to much discussion and division of opinion. One copy was immediately sent to Darien, another to Ebenezer, and another to Frederica. The Highlanders of Darien, led by John Mohr M'Intosh, refused to sign the petition; the malcontents accused Oglethorpe of bribing the Highlanders not to sign it. The Germans of Ebenezer, led by their pastors, Bolzius and Gronau, opposed slavery and refused to sign the representation. When the petition reached Frederica, the inhabitants were called together and informed that the inhabitants of Savannah were going to throw off the government of the Trustees. They were advised "to beware of any snare that might be laid by these people, which if they were caught

---

[35] "Petition of the Inhabitants of Savannah to the Trustees," *Colonial Records,* III, 424–425.

in would ruin them."[36]   Thus the design of the representation was defeated in Darien, Ebenezer, and Frederica. The opposition of the Scots of Darien and the Germans of Ebenezer to slavery obstructed for a number of years the agitation of the English colonists for negroes.   These people were accustomed to hard labor in their own country and they were persistent in their opposition to slavery. The Darien Highlanders and the Ebenezer Salzburgers not only refused to sign the petition of 1738 for negroes but they drew up counter-petitions of their own which they sent to Oglethorpe.   They protested the great danger to the province from the vicinity of the Spaniards who had proclaimed freedom to all slaves who should resort to them, and that they would be exposed to a dangerous enemy without and a still more dangerous one within.[37]   The Salzburgers insisted that negroes were unnecessary; that they were raising too much produce for their own consumption without the aid of negroes.[38]

On January 3, 1739, a formal counter-petition was drawn up and signed by the inhabitants of Darien in which objections to the introduction of slaves were recounted.   It was addressed to the Governor-General praying that he give no heed to the constant appeal of Savannah and the other settlements for negroes; they protested insistently against the introduction of negro slaves.   The petition read: "To his excellency General Oglethorpe: We are informed, that our Neighbors of Savannah have petitioned your Excellency for the Liberty of having Slaves. We hope, and earnestly entreat, that before such Proposals are hearkened unto, your Excellency will consider our situation, and of what dangerous and bad Consequence such Liberty would be of to us, for many Reasons."[39]   There followed a list of reasons as to why they opposed negro slavery: (1)

---

[36] Patrick Tailfer, Hugh Anderson, David Douglas and Others, *Op. cit.*, II, 223.
[37] *Ibid*, II, 300.
[38] "Letter of the Inhabitants of Ebenezer to Oglethorpe," *Colonial Records*, III, 429–430.
[39] "Petition of the Inhabitants of Darien to General Oglethorpe," *Colonial Records*, III, 427.

the nearness of the Spaniards, who had proclaimed freedom to all slaves who ran away from their masters, made it impossible to keep negroes without "more labor in watching than we would be at to do their work;" (2) The Highlanders were industrious and believed that white labor was more profitable than negro labor; that in a year a white man's labor was more than that of a slave; (3) the settlers were poor and would become debtors for the slaves and the masters would thus become slaves to the slave traders for them; (4) it would necessitate a guard duty as severe as if an invasion were daily expected; it would be a miserable feeling to the planters and to their wives and children, to have an enemy without and a still more dangerous one within; and (5) they declared that slavery was shocking to human nature, and opposed to justice and morality. "It's shocking to human Nature, [sic] that any Race of Mankind, and their Posterity, Should be sentenced to perpetual slavery; nor in Justice can we think otherwise of it, than they are thrown amongst us to be our Scourge one Day or another for our Sins; and as Freedom to them must be as dear as to us, what a Scene of Horror must it bring about!"[40]   This quotation shows that there was a humanitarian and moral reason behind the opposition of the people of Darien to slavery. The people considered slavery a crime that ought not to be tolerated. On the other hand the malcontents who petitioned for the use of slaves denied that the people of Darien were content. They accused them of having been bought with a number of cattle and extensive promises of future rewards when they signed their petition against negroes.[41]

On March 13, 1739, another formal counter petition, which protested vigorously against the introduction of negroes, was drawn up by the inhabitants of Ebenezer and

---

[40] "Petition of the Inhabitants of Darien to General Oglethorpe," *Colonial Records*, III, 427.
[41] "A Brief Account of the Causes that have Retarded the Progress of the Colony of Georgia in America," *Georgia Historical Collections*, II, 117–118, 119–120.

sent to Oglethorpe.[42] The Salzburgers endorsed the protest of the people of Darien; they commended their own industry and success; they expressed their satisfaction with white servants; they asked that another transport of Germans be sent to Ebenezer; they gave an account of how their time and money were spent; and they urgently requested that no negroes be allowed near them. Led by their faithful pastors, Bolzius and Gronau, these devout Salzburgers requested that no negroes be allowed in the colony; they stated that they were contented under the present laws and wished no change; they prayed that at least no negroes be allowed near them. It read: "We humbly beseech the honorable Trustees not to allow it, that any Negro might be brought to our Place, [sic] or to our Neighborhood, knowing by Experience, that Houses and Gardens will be robbed always by them, and White People are in Danger of Life because of them, besides other great inconveniences."[43] The counter-petition was signed by the inhabitants of Ebenezer and then countersigned by Bolzius and Gronau who added this postscript: "We the ministers of the congregation at Ebenezer, join with the Salzburgers in this petition, and verify, that every one of them has signed it with the greatest readiness and satisfaction."[44] In view of this disagreement among the colonists the Trustees, who were already strongly opposed to slavery, refused to alter their rules on the subject.

A copy of the petition of 1738 was sent to Oglethorpe accompanied by an urgent letter to him.[45] This letter gave a view of the situation of the colony at that time. It quoted the motives for the founding of the colony: (1) the establishment of a frontier colony to protect British America; (2) to employ those persons who were least useful

---

[42] "Petition of the Inhabitants of Ebenezer to General Oglethorpe," *Colonial Records*, III, 428–431.
[43] "Petition of the Inhabitants of Ebenezer to General Oglethorpe," *Colonial Records*, III, 430.
[44] *Ibid.*
[45] Patrick Tailfer, Hugh Anderson, David Douglas and Others, *Op. cit.*, II, 223–231.

at home; (3) to restore liberty and happiness to those who were incapable of serving themselves or their country at home; and (4) to establish new manufactures which would support the colony and rectify the balance of trade of Great Britain.   Then it was shown that each of these motives was frustrated by the plans of the Trustees.   The remedy suggested was that negroes should be admitted—not an unlimited use of them but with prudent regulations.[46] Oglethorpe was urged to sign the petition and to consider the consequences of his refusal to sign.   The letter was written anonymously and signed "The Plain Dealer." However it was attributed to the pen of Patrick Tailfer.[47] When Oglethorpe received this letter he had devoted six years of the prime of his life to service in Georgia; he had crossed the ocean five times; he had exposed himself to the hardships of pioneer life—to the dangers of an inhospitable climate and to the dangers of the sea; he had secluded himself from the society of a court which he might have enjoyed in affluence and luxury.   He had received no material reward for his services.   Believing that the introduction of slavery would be ruinous to the colony in its present situation, he determined to persevere in the prohibition of negroes.[48] Oglethorpe continued to refuse every petition for negroes. Many people began to despair of having a favorable answer to their petition and left the colony.   The colonists were so discouraged that Oglethorpe in 1739 tried to encourage them by offering a prize of two shillings for each bushel of potatoes and peas raised in the county of Savannah.[49] But even this attempt to arouse the colonists to greater effort failed.

On June 20, 1739, the Trustees, through their secretary, Benjamin Martyn, returned a firm though dignified refusal to the petition for negroes of December, 1738.   The letter was adressed to the magistrates of the town of Savannah.

---

[46] *Ibid*, II, 226.
[47] Hugh McCall, *History of Georgia*, I, 82.
[48] *Ibid*, 82–83.
[49] Patrick Tailfer, Hugh Anderson, David Douglas and Others, *Op. cit.*, II, 231.

The Trustees acknowledged the receipt of the petition. They expressed surprise that the magistrates of the town, appointed to be the guardians of the people, should so far forget their duty as to place themselves at the head of the attempt to introduce negroes. The magistrates were directed to give to the complainants this answer from the Trustees: "That they should deem themselves very unfit for the Trust reposed in them by his Majesty on their Behalf, [sic] if they could be prevailed upon by such an irrational Attempt, to give up a Constitution, framed with the greatest Caution for the Preservation of Liberty and Property, and of which the laws against the Use of Slaves, and for the Entail for Lands, are the surest Foundation."[50] They further declared that they could not and would not break the constitution by an introduction of slavery in blacks. In this reply the Trustees gave reasons for their refusal to allow negroes; (1) that they had received counter-petitions from Darien and other parts of the province representing the inconvenience and dangers which might arise from the introduction of negroes; (2) that the Trustees were convinced that it would destroy all industry among the white inhabitants; (3) the colony would soon be like its neighbors, void of white inhabitants and filled with blacks; (4) the colony would be held by a few landholders who would be exposed to domestic treachery and foreign invasion, "and therefore the Trustees cannot be supposed to be in any disposition of granting this Request."[51] In the Journal of the Trustees for June 27, 1739, we find the following minute: "Ordered: That the Seal of the Corporation be affixed to the Trustees' Answer to the Representation from Savannah of the 9th of December, 1738, for altering the Tenure of the Lands, and introducing Negroes into Georgia."[52] And in the Minutes of the Common Council of the Trustees for the same date we find: "Resolved:

---

[50] "Letter of the Trustees to the Magistrates of Savannah," *Colonial Records,* III, 431–432.
[51] *Ibid,* III, 432.
[52] "Journal of the Trustees," *Ibid,* I, 352.

that two hundred Copies of the Trustees Answer to the
Representation from Savannah about the Tenure of Lands
and Negroes be printed and sent to Georgia for the Information of the Inhabitants."[53]

From 1735, the date of the first petition for negroes, to
1749, the date of the last petition, the Trustees refused to
listen to any petitions except to condemn them.   For a
time the law relating to negroes was rigidly enforced.
Any negro found in Georgia, unless speedily reclaimed, was
sold back to Carolina.   Stephens, in his Journal, mentions
two instances of this where the negroes were sold at public
auction in Savannah, the first in 1740,[54] and the second in
1741.[55]   At another time a negro was apprehended at work
on a Mr. Upton's farm.   He was taken and sold for thirteen
pounds.[56]   The negroes who had already entered Georgia
with their masters from South Carolina were banished according to the terms of the Negro Act which Georgia constables were charged with executing.[57]   Oglethorpe himself
broke up at least one plantation begun by the South Carolinians who had brought in several negroes.[58]   Negroes were
forbidden to peddle wares along the waterfront of Savannah.[59]   So effective was the ban on negroes for several
years that the writer of "A Brief Account of the Causes
that Have Retarded the Progress of the Colony of Georgia
in America" complained that the importation, use or even
sight of negroes was prohibited.[60]   After the Trustees
refused to grant the petition of 1738 for negroes, a short
period of calm followed.   Colonel Stephens wrote, on July
26, 1739, that few people troubled themselves more about
negroes.   He said: "And as for Negroes, I always thought

[53] "Minutes of the Common Council of the Trustees," *Ibid*, II, 290.
[54] "Stephens' Journal," *Ibid*, IV, 523–524.
[55] *Ibid*, Supplement to Volume IV, 161–162.
[56] "Journal of the Earl of Egmont," *Colonial Records*, V, 481.
[57] "Minutes of the Common Council of the Trustees," *Colonial Records*, II, 120.
[58] "General Oglethorpe to the Trustees," *Georgia Historical Collections*, III,
    36; *Colonial Records*, XXI, 161–162.
[59] "Thomas Causton to the Trustees," *Colonial Records*, XXI, 402.
[60] Thomas Stephens, "A Brief Account of the Causes that have Retarded the
    Progress of the Colony of Georgia in America," (London, 1743), *Georgia
    Historical Collections*, II, 87–161.

it an impudent attempt to subvert the original constitution of the Colony, in all such as nothing less would please; but there are few left now, hardly enough to dwell upon that any longer; & I think under those marks of indulgence so evidently shown, we shall at last grow wiser, and quickly betake our selves to such Industry and Labour, as most undoubtedly ought to be the view of all such as come to live here."[61]

On the 20th of October General Oglethorpe informed the Trustees that their reply had been received and published and that their answer had had the best effects in the colony. He began: "The Order relating to Negroes is arrived and published & hath had a very good effect. The Resolution shown by the Trust hath in a great measure quelled the troublesome spirit. The remainder of the Idle Walkers and Doctor Tailfer are preparing to leave the Colony but several industrious people are settling. This week above eight Lotts have been taken up."[62]

On March 25, 1740, the Trustees, through their secretary, wrote a letter to Andrew Grant, David Douglass, and Thomas Baillie at Savannah and again protested against the importation of negroes.[63] The Trustees repeated the fact that they would not break into the constitution of the province by an introduction of slavery in blacks. They called to mind the recent insurrection of negroes in South Carolina, and the fact that Georgia would be in more imminent danger because of its location on the frontier. In answer to this letter another petition, dated August 10, 1740, and signed by Grant, Stirling, Douglas, and Baillie, was sent to the Trustees. This document was a plea for the admission of negroes and a recognition of the Trustees' reply to the former petition. It said:

"Because our Neighboring Province (of which you are pleas'd to Take Notice) has by an Introduction of Too [sic]

---

[61] "William Stephens Esq. to Mr. Harman Verelst," *Colonial Records*, XXII, Part II, 189–190.
[62] "Oglethorpe to the Trustees," *Georgia Historical Collections*, III, 89.
[63] *Ibid*, II, 241–242.

great numbers abus'd the Use of Negroes: or Because an
Undoubted property in our Land possessions might prove
Detrimental or hurtfull to Idle, profligate and abandon'd
people; it does not at all follow, that we should be debarred
the use of Negroes for the Field or the more Laborious parts
of Culture, under prudent Limitations: Or that sober and
virtuous men shou'd be Depriv'd of Just Titles To their
propertys."[64]

The petitioners accused the people of Darien of having
been bribed to sign the counter-petition of 1738. They
blamed the low condition of the colony to the refusal of
the Trustees to admit negroes. They accused the Trustees
of having been deluded and of having pursued policies
which were inconsistent with the welfare and prosperity
of the colony. They even threatened to present the question to the British Parliament which would institute an
investigation.[65]   The document plead loudly for the admission of negroes and indulged in a bitter denunciation
of Oglethorpe.   The Earl of Egmont, on December 19,
1740, recorded in his Journal that: "This day arrived a
very sawcy [sic] letter from four of the St. Andrews Club
viz. Tho. Baillie, Will. Sterling, Andrew Grant, and David
Douglass, vilifying Col. Oglethorpe, and divers of the
Trustees for not allowing them Negroes: dat. 10 Aug.
1740."[66]

In the same year 1740, another petition was sent to the
Trustees. This representation, signed by sixty-three land
holders of Savannah, demanded and insisted on the use
of negroes.[67] On November 27, 1740, Colonel Stephens
wrote the Trustees that a representation had been drawn
up in which the inhabitants demanded absolutely the use of
negroes but with some limitation.[68] Three copies of this
petition were sent to England: one copy for the Trustees,

---

[64] "Grant, Douglas, Stirling and Baillie to the Trustees," *Colonial Records,*
    XXII, Part II, 411–412.
[65] *Ibid,* XXII, Part II, 416.
[66] "Journal of the Earl of Egmont," *Colonial Records,* V, 413.
[67] *Ibid,* V, 407.
[68] "Mr. Stephens to the Trustees," *Ibid,* XXII, Part II, 449.

one for Parliament, and one for the King.[69] The Trustees however paid no attention to the demand and continued in their opposition to the importation of negroes. Public opinion in Georgia was still divided and the Trustees did not yet see fit to relent. The clamoring for negroes was to continue for several years yet before the Trustees would finally agree to the repeal of the prohibition. How the prohibitive statute was finally removed and the importation of negroes was freely allowed will be shown in the following chapter.

---

[69] "Journal of the Earl of Egmont," *Ibid*, V, 408.

CHAPTER III

THE ADMISSION OF NEGROES INTO GEORGIA

In Chapter II was discussed: (1) the early attempts to import negroes into the province, (2) the dissatisfaction of the colonists which led to their desire for slaves, and (3) the many petitions and counter-petitions for and against slavery. In this chapter will be discussed: (1) the internal dissentions in the province concerning slavery, (2) the final admission of negroes, and (3) the immediate results of the action.

There was still much opposition to slavery in 1740. Public opinion in the province of Georgia was not united on the negro question. In that year a petition against negroes was drawn up at Frederica; however, it was decided not to present it to the Trustees but to wait and see what action the authorities might take.[1] Some of the Scots at Darien wished for negroes,[2] but the majority was still opposed to their introduction. The Salzburgers of Ebenezer still opposed negro slavery. Bolzius, in a letter to Whitefield of December 24, 1745, expressed a determined opposition to the introduction of negroes into the colony.[3] He refuted all of Whitefield's arguments and stated his ardent desire to see the colony settled with white people. These internal dissentions were a great handicap to Oglethorpe at this time. Preparations for war and an invasion of Florida were going on when the agitation against the Laws of the Trustees in regard to slavery was at its height. Large numbers of the settlers deserted the colony; most of the deserters went to South Carolina where conditions were

---

[1] "Journal of the Earl of Egmont," *Colonial Records*, V, 348.
[2] *Ibid.*
[3] "Bolzius to Whitefield," *Colonial Records*, XXIV, 434–444.

more favorable. Of the five thousand souls who had immigrated to Georgia from 1733 to 1740, scarce as many hundreds remained.[4] During the following two years the malcontents were extremely active and had many witnesses in England.

Those who desired negroes continued to send petitions, but the Trustees were persistent in their opposition. As late as March, 1748, we find the following record in the Journal of the Trustees:

> "Resolved: That an Instruction be prepared and afterwards seal'd and counter-signed by the Secretary to the President and Assistants to the following Purport. That, after so many Declarations that the Introduction and Use of Negroes in the Colony is not only inconsistent with the Intention of His Majesty's Charter, but also directly contrary to an Express Act approv'd by his Majesty in Council in the Year 1735 for the Year 1735 for prohibiting the Importation and Use of Negroes, Declaring the Meaning and Intention of the said Charter: The Trustees are surpris'd any Expectations of them can yet remain at Savannah, and in other Parts of the Colony: And therefore it must be, and is, upon that foundation, a Resolution of the Trustees never to permit the Introduction of Negroes into the Colony of Georgia, as the danger which must arise from them in a Frontier Town is so evident; And as the People Who continue to clamour for Negroes declare that the Colony can never succeed without the use of them, it is evident they don't intend by their own Industry to contribute to its Success, and must therefore rather hinder than promote it; The Trustees therefore require it may be signified to all the inhabitants of the Colony, that if any of them persist in declaring they cannot succeed without Negroes, it would be of service to the Colony as well as themselves for them to retire into any other Province, where they will be freely allow'd the Use of Negroes."[5]

---

[4] Patrick Tailfer, Hugh Anderson, David Douglas, and Others, "A True and Historical Narrative of the Colony of Georgia in America, from the First Settlement thereof until This Present Period," *Georgia Historical Collections*, II, 248–249.

[5] "Journal of the Trustees," *Colonial Records*, I, 506–507.

This resolution received the official seal on March 25, 1748.[6]

From 1740 Parliament began to consider the question of admitting negroes; for the first time they began seriously to consider the repeal of the anti-slavery law. Several of the members were violent partisans of negro slavery; others were opposed to it but did not believe the colony could succeed without negroes. Lord Gage and LaRoche were willing to admit negroes and were anxious that the many complaints should be investigated.[7] LaRoche pointed out that the presence of free negroes in Georgia would tend to encourage runaways from South Carolina.[8] The Earl of Egmont persistently opposed the admission of negroes. He feared that cheap negro labor would discourage and drive away white servants.[9] In his Journal the Earl frequently alludes to his opposition to slaves.[10] Egmont thought that the best way to end the clamors in Georgia would be to have Parliament formally recognize the necessity for the exclusion of negroes.[11] All were desirous of the prosperity of Georgia and wished to know the truth concerning the province. Sir John Barnard was opposed to slavery but believed that the introduction of negroes was necessary to the prosperity of the province. He wished that none of the plantations found it necessary to have any. "But since Carolina (which can raise all the produces that Georgia proposes) is so near a Neighbor[sic] to the latter & uses the labour of Negroes, it appear'd impossible to him that Georgia should ever be able to support itself without Negroes because Carolina would undersell them."[12] Vernon advocated the admission of negroes. He interpreted the negro act to mean that no negroes were to be excluded except slaves.[13] In March, 1742, the House of Commons

---

[6] *Ibid*, I, 509.
[7] "Journal of the Earl of Egmont," *Ibid*, V, 299–300.
[8] *Ibid*, V, 378.
[9] *Ibid*, V, 378–379.
[10] *Ibid*, V, 301, 304, 378–379, 583, 584.
[11] *Ibid*, V, 577.
[12] *Ibid*, V, 301.
[13] *Ibid*, V, 378–379.

yielded to the enemies of the colony and refused an appropriation for its support.[14] It seemed that the Trustees must yield. Many witnesses were examined by the Commons Committee. However, on June 29, 1742, the House rejected the application for the admission of negroes by a vote of 43 to 34.[15] Many members declared themselves opposed to any further appropriation until negroes should be admitted.[16] The Earl of Egmont, still persistent in his opposition to slavery, tendered his resignation.[17] The Trustees indicated that they were willing to investigate the feasibility of admitting negroes, probably under limitations.[18] William Stephens wrote from Georgia that their limited use could be begun as soon as the Spanish difficulties ceased on the frontier.[19]

Meanwhile negroes were being illegally admitted into Georgia. Evasions and infractions of the laws became frequent and notorious. Purchases from negro traders were openly concluded in Savannah.[20] Some seizures were made by those who opposed the principle. But since a majority of the magistrates were favorable to the introduction of slaves into the province, legal decisions were suspended from time to time, and a strong disposition was evidenced by the courts to evade the operation of the law.[21] Letters were written during this period which acknowledged the existence of negroes in the province. On May 11, 1748, Colonel Alexander Heron, after stating that his opinion was for the admission of negroes and that the colony would not prosper without them, boldly said: "It's well known to every one in the Colony [sic] that Negroes have been in and about Savannah for these several Years, that the Magistrates knew and wink'd at it and that their constant Toast is (the one thing needful) by which is meant Negroes."[22]

---

[14] *Ibid*, V, 607.
[15] *Ibid*, V, 639.
[16] *Ibid*, V, 639–640.
[17] *Manuscripts of the Earl of Egmont*, (London, 1923), III, 265.
[18] "Journal of the Trustees," *Colonial Records*, I, 400–401.
[19] "Journal of the Earl of Egmont," *Ibid*, V, 657.
[20] Charles C. Jones, *History of Savannah, Georgia*, (Syracuse, 1890), 143.
[21] Hugh McCall, *History of Georgia*, (Savannah, 1811), I, 206–207.
[22] "Letter from Alexander Heron," *Colonial Records*, XXV, 295.

Colonists who emigrated from Carolina brought their negroes with them.[23]   They moved over to the Georgia side and cultivated their plantations in the same manner as before.   A letter from the Reverend Mr. Bolzius of Ebenezer on May 20, 1748, severely denounced the colonists for this illegal introduction of negroes.[24]   It seems that there was very little effort at this time to enforce the law.

During this time slavery was allowed, perhaps knowingly, by the officials.   The employment of negro slaves on the Georgia side of the Savannah river went on covertly. In 1741 William Stephens ridiculed the idea that a hundred negroes were being worked on Georgia plantations.   "What they so positively affirm, that there are at least 100 Negroes made use of by the Inhabitants of Augusta, without which, not one Settler would live on that Side of the River; is another Instance of their Labour to magnify Molehills into Mountains; for . . . I could never make such a discovery."[25]

In December, 1746, the Trustees learned that the Reverend Thomas Bosomworth, who had married the celebrated half breed, Mrs. Mary Matthews (Mary Musgrove), had sent to Carolina for six negroes to cultivate his wife's plantation at the Forks of the Altamaha, and also that negroes had been creeping into the colony at Augusta and other remote places.[26]   The Secretary was ordered to write to Mr. Stephens and to acquaint him that the Trustees were surprised that he, as President, and the assistants had not taken any steps to punish and put a stop to such a violation of the law against negroes; and that they had not proposed any means for the Trustees doing it, but that they had contented themselves with seeing, and complaining of it.[27]   In October, 1747, the president and the assistants in a letter to Secretary Benjamin Martyn denied all complicity with the negro movement.   They wrote:

---

[23] "Letter from the President and Assistants to Mr. Martyn," *Ibid*, XXV, 237.
[24] "Letter from the Rev. John Martin Bolzius to Mr. John Dobell," *Ibid*, XXV, 284–285.
[25] "Mr. Stephens to the Trustees," *Colonial Records*, XXIII, 185.
[26] "Journal of the Trustees," *Ibid*, I, 495.
[27] *Ibid*.

We are afraid Sir from what you have wrote in Relation to Negroes, That the Honble Trustees have been misinformed as to our Conduct relating thereto: for We can with great Assurance assert, that this Board has always acted an uniform Part in discouraging the Use of Negroes in this Colony, well knowing it to be disagreeable to the Trust as well as contrary to an Act existing for Prohibition of them, and always give it in Charge to those Whom We have put in Possession of Lands not to Attempt the Introduction or Use of Negroes; but notwithstanding our great Caution some People from Carolina soon after their Settling Lands on the Little Ogeechee, found Means of bringing and employing a few Negroes on the said Lands sometime before it was discovered to Us; Upon which Discovery they thought it high time to withdraw them for fear of their being seized and soon after withdrew themselves and Families out of the Colony; Which appears to Us at present to be the Resolution of divers Others, particularly the whole Inhabitants of Augusta who have had Negroes among them for many years past, and now declare that if they cannot obtain that Liberty, they will remove to the Carolina Side, where they can carry on their Trade and Plantations with the same advantage as where they now are; and several others of late (finding Us strenuous in endeavoring to see the Trustees Orders fulfilled) express themselves in the same Strain.

We are thoroughly sensible Sir that what we have now wrote relating to Negroes must be very disagreeable to the Trustees, and it is with the greatest Reluctance that We are driven to this Necessity, but it being a Matter of such Importance, We thought it highly incumbent on Us to acquaint their Honours therewith for fear we might incurr their high Displeasure if we should conceal any thing from them, that was consistent with our Duty to Lay before them.

We are Sir
Your Most humble Servants

Signed
{
WILL STEPHENS
HENRY PARKER
WILLM: SPENCER
SAML: MARCER
PAT: GRAHAM.[28]
}

---

[28] "Letter from the President and Assistants to Mr. Martyn," *Colonial Records*, XXV, 236–237.

This letter is proof that the Savannah officials knew that negroes were creeping into the colony. They made little effort to enforce an unpopular statute. They concealed, as far as possible, from the Trustees the fact of the negroes' presence in the colony. It seems that they waited for the introduction of negroes to become an actuality, and then plead the impossibility of ridding the province of them, and the terrible consequences likely to follow. When concealment was no longer possible, fearing the displeasure of the Trustees, and attempting to vindicate themselves, they acknowledged that negroes had been introduced many years before and were employed at Augusta in spite of parliament and the Trustees.

Some of the colonists disregarded altogether the injunction of the Trustees. The promised lucrative returns from negro labor were more powerful than the respect for the law. The Georgia planters began to hire slaves from the South Carolina planters, with the promise that if any attempt should be made by the Georgia authorities to enforce the regulations of the Trustees, then the owner of the slave would be notified so that he might come forward and claim his property. Finding that this plan of evading the law succeeded, the colonists even went so far as to hire slaves for a period of one hundred years, or during life, paying in advance a sum equal to the full value of the negro. The former owners agreed to come forward and exhibit their claim in case the authorities of the colony interfered.[29] Finally, purchases were openly made in Savannah from African traders. "It was not long before slaves direct from Africa were landed at Savannah, while the laws against their introduction ceased to be observed."[30] Some seizures were made by those who opposed the principle, but as the majority of the magistrates were favorable to the introduction of slaves into the province, legal decisions were suspended from time to time, and the courts showed a disposition to evade the operation of the law altogether.[31]

[29] Charles C. Jones, *History of Georgia*, I, 420.
[30] James Ford Rhodes, *History of the United States*, (New York, 1892), I, 5.
[31] McCall, *History of Georgia*, I, 143–144.

The activity of Thomas Stephens in behalf of the malcontents brought the issue to its climax. Determined to
make one more effort some of the landholders and settlers
decided to send a personal representative to England to
represent their cause to the proper authorities. So Thomas
Stephens, son of President William Stephens, was chosen for
this office much to the embarrassment of his aged father who
was not in sympathy with his errand. A committee of five
persons was appointed to correspond with Mr. Stephens.[32]
These proceedings were accomplished at a meeting held at
Savannah on October 7, 1741, and were signed by one hundred and twenty-three land holders in the province.[33]
In the instructions given to Mr. Stephens he was desired,
on his arrival in England, to "apply, petition, and solicit
for redress of grievances, in such manner as you shall think
most advisable, (application to the Trustees only excepted)."[34] Among other things he was to petition "That
the use of negroes, under such restrictions as shall be thought
proper, be allowed for cultivating our lands."[35] And, if he
was unsuccessful in this, he was to pray "that the money,
which may hereafter be granted for the use of the colony,
may be applied for removing them to some other part of
his Majesty's dominions, where they may be able to support themselves and families, and be of use to the public,
instead of a burthen to it as they are now."[36]

Thus furnished with these instructions Mr. Stephens
sailed for England in order to present his petition to the
king. The petition represented the deplorable condition
of the colony and stated that many former petitions had
been sent to the Trustees without any redress of grievances. It was formally presented to the king and then it
was referred by the king to the Lords of the Committee of

[32] "Stephens' Journal," *Colonial Records*, Supplement to Volume IV, 263–264.
[33] "A Brief Account of the Causes that Have Retarded the Progress of the
    Colony of Georgia in America," *Georgia Historical Collections*, II, Ap-
    pendix XXXIV, 153–154.
[34] *Ibid*, II, 154–155.
[35] *Ibid*, II, 155.
[36] *Ibid*.

Council for Plantation Affairs.[37]   This committee then sent
a copy to the Trustees who were required to answer it as
speedily as possible.   This answer was read before the
Trustees on May 3, 1742, and referred back to the former
committee.[38]   Stephens also presented a petition to parliament.   He criticized the Trustees for their mismanagement
of the colony.   He accused them of refusing to listen to the
representations of the people, of misapplication of public
funds, of delays in discharging debts, and other abuses.
He closed with an appeal to the Commons to grant such
redress of grievances as they should see fit.[39]   The House
determined to investigate the charges, and asked that all
former petitions be laid before them.   This was done and
the House began a thorough investigation of the conduct
of the Trustees.   Witnesses before the House of Commons
were of the opinion that the colony of Georgia should be
further supported but with a change in the system of administration which would allow the use of slaves and modify
the system of land tenure.[40]   At this time Bladen of the
Board of Trade and Horace Walpole were among the champions for the admission of slavery to Georgia.[41]   Three
solemn hearings were held before the House of Commons.
It had been agreed that both sides should be allowed to
introduce evidence, so the defense of the Trustees was presented.   After hearing the counsel for both sides the members of the House adopted resolutions to embody their
findings in the case.   They condemned the petition of
Stephens as containing false and malicious charges, but they
reported in favor of modifying some of the regulations of the
Trustees.   Thomas Stephens was made to kneel before the
House of Commons and he was severely reprimanded for
his part in trying to attack and criticize the characters of
the Trustees.[42]   The Trustees were exonerated, but the

---

[37] "Journal of the Trustees," *Colonial Records*, I, 396.
[38] *Ibid*, I, 397.
[39] "Journal of the House of Commons," 1742, quoted by William Bacon
    Stevens, *History of Georgia*, I, 302.
[40] "Journal of the Earl of Egmont," *Colonial Records*, V, 619–620.
[41] *Ibid*, V, 639–640.
[42] Knight, *A Standard History of Georgia and Georgians*, 167.

inquiry caused them to see the necessity of relaxing some of their laws. Accordingly, they decided to consider the petitions and to find out from the colonists on what conditions and restrictions they would agree to the admission of negroes. On July 14, 1742, the Trustees ordered: that instructions should be sent to William Stephens Esquire, President of the colony, that he should make an inquiry among the people of the province as to whether or not it was their general opinion that it was proper to admit "the Use and Introduction of Negroes in the said Province; And that he do as soon as he can certify their Opinion and his own how far it may be proper under any, and under what Limitations and Restrictions."[43]

The Salzburgers, under the leadership of Bolzius, were still skeptical about the introduction of negroes. On March 20, 1748, Bolzius wrote that since the settlers had introduced negroes in defiance of the orders of the Trustees, "how can we believe they would regard any restrictions under which they would have Negroes [sic] allowed?"[44] But the Salzburgers finally relented. In a letter written May 3, 1748, Mr. Bolzius stated that he and the Germans withdrew the objections they had made to the use of slaves.

> Things being now here in such a melancholy situation I most humbly beseech their Honors not to regard any more our or our Friend's [sic] Petition against Negroes but if they are bountifully disposed to forgive the present bold step of several Inhabitants in bringing over black Slaves from Carolina to our Province and to allow the introduction of them We beg humbly to lay the use of them under such wise restrictions that it be not a discouragement but rather an encouragement to poor white Industrious people to settle and live in this happy Climate.[45]

Thus, when the leading Salzburger minister joined with the majority, there was little opportunity for the Trustees

---

[43] "Journal of the Trustees," *Colonial Records*, I, 400–401.
[44] "Letter from the Rev. Mr. John Martin Bolzius to Mr. John Dobell," *Ibid*, XXV, 285.
[45] "Letter from the Rev. Mr. John Martin Bolzius to Mr. Verelst," *Ibid*, XXV, 289.

to hold out longer. Even the Scotch Highlanders no longer interposed an objection.

On May 16, 1749, the president, the assistants, and a large number of the inhabitants sent to the Trustees a final petition, to which the town seal was affixed, setting forth several restrictions and regulations under which they prayed that negroes might be permitted in the colony.[46] It stated: that an abundance of people had applied to them for grants of land in Georgia; that numbers of negroes had been introduced into the province; that they had taken methods to drive the negroes out of the province but ineffectually; that any further attempts to put the act against negroes into execution would in their apprehension dispeople the colony; and they gave reasons why they hoped that the Trustees might be induced to permit negroes in the province under restrictions.[47] This representation was considered by the Board of Trustees May 17, 1749, seven members being present. Mr. Vernon presided over the meeting. It was officially decided to ask for a repeal of the act. They did not forget their obligations to a frontier colony. Steps were taken to prevent the Spanish authorities from inveigling slaves from British owners.[48] It was resolved that a committee should prepare an act to be laid before the king for repealing the law against negroes.[49]

The Trustees were persuaded that the time had come when they must give their consent to the introduction of negroes. After duly considering the subject the Trustees directed their secretary, Mr. Benjamin Martyn, to write to William Stephens, President of the colony, instructing him to call a convention of the most able persons and to send him their opinion as to what regulations were necessary. The various districts were called upon to choose delegates who were considered capable of giving the true sentiments of a majority of the people upon the introduction of slavery.

---

[46] "Journal of the Trustees," *Colonial Records,* I, 530, 531.
[47] *Ibid,* I, 530.
[48] "Journal of the Trustees," *Colonial Records,* I, 530–533.
[49] *Ibid,* I, 531–532.

Mr. Martyn stated the regulations which the Trustees had adopted in regard to the admission of negroes. The substance of these regulations was as follows:

1. That on account of the colony's exposed and frontier condition a negro owner must keep for every four male negroes above the age of fourteen one white male servant between twenty and twenty-five years of age;

2. No negro was to be hired as an apprentice, but they were to be used in cultivating the plantations of the province;

3. Owners of negroes should not have unlimited power over them, and inhuman treatment was not to be allowed;

4. All negroes (born, sold, or imported into Georgia) must be registered;

5. Quarantines must be established at proper places to prevent the spread of contagious diseases;

6. Negroes were not to be permitted to work on the Sabbath but they were to be instructed in the christian religion; inter-marriage between races was prohibited;

7. Since silk raising was to be the leading industry, each slave owner must for every four male negroes keep one female negro skilled in the art of winding silk; every hundred acres of land must have one thousand mulberry trees, and a like proportion must be made for smaller grants;

8. An import duty was to be laid on negroes, and an annual per capita tax thereafter.[50]

These regulations were nearly identical with those proposed from Savannah, and they were the restrictions under which slavery was finally permitted. They were included in the act which repealed the prohibitory act of 1735 and which allowed the introduction of negroes under certain restrictions.[51]

According to Mr. Martyn's suggestion, a convention was held in Savannah to decide what restrictions the colonists would agree to adopt in regard to the importation of negroes.

[50] British Public Records Office, Georgia Board of Trade, X, Quoted by, Charles C. Jones, *History of Georgia*, I, 422–425.
[51] "By-Laws and Laws," *Colonial Records*, I, 56–62.

Major Horton of Frederica presided over the convention. Resolutions were passed stating upon what conditions the colonists would like to have slaves among them. On October 26, 1749, they signed the representation which had been drawn up, and urged that under the limitations mentioned, slavery should be immediately allowed in the province. This document, signed by President Stephens and the members of the convention, was forwarded at the earliest opportunity to the Trustees who approved it with a few modifications and additions.[52]   It was referred by the Trustees to a committee which was to prepare an act to be presented to the king which would permit the importation and use of negroes in the province..[53]   This committee drew up the act entitled: "An Act for repealing an Act Intituled (An Act for rendering the Colony of Georgia more defensible by prohibiting the Importation and Use of Black Slaves or Negroes into the same) & for permitting the Importation and Use of them in the Colony under proper Restrictions and Regulations, and for other Purposes therein mentioned."[54]   This act received the royal signature and formally became a law on August 8, 1750.[55] The colony was now placed on the same footing with regard to negroes as the other colonies.   The anti-slavery restriction was removed and slavery became a recognized institution in Georgia after 1750.

The Trustees were beaten.   After having prevented the introduction of negroes for a period of eighteen years, the benevolent Trustees were finally made to realize that resistance was no longer a virtue.   Their own officials had been in sympathy with the enemies of the board.   All the other colonies were slave holding.   A large number of the colonists of Georgia had opposed and defied the laws. Oglethorpe was no longer in Georgia to lend a hand in enforcing the laws.   Parliament had refused appropriations

[52] "Minutes of the Common Council of the Trustees," *Colonial Records*, II, 504–505.
[53] *Ibid*, II, 504.
[54] "By-Laws and Laws," *Colonial Records*, I, 56.
[55] *Ibid*, I, 62.

chiefly because of the non-admission of negroes. New England merchants were busy plying the slave trade between Africa and the colonies. We wonder that the Trustees held out so long. Thus the Trustees, at the end of their administration, found themselves compelled to abandon their most cherished ideal—the prohibition of negroes in Georgia. The philanthropic Trustees had sought to impose upon the colony a code of morals higher than the colonists wished. The economic advantages of slavery out weighed the political, moral, and economic objections of the founders. Thus Georgia, after a struggle of eighteen years (1732–1750), acquired the right, long enjoyed by her sister colonies, of owning and using negro slaves. The founders of Georgia had sought to make that province unlike its neighbors, but they were thwarted by the dictates of geography. The most industrious settlers in Georgia were entirely opposed to the introduction of slavery into the colony, but they were overruled by the discontented element who were in the majority. This element finally convinced the Trustees of the necessity of admitting negroes. Thus Georgia surrendered her position as a free colony—a distinction to which no other English-American colony could aspire.

CHAPTER IV

OPINIONS OF GEORGIA LEADERS

In the preceding chapters it has been shown that Georgia was founded as a free colony; that according to the early law of 1735 slavery was excluded; that as the colony grew and conditions changed the colonists began to demand negroes; that many representations were sent to the Trustees petitioning for the admission of negroes; that the Trustees were persistent in their opposition but reluctantly yielded; and that the restriction was finally removed in 1750. Before considering the new conditions and problems that arose as a result of the admission of negroes, it will be advisable to consider here the various opinions of the leaders of Georgia at that time.

Oglethorpe, "the father of Georgia," was opposed to slavery and, although he finally agreed to the removal of the restriction, he never changed his opinion in that regard. Oglethorpe was the leader in the founding of Georgia; he lived to see it flourish and become of consequence to the commerce of Great Britain; he saw it in a state of resistance and at length independent of the mother country; and he lived to see it as an independent state and of great importance in its quarter of the globe. A careful perusal of Oglethorpe's letters to the Trustees and others shows his determined persistance in opposing the introduction of negro slavery into Georgia. He opposed slavery from the very beginning. By his stubborn persistance he succeeded in keeping it out for a period of eighteen years until his wishes were finally overruled by both the colonists and the home government. In a letter written from Savannah on March 12, 1739, he warns the Trustees against the introduction of negroes.[1] Later in a letter to the Trustees, dated June 29, 1741, he accused the Spaniards of stirring up discontent among the people; he stated that if negroes were admitted they would become friends to the Spaniards. He continues: "The way to overcome all this is to persist in allowing no slaves.[2] Oglethorpe declared openly in the court-house of Savannah that as long as he had anything to do with the colony there should be no allowance of negroes, and that if such a thing should happen he would have no further concern with it.[3] In the Journal of the Earl of Egmont for January 17, 1739, we find the following entry:

> Col. Oglethorpe wrote again to the Trustees, to show further inconveniences arising from the allowing the use of Negroes, viz.
>
> 1. That it is against the principles by which the Trustees associated together, which was to relieve the distressed, whereas we should occasion the misery of thousands in Africa, by setting Men upon using arts to buy and bring into perpetual slavery the poor people, who now live free there.
>
> 2. Instead of strengthening, we should weaken the Frontiers of America.
>
> 3. Give away to the Owners of slaves that land which was design'd as a Refuge to persecuted Protestants.
>
> 4. Prevent all improvements of silk and wine.
>
> 5. And glut the Markets with more of the American Commodities, which do already but too much interfere with the English produce.[4]

This letter shows that Oglethorpe was actuated by humanitarian as well as by political and economic motives in his opposition to negroes. And yet we find that even Oglethorpe owned a plantation and negroes in South Carolina, about forty miles from Savannah.[5] He was also

---

[1] "General Oglethorpe to the Trustees," *Georgia Historical Collections*, III, 70–71.
[2] *Ibid*, III, 117.
[3] Patrick Tailfer, Hugh Anderson, David Douglas, and Others, *Ibid*, II, 215.
[4] "Journal of the Earl of Egmont," *Colonial Records*, V, 95–96.
[5] "Stephens' Journal," *Colonial Records*, Supplement to Volume IV, 201.

Deputy Governor of the Royal African Company which
had the sole right of planting forts and trading on the coast
of Africa.[6]   Since the slave trade would have benefited
him economically, his humanitarian motives must have
been predominant in his opposition to negroes in Georgia.
Oglethorpe stated that slavery was against the gospel,
and the fundamental law of England, and that the Trustees
refused to make a law permitting such a horrid crime.[7]
Instead of allowing negroes, Oglethorpe urged the Trust
to encourage the further importation of Germans and married recruits.[8]

Further proof of Oglethorpe's humanitarian motives in
his opposition to slavery is given in the story of the negro,
Job.   This young African prince, Job Ben Solomon of
Gambia, had been sold by his enemies to an African slave
trader.   He was brought to America and sold into slavery
in Maryland.   Job could not speak the English language
and he found it hard to adjust himself to his new conditions
and surroundings.   Finally he decided to run away.   Having
no passport he was intercepted, placed in prison, and then
returned to his former master.   Slavery in any form was
intolerable to Job.   He wrote a letter in Arabic to his
father, stating all his circumstances.   The letter was to be
sent to Africa through London; it was ultimately laid before
General Oglethorpe, the deputy governor of the Royal
African Company.   Oglethorpe sent the letter to Oxford
to be translated and thus he became acquainted with the
story of the captivity of the native African prince.   Consequently, the benevolent Oglethorpe undertook the ransom
of Job.   The negro was brought to England where he lived
in state for a whole year; then he was loaded with gifts
and was finally returned to his home as a free man in 1734.[9]

---

[6] William Bacon Stevens, *History of Georgia*, I, 287.
[7] *The African Repository* (Washington, 1826), II, 104–105; George Bancroft,
    History of the United States, II, 287; Henry Bruce, *Life of General Ogle-
    thorpe*, 99.
[8] "Journal of the Earl of Egmont," *Colonial Records*, V, 522–523.
[9] Henry Bruce, *Life of General Oglethorpe*, 132–138; Ulrich Bonnell Phillips,
    American Negro Slavery (New York, 1918), 31–32.

Job was sent back to his homeland under British escort
in a Royal African Ship with credentials requiring the governor and other officials to show him every respect. This
incident shows that the humanitarianism of Oglethorpe
was not confined to members of his own race; his interest
in this individual case may have directed his attention more
particularly to the subject of slavery and intensified the
objections to it which he already felt. At any rate he continued his refusal to alter the laws prohibiting slavery in the
colony.

Oglethorpe continued to oppose every petition for negroes.
His views in regard to the petition of 1738 and the counter-
petitions were embodied in his letter to the Trustees, March
12, 1739.[10] He accused Mr. Williams, a merchant who was
dealing in negro traffic, of persuading the poor people of
Savannah, many of whom were deeply in debt to him,
to sign the petition for negroes. He stated that the assertion of the need of negroes and the disability of white
people to work in Georgia could be disproved by hundreds
of witnesses, by all Salzburgers, by the people of Darien,
by many at Frederica and Savannah, and by all in the
province who were industriously inclined. "The idle
ones," he adds "are indeed for Negroes. If the Petition
is countenanced, the Province is ruined."[11] He continued,
"Mr Williams and Doctor Talfeur will buy most of the
Lands at Savannah with Debts due to them and the Inhabitants must go off and be succeeded by Negroes. Yet
the very debtors have been weak enough to sign their
Desire of Leave to sell."[12] In a letter of July 16, 1739
Oglethorpe again refers to the subject in the following
manner:

> There is one Tailfeur an Apothecary Surgeon who gives
> Physick and one Williams of whom I wrote to you formerly,
> a Merchant who quitted planting to sell rum. To these two,

---

[10] "General Oglethorpe to the Trustees," *Georgia Historical Collections*, III,
70–71.
[11] *Ibid*, III, 71.
[12] *Ibid*.

almost all the Town is in debt for Physick & Rum and they
have raised a strong spirit to desire that Lands may be
alienable and then they would take the Lands for the Debts,
monopolize the Country and settle it with Negroes. They
have a vast deal of Art and if they think they cannot carry
this, they would apply for any other alteration since they
hope thereby to bring confusion and you cannot imagine
how much uneasiness I have had here. I hope therefore
you will make no alterations. [13]

The fact that Oglethorpe was bitterly opposed to the
institution of slavery is shown by a letter written long after
his active association with the colony had ceased—after
the American Revolution had begun and the Declaration
of Independence had been signed. In a letter to Granville
Sharp, dated October 13, 1776, he says:

My friends and I settled the colony of Georgia, and by
charter were established trustees, to make laws, &c. *We
determined not to suffer slavery there.* But the slave merchants
and their adherents occasioned us not only much trouble,
but at last got the then government to favor them. *We
would not suffer slavery, (which is against the Gospel, as well as
the fundamental law of England,) to be authorized under our
authority; we refused, as trustees, to make a law permitting
such a horrid crime.* The government, finding the Trustees
resolved firmly not to concur with what they believed un-
just, took away the charter by which no law could be passed
without our consent. [14]

And further on in the same letter Oglethorpe says:

You mention an argument urged by Hume, that the Africans
were incapable of liberty, and that no man capable of government was ever produced by Africa. What a historian!
He must never have heard of Shishak, the great Sesostris,
of Hannibal, or of Tirhaka, king of Ethiopia, whose very
name frightened the mighty Assyrian monarch, (2 Kings,
XIX, 9.) Is it possible he never should have seen Herodotus,
where the mighty works of the Pyramids, remaining to this

---

[13] *Ibid,* III, 79–80.
[14] *The African Repository,* II, 104–105.

day, are mentioned; and in ——the answer of the king of Ethiopia to Cambyses. In Leo the African's geographical description of Africa, he would have found that Africa had produced a race of heroes. [15]

Evidently Oglethorpe had faith in the negro and his capacity for liberty. He did not look upon him as an inferior being who was incapable of acquiring for himself a high degree of civilization.

Granville Sharp, in his reply to the above letter, commended Oglethorpe for the decided stand he had assumed against slavery. Oglethorpe had confided his anti-slavery sentiments to his friend; in return Sharp expressed his appreciation of the confidence placed in him. The views of the two men were similar in respect to slavery.

> The noble principles on which that undertaking (the founding of Georgia) was at first set on foot, and your own truly disinterested and prudent conduct in establishing, as well as your brave and successful behavior in defending it, form altogether a most instructive and exemplary piece of history for the imitation of the present and future ages; and as example and practice are infinitely superior to theory and precepts, you certainly enjoy the heartfelt satisfaction, of having really practiced and set forth in a conspicuous active life, those disinterested principles and duties, which, in my humble station, I have only been able to recommend in theory. [16]

Bolzius and Gronau, ministers at Ebenezer, were very much opposed to slavery. They had a powerful influence over their congregations and wielded it in favor of the Trustees' policy. They were the leaders in drawing up the anti-slavery petition of 1739. The Reverend Mr. Bolzius was uniform in his opposition to the principles of slavery. He expressed his fears that idleness and dissipation would grow out of the change to the destruction of the people's morals. His many letters express his opposition to the introduction of negroes. Indeed his final yielding seems

---

[15] *Ibid*, II, 105.
[16] *Ibid*, II, 106–107.

to have resulted from the apprehension of civil war rather than from any conviction which had changed his opinion in regard to the justice or propriety of the measure. He eventually yielded because affairs were in "such a melancholy state." [17]

The opposition of Bolzius to negroes and his influence over the Salzburgers brought upon him much criticism and many insults from the inhabitants of Savannah who were so enthusiastic in their desire for negroes. The pro-slavery party placed upon him the charge that through his tyrannical influence the Salzburgers were prevented from signing the petition for negroes. He was accused of exercising a spiritual tyranny over a people who were unacquainted with the privilege of choosing for themselves. [18] John Speilbeigler of Ebenezer said:

> That the inhabitants in general of the said Ebenezer, have often said to him, that they wanted and would be glad of negroes, because they found that they were unable to raise provisions for their support by their own labor. That the said inhabitants were called together by the said Bolzius to sign their petition, dated March 13, 1739, and that they, or many of them, would not have signed it had they not been compelled to do it by the said Bolzius, as they after told this deponent, and repenting their signing it, did several of them leave the colony as this deponent believes the rest would do, were they able; for they were very uneasy under the arbitrary government of the said Bolzius, who judges in all causes, gives to and takes from whom he pleases, the said inhabitants being deprived the benefits of any courts of judicature, or magistrates, having no such among them, except the said Bolzius, who takes upon him to act as king, priest and prophet . . . . [19]

Three Salzburgers (Ortman, Riser, and Bicker) made oath October 20, 1741, that they and most of their people

---

[17] "Letter from the Rev. Mr. John Martin Bolzius to Mr. Verelst," *Colonial Records,* XXV, 289.
[18] "A Brief Account of the Causes That Have Retarded the Progress of the Colony of Georgia in America," *Georgia Historical Collections,* II, 93.
[19] *Ibid,* II, 122.

desired negroes but feared Bolzius too much to sign the negro petition. They concluded:

> And further, that the inhabitants in general of the said Ebenezer, are desirous of negroes. That they were called together to sign their said petition, and many of them have been heard by us to say, that they would not have done it, but that our minister would have been angry with them, if they had refused to do so. That they would yet sign a petition for negroes, were it not that Mr. Bolzius, our minister, who exercises an arbitrary power over us, might make them very uneasy.[20]

Bolzius thus received the blame for the refusal of the Salzburgers to sign the petition of 1738 for negroes. The subscribers appointed some of the Salzburgers to wait upon him and to present the representation to him. This was done. Mr. Bolzius agreed to consult his people and to bring their answer; this he never did. Later, when he was questioned in the presence of others, he stated that Oglethorpe had given him satisfaction and had engaged him to write home to Germany for a further supply of his countrymen.[21] The insults heaped upon Mr. Bolzius increased, but his firm opposition to the introduction of negroes continued. Writing of this in 1747 to his friend Van Munch at Augsburg he says:

> I am still of the same Sentiments that the Introduction of Negroes will not be a means to make the Colonie flourish or the Inhabitants happy: if at any Time Leave should be given for it, or Liberty to buy or sell the Land, as every one pleaseth, surely the prerogatives which this Colonie is blessed with before South and North Carolina, and more particularly Savannah before Charles-Town, will draw numbers of Merchants from thence hither, which will buy the best Districts of Land imploy Negroes in all necessary Worck and refuse to pay a greater price to the White People for their Labor than to Negroes, by which they can't possibly subsist or maintain themselves, but will be forced to leave the Colonie,

---

[20] *Ibid*, II, 123.
[21] Patrick Tailfer, Hugh Anderson, David Douglas and Others, *Ibid*, II, 222.

not to mention the great Danger of Life, nor the Robberies of Fields and Orchards; that must be expected from those savage and hungry Creatures.[22]

On August 29, 1747, Bolzius wrote to Benjamin Martyn and complained of the many reproaches heaped upon him only on account of his dutiful attachment to the Trustees and their wise scheme. The wrath of the people was so kindled against him that they called him "The Fountain of all Evils" because of his attempt to carry out the prohibition of negroes. He continued:

> They curse me in a very scandalous manner, and threaten to do me a mischief, if it was in their power. I can appeal to God & my conscience, that I aime by my preaching, prayers, Labours & writing to our dear Benefactors in England & Germany at nothing else, but at the sincere promoting of the Prosperity of our Settlement, nay if possible of this whole Province by using all possible honest means for bringing their wise Scheme into execution, Viz. to make this Colony not a harbour of black Slaves, but an Asylum for poor Distressed & Labouring Protestants of any denomination, for which, as I am told, it was intended from the very first beginning.[23]

In this same letter Mr. Bolzius contradicted the statements which had been made accusing him of thwarting the desire of the Salzburgers for negroes. He even employed a Mr. Meyer to speak to the Salzburgers and to urge them to speak frankly.[24]

Bolzius then stated that he was assured by Mr. Meyer that there was not a man in Ebenezer who did not show his abhorrence for negroes. Bolzius said that, although the Salzburgers were almost without exception opposed to negroes, yet if their benefactors, the Trustees, thought it necessary for the prosperity of the colony to introduce negroes, from gratitude to them, "We & our friends in

---

[22] "Letter from the Rev. Mr. Bolzius to Mr. Van Munch," *Colonial Records,* XXV, 168.
[23] "Letter from Mr. Bolzius to Mr. Martyn," *Ibid,* XXV, 200–201.
[24] *Ibid,* 203–204.

Germany will say not a word against it, but rely intirely [sic] upon God's & their Honours favours being in confidence, that merciful God will protect & bless us notwithstanding."[25]

Bolzius said in a letter to Mr. Verelst, dated August 29, 1747, that the calumniators had charged every sort of wickedness upon him. Even the Trustees' kind mention of him in their letters to Georgia had acted like "emetictartar in some people's stomach." He had even been styled "A Mercinary slave of the Georgian Trustees."[26] He begged, therefore, that the Trustees would make no mention of him or of the Salzburgers in their letters to the Savannah officials.

John Dobell, who had been of great service in Georgia but later returned to England, was opposed to the introduction of negroes. In one of his letters, written from Charles-Town in 1748, he condemned the officials in Georgia because of their lack of sympathy with the schemes of the Trustees. He said that they were men of opposite sentiments to the cause which they were supposed to support; that they were unpeopling Georgia; and that the colony would perish unless the Trustees interposed. He said also that sufficient proofs existed to show that white people were able to live prosperously without the use of negroes. He gave as instances of this, the towns of Orangeburgh, a German township, and Williamsburgh, an Irish township.[27] In this letter was enclosed a copy of a letter from Mr. Bolzius who stated that he was resolved to suffer any kind of hardships, revilings, and reproaches, in order to oppose the introduction of negroes. "I am in Christ's Name resolved rather to suffer hardships heinous reflectings revilings reproaches and I don't know what else than lend the least finger to promote the Introduction of Black

---

[25] *Ibid*, XXV, 205.
[26] "Letter from Mr. Bolzius to Mr. Verelst," *Colonial Records*, XXV, 210.
[27] "Letter from Mr. John Dobell," *Ibid*, XXV, 281.

Slaves to the apparent destruction of our Well Situated and Fertile Province. . . . [28]

But if the Salzburgers, led by their faithful pastors, so steadily opposed the introduction of negroes, they were not seconded by the English or Scotch clergy so far as we know. These latter seem either to have joined with the Trustees' enemies, or to have kept quiet in the controversy. The Scotch minister, John McLeod of Darien, favored the admission of negroes. Although the majority of the people of Darien were decidedly opposed to slavery and had signed the counter-petition against their importation in January, 1739, there was a minority, led by McLeod, who desired slaves. He stated that the people of Darien desired negroes in spite of the counter-petition of 1739. An affidavit of his, made on November 12, 1741, declared that the Darien people desired negroes but were cajoled into signing the counter-petition. They were virtually prisoners held in the colony and unable to leave, though desirous of doing so. He declared that the petition against negroes was written by a non-resident of Darien, an officer in Oglethorpe's regiment, who had been sent to Darien for that purpose.[29]

John and Charles Wesley came to Georgia in 1736, but neither remained as long as two years. John Wesley, after his return to England, pondered deeply on the cruelty of slavery as he had seen it in America. He characterized the slave trade as "that execrable sum of all villainies." The Journal of John Wesley while in Georgia frequently alludes to slaves. His chief interest seemed to have been in the spiritual salvation of the negro. He pictured the cruelty toward the slaves and the inhumaneness of the institution. In regard to slavery he said: "Alas for those whose lives were here viley cast away through oppression,

---

[28] "Letter from Mr. John Martin Bolzius to Mr. John Dobell," *Ibid*, XXV, 283.
[29] "A Brief Account of the Causes That Have Retarded the Progress of the Colony of Georgia in America," *Georgia Historical Collections*, II, Appendix IV, 113–114.

through divers plagues and troubles! O earth! how long wilt thou hide their blood! How long wilt thou cover thy slain?"[30] In his pamphlet entitled *Thoughts on Slavery*, John Wesley denounced the practice in unmeasured terms; it was a stirring appeal to the justice and humanity of England and the colonies. In his tract he combated the institution with earnestness and experience. He made the slave holders appear pitiful and mean. He compared them to the champions of liberty. He characterized slavery as "the worst that ever saw the sun; it is the sum of all villainies."[31]

The celebrated Whitefield did not hesitate to express himself in favor of negro slaves for Georgia. He upheld slavery on the ground that it was the Christian duty to bring the slave of a heathen master in Africa to America and to place him under the influence of a Christian Master. He believed that slavery was an ordinance of God designed for the eventual good of the African. He also had an eye to the economic advantage to the colonist and he argued earnestly that slavery might be permitted in Georgia.[32] One cause of divergence between Whitefield and Wesley was the attitude assumed by the former in regard to slavery. Wesley could not understand Whitefield's part in the campaign to introduce negro slavery into Georgia. "All that might be said about the slaves being brought to salvation did not mitigate their being brought also to a condition too similar to that of beasts of burden."[33]

Whitefield's opinions on slavery involved him in arguments with Bolzius who assumed the opposite position. A verbal slavery and anti-slavery combat took place between the two men. A letter from Bolzius to Whitefield, dated December 24, 1745, contains a summary of the latter's arguments in favor of the introduction of negroes: (1)

---

[30] *Journal of the Reverend John Wesley* (London, 1788), I, 48.
[31] John Wesley, *Thoughts on Slavery*, (Pamphlet, 1774), 22–23. For further discussion of Wesley's views, see Appendix I.
[32] James Ford Rhodes, *History of the United States*, I, 5.
[33] John Donald Wade, *John Wesley* (New York, 1930), 104.

the Providence of God appointed the colony of Georgia for the work of black slaves because of the excessive heat of the climate; (2) the Trustees had already spent 250,000 pounds sterling for establishing the colony, and this would be to no purpose unless negroes were introduced; (3) it was impossible to continue the orphanage of Bethesda without negroes; (4) it would be a means of bringing the negroes to a knowledge of Christ. Bolzius, the author of the letter, refutes each of Whitefield's arguments and upholds his own position in opposition to slavery. He said: (1) that if the weather was too hot in the summer months, the white man could choose the morning and afternoon hours for laboring in the field (this was the method practiced in Ebenezer and had proved very successful); (2) the colony was not a failure and a single letter would bring over enough Germans to settle the colony; (3) it was better to give up the orphan house than to drive the poor out of the colony; and (4) that if a minister had a call to bring negroes to a knowledge of Christ, he had in Carolina a large field.[34] Bolzius charged Whitefield with harboring sentiments which were destructive to industry and morality. He invoked the vengeance of heaven against those who were instrumental in bringing a people under the yoke of slavery. No two people were more instrumental in prevailing upon the Trustees to permit Georgia the right, long enjoyed by her sister colonies, of owning and using negro slaves than the Reverend George Whitefield and the Honorable James Habersham. Whitefield asserted that the transportation of the African from his home of barbarism to a Christian land was advantageous. Habersham affirmed that the colony could not prosper without the intervention of slave labor.[35]

During Whitefield's stay in Georgia he interested himself deeply in the amelioration of the condition of the slaves. One of his first publications was a letter addressed to the

---

[34] "Letter from Bolzius to Whitefield," *Colonial Records*, XXIV, 434–442.
[35] Jones and Dutcher, *History of Augusta*, 35.

planters of Virginia, Maryland, and the Carolinas, on the
cruelties inflicted on their negro slaves. So successfully did
he advocate the interest of the negroes that he even (un-
consciously) persuaded a number of the planters to emancipate their slaves.[36] Whitefield himself owned a plantation
on which, at the time of his death, there were seventy-five
slaves. Extracts from one of Whitefield's letters in 1751
show his attitude toward slavery. He wrote:

> As for the lawfulness of keeping slaves I have no doubt.
> It is plain that hot countries cannot be cultivated without
> negroes. What a flourishing country Georgia might have
> been, had the use of them been permitted years ago . . .
> Though it is true they are brought in a wrong way from their
> own country, and it is a trade not to be approved of, yet
> as it will be carried on whether we will or not, I should think
> myself highly favored if I could purchase a good number of
> them in order to make their lives comfortable, and lay a
> foundation for breeding up their posterity in the nurture
> and admonition of the Lord. I had no hand in bringing
> them into Georgia, though my judgement was for it.[37]

Lieutenant Horton of Frederica, a military leader who
did great service in Georgia, was opposed to slavery. He
said to the Earl of Egmont on May 9, 1740, that if negroes
were introduced it would be the absolute ruin of the colony
and that the people were all sensible of it.[38] He added later
that he believed that the colony would be endangered
by employing negroes and that industrious people could
live comfortably without them, but could not grow rich.[39]
The inhabitants of Frederica prepared a petition against
negroes and gave it to Lieutenant Horton. He, however,
advised them to drop it as entirely unnecessary since there
was a law against the importation of negroes which he
was sure the Trustees would not repeal.[40] When Thomas

---

[36] J. S. Buckingham, *The Slave States of America* (London, 1842), I, 107.
[37] Tyerman, *Life and Times of John Wesley*, quoted by James Ford Rhodes,
    History of the United States, I, 5.
[38] "Journal of the Earl of Egmont," *Colonial Records*, V, 348.
[39] *Ibid*, V, 381.
[40] *Ibid*, V, 348.

Christie signed his lease for two hundred acres in Georgia, he said (on that occasion) that there would be no security to the province if negroes were allowed while Augustine remained in the hands of the Spaniards.[41]   Mr. Kenneth Baillie, who had escaped to England after his capture by the Spanish at Fort Moosa, expressed the same opinion but added that if St. Augustine should be taken, negroes would be necessary because of the inability of the white man to endure the heat.[42]

But the Earl of Egmont, member of Parliament and first president of "The Trustees for establishing the Colony of Georgia in America" opposed slavery to the utmost.   In a letter from Colonel William Byrd II to the Earl of Egmont, dated July 12, 1736, Colonel Byrd commends the Earl for his stand on slavery.   "Your Lord's Opinion concerning Rum and Negroes is certainly very just, and your excludeing both of them from your Colony of Georgia will be very happy . . . . "[43]   In the letter to the Earl of Egmont from Colonel Byrd mentioned above, the latter expresses himself in entire agreement with the Earl's attitude concerning slavery.   This attitude may be summed up as:

> I am sensible of many bad consequences of multiplying these Ethiopians amongst us.   They blow up the pride, and ruin the Industry of our White People, who seeing a Rank of poor Creatures below them, detest work for fear it should make them look like Slaves.   Then that poverty which will ever attend upon Idleness, disposes them as much to pilfer as it dos [sic] the Portuguese, who account it much more like a Gentleman to steal, than to dirty their hands with Labour of any kind.
>
> Another unhappy Effect of Many Negroes is the necessity of being severe.   Numbers make them insolent, and then foul Means must do what fair will not.   We have however nothing like the Inhumanity here that is practiced in the Islands, and God forbid we ever should.   But these base

---

[41] *Ibid*, V, 464.
[42] *Ibid*, V, 605–606.
[43] "Colonel Byrd to the Earl of Egmont," *American Historical Review*, I, 88.

Tempters require to be rid with a tort Rein, or they will be apt to throw their Rider. Yet even this is terrible to a good natured Man, who must submit to be either a Fool or a Fury. And this will be more our unhappy case the more Negroes are increast amongst us.[44]

In a conference with Thomas Stephens on February 2, 1740, the Earl of Egmont quotes himself as saying:

I reply'd that Negroes would never be allow'd for we wanted them not for the works & produces we intended to carry on & raise, Besides our nearness to the Spaniards would endanger the throats of all white men to be cut by Negroes, especially now that the Spaniards give protection to Runaway Negroes. That Col. Stephens his father, on whose wisdom the Trustees greatly relyed, had over & over in his letters expressed his aversion to Negroes, and certainly if they had rose lately in Carolina & kill'd 34 white men (for which 50 of them were put to death) there could be nothing more dangerous than to allow them in our Colony, so thinly inhabited and so near to Augustine as it is.[45]

In continuing the argument the Earl adds that the poor inhabitants of Georgia would not be able to afford negroes, that they might become debtors to the negro merchants for them, that the land would fall into hands of a few rich men, and that Georgia would cease to be a barrier province.[46] On January 8, 1742, the Earl adds that the Trustees will not petition the king for negroes.[47] He gave as his reasons the fact that Georgia lay so near to the Spaniards who had proclaimed liberty and protection and had promised lands to all negroes who would escape to them, that several parts of the colony had petitioned against negroes, that they were desired only by the idle settlers, and that it would defeat the military purpose in making Georgia a frontier province. But he adds: "That for the rest, we had no Interest in denying the people Negroes, and if

[44] *Ibid*, I, 89.
[45] "Journal of the Earl of Egmont," *Colonial Records*, V, 303.
[46] *Ibid*, V, 304.
[47] *Ibid*, V, 583–584.

the Parliament or his Majesty thought them necessary, and would take that hazard upon them, we should be satisfied."[48] When members of Parliament refused appropriations to Georgia until negroes should be admitted, the Earl of Egmont, persistent in his opposition to slavery and refusing to be appeased, became disgusted. Accordingly he tendered his resignation on July 7, 1742.[49]

John Mohr McIntosh of New Inverness opposed slavery. He was the first to sign the counter-petition of January, 1739, which opposed the introduction of slavery.[50] He and the Reverend John Martin Bolzius were the leaders of the losing party—those who upheld the policy of the Trustees and **opp**osed slavery. They wrote, signed, and published the first protest against the use of African slaves issued in the history of the New World.[51]

Mr. Thomas Spalding of McIntosh County (born in 1774) opposed slavery. He had pondered deeply upon the dangers to the Union as threatened by the institution. He was a slave holder by inheritance, but he was keenly aware of the evils foretold by his grandfather. He watched the growth of the new free states. He interested himself in the amelioration of the conditions of slavery and in awaiting events. When a member of the state legislature he introduced and pressed the enactment of a law which would prevent the slave from being removed from the estate on which he was born through any process of sale. In that way he hoped to prevent the separation of families.[52] He strove to teach the principle of self-reliance to his slaves. He gave them the means, tools, and leisure in which to improve their houses or cottages. He had confidence in their loyalty. During the war of 1812 he applied to the governor for arms and received eighty muskets with which

---

[48] *Ibid,* V, 584.
[49] *Manuscripts of the Earl of Egmont,* III, 265.
[50] "Journal of the Trustees," *Colonial Records,* III, 427.
[51] Charles Spalding Wylly, *The Seed That Was Sown in the Colony of Georgia,* (New York, 1910), 34.
[52] *Ibid,* 51.

he armed and drilled his negro men.[53]   Mr. Spalding was
seventy-seven years of age when the Secession Convention
met in Milledgeville in 1850.   He was chosen president
of the convention, used his conservative influence in maintaining the union, and died on his return to his home.[54]

These early leaders of Georgia opposed slavery.   They
used their influence to uphold the policy of the Trustees
and to continue to prohibit the introduction of negroes
into the colony.   But the majority of the colonists demanded
negro slaves and were able to overcome the opposition
of the minority.   When slavery was finally introduced
these leaders calmly accepted the situation; they then
strove to uphold the regulations under which negroes were
to be introduced.   They accepted the evil, but strove to
limit the dangers to which the presence of negroes might
lead them.

---

[53] *Ibid*, 52.
[54] *Ibid*, 69.

CHAPTER V

GEORGIA UNDER THE SLAVE SYSTEM

In the preceding chapters has been told the result of the struggle between the spirit in which the colony of Georgia was founded and the inharmonious beliefs and desires of a majority of her citizens. Negro slavery was legally introduced in 1750. The Trustees resigned in 1752 feeling that they had failed in their scheme of government. The year 1752 brought a new era of government to Georgia. At first the province was placed under a provisional government, but in 1754 Georgia came under the direct control of the crown. A governor and council were appointed by royal commission. With the passing away of the restrictions regarding slavery and land tenure, there followed a period of renewed energy. The early regulations of the Trustees were not adapted to the circumstances of the colonists. Although these rules were made with the best of intentions, they were detrimental to the prosperity of the settlers, and they were hostile to the results desired by the benevolent founders.

When the Trustees were forced by the discontent of the people to allow slaves to be introduced, they felt that their original plans for the colony had failed. Furthermore interest in the colony had declined in England; gifts of money by private persons and charities had ceased; Parliament had failed to make the necessary appropriations; and many of the inhabitants had failed to exhibit the necessary exertions. After an experiment of nearly twenty years the Trustees found themselves incapable of longer supporting their charge.[1] The Trust would have ended in June, 1753,

---

[1] Charles C. Jones, *History of Georgia*, I, 468.

by the terms of the charter; but the Trustees resigned in June, 1752, feeling that they could be of no further use, and wishing to place on other shoulders the burden of managing the colony. Upon the surrender of the Trust, the Trustees offered several recommendations for the government of the province.[2] Thus the Trustees, at the end of their administration found themselves compelled to give up their views concerning slavery and government.

In 1752 Georgia became a royal province and passed under the direct control of the crown. The change in the tenure of land grants and the permission to hold slaves led to immediate prosperity in Georgia. New settlers came into the colony. Lands were cleared and cultivated. A flourishing export trade grew up with England and the West Indies. The population increased rapidly. The regulations under which negroes were admitted were not strictly carried out. July 19, 1750, President Stephens and his assistants reported: "By an exact List [sic] taken this Month it appears that there are in this Province three Hundred and Forty-Nine working Negroes, namely two Hundred and two Men, and one Hundred and Forty-Seven Women, besides children too young for Labour."[3] John Gerar William DeBrahm, in his contemporary account, comments on the immediate and rapid increase of negroes in Georgia.[4]

A new era of prosperity and security dawned for Georgia with the treaty of Paris in 1763. There was no longer any fear of French aggression. Florida was ceded to Great Britain, and there was no longer any fear of a jealous, intriguing neighbor on Georgia's southern frontier. There was no longer any fear of Spanish officials encouraging Georgia negroes to run away to Florida; the laws pertaining to negroes refugeeing to that province became null. The two provinces now had the same interests and acknowledged

[3] "Journal of the Trustees," *Colonial Records*, I, 513–515.
"Letter from William Stephens and Assistants to Benjamin Martyn," *Ibid*, XXVI, 22.
[4] John Jerar William Debrahm, *History of the Province of Georgia*, (Savannah. 1849), 50.

the same king. St. Augustine, so long the nightmare of the Southern colonies, was no longer a menace, but meekly accepted British rule. It was the treaty of Paris in 1763 that gave England the monopoly of the slave trade; any excess of supply was "dumped" on the colonies, so that the number of Africans imported to the colonies each year increased.

The introduction of negroes into the colony introduced an immense and ever increasing body of statutes into Georgia's code. One of the first ordinances passed by the new government was that of 1754 which provided that "all offenses committed by slaves were to be tried by a single justice without a jury, who was to award execution, and, in capital cases to set a value on the slave, to be paid out of the public treasury."[5]   The first enactment regulating the status of slaves in Georgia was approved by the crown in 1755 to be in force for three years. It was entitled: "An Act For the Better Ordering and Governing Negroes and other Slaves in this Province."[6]   This act was re-enacted in 1759 to extend to 1764.[7]   It was continued with some modifications by a law of 1765.[8]   The law of 1765 was further changed in some details in 1768.[9]   It was re-enacted with modifications in 1770.[10]   After Georgia became an independent state a somewhat lightened system of slave law was continued by state authority. The severity of these laws shows how dangerous slavery was considered to the peace of the colony.

The law of 1755 explained what persons were deemed slaves. All negroes, mulattoes, mestizoes, and other persons of color, except Indians in amity with the colony,

---

[5] John Codman Hurd, *The Law of Freedom and Bondage* (New York, 1858) I, 310.
[6] *Colonial Acts of Georgia,* 1755–1774 (Wormsloe Print, Savannah, 1881), 73–99.
[7] *Ibid,* 164; Robert and George Watkins, *Digest of the Laws of Georgia* (Philadelphia, 1800), 61; Hereafter referred to as Watkins *Digest.*
[8] Oliver H. Prince, *Digest of the Laws of Georgia to 1820* (Milledgeville, 1822), 441–444; Hereafter referred to as Prince, *Digest.*
[9] *Ibid,* 445.
[10] *Ibid,* 446–455.

"Who now are or shall hereafter be in this Province [sic] and all their Issue and Offspring Born or to be Born shall be and they are hereby declared to be and remain for ever hereafter absolute Slaves and shall follow the Condition of the Mother and shall be deemed in Law to be Chattels personal in the Hands of their Owners and possessors and their Executors Administrators and Assigns to all intents and purposes whatsoever."[11]   Slaves were considered as personal property subject to the will of the master. "Slaves shall be deemed, sold, taken, reputed and adjudged in law to be chattels personal in the hands of their owners and possessors, and their executors, administrators and assigns, to all intents, constructions and purposes whatsoever."[12] If any slave wished to sue for his freedom a guardian should be appointed for that purpose; the guardian of the slave could bring an action of trespass against the person in possession of the negro.[13]   If he failed to win his case in court the slave was to resume his servile condition.[14]   The fact that slaves were even allowed to sue for their freedom shows that slaves were being freed in Georgia and that the laws were upheld by public opinion.

South Carolina had had a great deal of trouble with slave insurrections, so that when slavery was allowed in Georgia the Assembly drew up rigid rules for the control of the negroes.   Slaves were not allowed to leave the plantation without a written permit from the owner.   If they were caught without such a permit they could be whipped. Slaves who refused to be examined by any white person should be corrected and, if they resisted, they could be lawfully killed.[15]   Any meeting of slaves which might prove dangerous to the peace and safety of the province could be dispersed.   By an act of 1770 slaves were forbidden

---

[11] *Colonial Acts of Georgia*, 74–75.
[12] Prince, *Digest*, 446.
[13] *Colonial Acts of Georgia*, 75.
[14] Prince, *Digest*, 446.
[15] *Colonial Acts of Georgia*, 75–76; Prince, *Digest*, 446–447; Thomas R. R. Cobb, *Digest of the Laws of the State of Georgia to 1851* (Athens, 1851), 785, 972.   Hereafter referred to as Cobb's, *Digest*.

to assemble on pretense of feasting; constables were commanded to disperse any assembly or meeting of slaves
which might disturb the peace or endanger the safety of
his Majesty's subjects; slaves found at such meetings were
to be immediately corrected or whipped.[16]   By an act of
1792, enacted to protect religious societies in the exercises
of their duties, it was required of every justice of the peace
to take into custody any person who should interrupt or
disturb a congregation of white persons and to impose a
fine on the offender; in default of payment the offender
could be imprisoned.   The same law prohibited any company of negroes, under pretense of divine worship, from
assembling contrary to the act regulating patrols.[17]   Justices
were authorized to search all suspected persons for arms,
ammunition, or stolen goods, and to apprehend any slaves
whom they might suspect of any crimes or offenses whatsoever.   Slaves were not allowed to buy, sell, or trade for
any goods without a license from the owner.   Slaves could
not be hired out except by the master.   Lest the master
should sometimes permit the slave to hire himself to another
for his own benefit, the state imposed a penalty of thirty
dollars for every weekly offense on the part of the master
unless the work was done on his own premises.[18]

Slaves who gave information of any design to poison were
to receive a reward of twenty shillings.   Slaves giving false
information were to be punished.   No slave was permitted to
administer medicine to a slave without the consent of the
owner.   Slaves were prohibited from carrying fire arms,
unless with the written consent of the owner of the slave.[19]
Under no circumstances could they have weapons between
Saturday evening and Monday morning.   Patrols were to
seize offensive weapons found in negro houses.[20]   The wilful
burning or destroying of a stack of corn, rice, or other grain,

---

[16] Prince, *Digest*, 447.
[17] *Ibid*, 342.
[18] *Ibid*, 453, 457.
[19] Prince, *Digest*, 447.
[20] *Ibid*, 445.

or setting fire to a tar kiln, or a barrel of pitch, tar, turpentine, or resin, was punishable by death. Death was also the penalty for killing a white person or for striking a white person,[21] (a second offense). It was provided: "If any slave shall presume to strike any white person, such slave, upon trial and conviction before the justice or justices, according to the directions of this Act, shall for the first offense suffer such punishment as the said justice or justices shall in his or their discretion think fit, not extending to life or limb; and for the second offense suffer Death."[22] Death was the penalty for attempting to raise an insurrection, or trying to persuade a fellow slave to run away.[23] Any person could apprehend a runaway slave and send him back to his master. If the master was unknown, the fugitive slave was to be sent to the constable of the precinct.[24] Fugitive slaves were to be maintained at the charge of the owners.[25] If a slave should harbor, conceal, or entertain another slave, being a runaway, he was subjected to corporal punishment, not affecting life and limb.[26] Slaves were not allowed to congregate in large numbers. Men slaves exceeding seven were not allowed to travel the highway without a white person.[27] It was lawful for any person who should see more than seven men slaves travelling on any road without a white person to apprehend such slaves, and to inflict a whipping upon each of them not exceeding twenty lashes apiece.[28] Slaves were subjected to severe punishment for other offenses. An Act of 1816 provided: "All other offenses committed by a slave or free person of colour, either against persons or property, or against another slave or person of colour, shall be punished at the discretion of the court, such court having in view the

---

[21] *Ibid*, 450–451.
[22] Prince, *Digest*, 450; Cobb's *Digest*, 976.
[23] *Colonial Acts of Georgia*, 81.
[24] *Ibid*, 85.
[25] Prince, *Digest*, 451.
[26] *Ibid*, 452.
[27] *Ibid*, 454–455.
[28] *Ibid*, 454.

principles of humanity in passing sentence; and in no case shall the same extend to life or limb."[29]

In addition to the laws of the state of Georgia there were local laws restricting slaves. In Athens, Georgia, no negroes were allowed to own a dog; negroes were forbidden to assemble on Sunday on porches or other public places; negroes were not allowed on the streets after nine o'clock at night without a pass; persons violating this latter act could be whipped or confined by the town marshal and the owner of the slave was to be whipped or fined one dollar or confined. Negroes were not allowed in a barroom at any time.[30]

A close patrol system was established as absolutely necessary for the safety of the province. The act of 1765 was called: "An Act for the establishing and regulating Patrols, and for preventing any Person from purchasing Provisions or any other commodities from, or selling such to any Slave, unless such Slave shall produce a Ticket from his or her Owner, Manager, or Employer."[31] The patrols were efficiently organized. Every commanding officer of a company militia was to divide his district into patrol divisions. Captains who failed to do this were to forfeit five pounds.[32] All males between the ages of sixteen and sixty were subject to patrol duty. Captains were to levy fines for misbehavior, for neglect of duty, and for disobedience. Every patrol was required to ride at least one night in fourteen, to correct slaves, to search for offensive weapons, and to apprehend fugitive slaves. The greatest caution was exercised to prevent insurrections or plots. Meetings of slaves were to be dispersed. At the same time it was provided that negroes whose fidelity had been tested and proved might be drilled and armed in case of invasion. Compensation was to be given to the slave owner if his slave should be killed or wounded in service. This act

---

[29] Cobb's *Digest*, 987.
[30] Augustus Longstreet Hull, *Annals of Athens, Georgia* (Athens, 1906), 128.
[31] Prince, *Digest*, 441–455; Watkins, *Digest*, 119–124.
[32] Prince, *Digest*, 441.

was amended and continued in 1768,[33] and again in 1770.[34]
The chief aim of the patrol system was to control the negroes
and to suppress any anticipated insurrections. The act
of 1770 was renewed in 1773.[35] In 1778 an act was passed
for the better regulating of the militia and for preventing
the dangerous consequences arising from an invasion.[36]
This act was continued and amended in 1781, 1784, 1786,
1787, and 1792.[37] Negro outbreaks in other states always
aroused Georgians and put them on guard. The following
appeared in an editorial in the Federal Union, Milledgeville, Georgia, on December 23, 1856:

> Patrols should sweep through every county in Georgia, be-
> tween this and New Year, and all assemblages of negroes be
> dispersed. The patrol system is an excellent one, and our
> friends in the country could see to it at once, that efficient
> bodies of men be dispatched through their neighborhoods
> to look after suspicious characters. Our city police should
> keep a strict watch upon the movements of the negroes
> during the Xmas holidays, and particularly at night, pro-
> vide against all assemblages of negroes. These precautionary
> steps are called for, by events that have lately transpired
> in neighboring and other Southern States, showing well
> concerted plans among the negroes in some localities, to
> rise in insurrection during Xmas. Forewarned is fore-
> armed.[38]

The slave laws contained many provisions for the pro
tection of the slave. Cruelty to the slaves was prohibited.
Any person found guilty of beating a slave without cause
was to pay a forfeit of six shillings sterling to the poor.[39]
If a slave was disabled from performing his work, the
offender had to pay two shillings sterling for each day of his
lost time, and also pay for the cure of such slave.[40] Per-

---

[33] Prince, *Digest*, 445; Watkins, *Digest*, 153–155.
[34] Watkins, *Digest*, 161.
[35] *Ibid*, 192.
[36] *Ibid*, 227.
[37] *Ibid*, 238, 299, 346, 363, 458–467.
[38] Ullrich Bonnell Phillips, *Plantation and Frontier Documents*, (Cleveland, 1909), II, 116.
[39] *Colonial Acts of Georgia*, 76–77.
[40] *Ibid*, 77.

sons who wilfully killed any slave were to be severely punished. If a person killed a slave in a sudden heat or passion, he was to forfeit fifty pounds sterling. Persons exercising any cruelty towards slaves were to forfeit the sum of ten pounds sterling.[41] It was illegal to work slaves on Sunday except in work of absolute necessity and domestic service.[42] An act of May 10, 1770, provided: "If any person shall on the Lord's day, commonly called Sunday, employ any slave in any work or labour, (Works of absolute necessity and the necessary occasions of the family only excepted,) every person so offending shall forfeit and pay the sum of ten shillings for every slave he, she or they shall so cause to work or labour."[43] As late as 1852 a bill was introduced into both Houses of the state legislature "to prohibit the owners, overseers, or employers of slaves in this State, from permitting said slaves to do unnecessary work on the Sabbath."[44] However, the bill was indefinitely postponed.

It was forbidden to sell whiskey or beer to a slave without the consent of the owner.[45] In 1852 a bill was introduced "to more effectually prevent the furnishing of intoxicating liquors to slaves."[46] The law provided that in case of the murder, malicious killing or maiming of a slave or free person of color the trial and punishment should be the same as if the victim had been a white person.[47] "Any person who shall maliciously dismember or deprive a slave of life, shall suffer such punishment as would be inflicted in case the like offense had been committed upon a free white person and on the like proof, except in case of insurrection of such slave, and unless such death should

---

[41] *Ibid*, 92.
[42] *Ibid*, 83.
[43] Prince, *Digest*, 455; Cobb's *Digest*, 981.
[44] *Journal of the House of Representatives*, 1851–52, 888–889. Hereafter referred to as *House Journal*.
[45] *Colonial Acts of Georgia*, 89.
[46] *House Journal*, 1851–52, 866.
[47] Horatio Marbury and William H. Crawford, *A Compilation of the Laws of Georgia, 1755–1800*, (Savannah, 1802), 443. Hereafter referred to as Marbury and Crawford, *Compilation*.

happen by accident in giving such slave moderate correction."[48] The unauthorized whipping or wounding of slaves or free persons of color was to be punished by a fine or by imprisonment.[49] According to an act of 1817, the excessive whipping or beating of a slave, the withholding of proper food and sustenance, the requiring greater labor from slaves than they were able to perform, the withholding of proper clothing whereby the health of the slave might be injured or impaired, or other like offenses were to be punishable by fines or imprisonment or both.[50]

Slaves might not be worked longer than sixteen hours per day. Offending persons had to pay a fine not exceeding three pounds sterling. Neglect on the part of the owner or employer to furnish a slave with sufficient clothing and food subjected the offender to a fine not exceeding three pounds sterling for each offense, the same, when collected, to be appropriated to the benefit of the poor of the district.[51] In cases of the trial of slaves, it was enacted that ordinary trials should be held before a justice of the peace, but cases involving capital punishment should be tried in the inferior county court. The right of trial by jury, with the privilege to the master of challenging seven persons on behalf of the slave, was expressly provided for.[52] There were laws guaranteeing protection and care to the old and infirm slaves. An act was passed in 1815 of a very novel character. This act placed upon the inferior courts of the state the duty of making inquiries into the situation of the slaves and, upon receiving information of any infirm slaves who were suffering from the neglect of the masters, to render such relief as was thought proper. The courts were authorized to sue and recover from the owners of the slaves the amount that was appropriated for relief.[53]

---

[48] Prince, *Digest*, 559; Cobb's *Digest*, 982.
[49] Prince, *Digest*, 376.
[50] *Ibid*, 376; Cobb's *Digest*, 827.
[51] *Colonial Acts of Georgia*, 93.
[52] Prince, *Digest*, 459.
[53] *Ibid*, 460; Cobb's *Digest*, 987.

The benefits of the education were withheld from the slave. Several statutes were enacted on that subject. In 1770 an act was passed which prohibited the instruction in reading and writing to slaves. Violations of this act were punishable by a fine of twenty pounds.[54] Negroes were prevented from being employed as handicraft tradesmen.[55] The employment of slaves as scribes was strictly prohibited.[56] In 1829 it was enacted that if any person should teach a slave to read or write, the slave should be punished by fine and whipping; the offending person who attempted to teach the slave was to be punished by fine not exceeding five hundred dollars and imprisonment.[57] It was also provided that: "If one free negro teach another, he is to be fined and whipped at the discretion of the court! Should a free negro presume to preach to, or exhort his companions, he may be seized without warrant, and whipped thirty-nine lashes, and the same number of lashes may be applied to each one of his congregation."[58] In 1833 it was further enacted that if any person should teach any slave, negro, or free person of color to read and write, or should procure, suffer, or permit any slave, negro, or person of color to transact business for him in writing, such person should be punished by fine or imprisonment or both.[59]

Besides the state laws the separate towns frequently passed ordinances on the subject. In 1818 an ordinance was passed by the city of Savannah which stated that any person who should engage himself to teach any person of color (slave or free) to read or write, or who should cause any such person to be so taught, was to be subjected to a fine of thirty dollars for each offense; and that every person of color who should keep a school in which reading or writing

---

[54] Cobb's *Digest*, 981; Prince, *Digest*, 445.
[55] *Colonial Acts of Georgia*, 149–152.
[56] *Ibid*, 94–95.
[57] Cobb's *Digest*, 1001.
[58] William Jay, *An Inquiry into the Character and Tendency of the American Colonization and American Anti-Slavery Societies*, (New York, 1835), 23. Cited hereafter as *Jay's Inquiry*.
[59] Cobb's *Digest*, 828.

was taught was to be subject to a fine of thirty dollars or to be imprisoned for ten days, and to be whipped thirty-nine lashes.[60] However, in Liberty County, Georgia, in the spring of 1831, there was formed a Society called "The Association for the Religious Instruction of the Negroes." This association did active work. It made an annual report of its activities. The association published thirteen of these annual reports, the last appearing in 1848. These documents testify to the concern felt by many southern planters for the spiritual welfare of the slaves.[61] This organization adopted wise measures, prosecuted them with zeal, and accomplished immediate results. Sabbath schools were organized for the negroes, plantation meetings were held, and a missionary was employed for preaching to the negroes on the Sabbath.[62] The missionary employed was the Reverend Charles C. Jones, father of the Georgia historian.

Strict laws were maintained for the regulation of the negroes. No one was permitted to have a plantation or settlement whereon slaves were worked without keeping a white person also on such plantation. Every owner of twenty slaves was required to retain a white servant capable of bearing arms. Owners of fifty slaves were compelled to have at least two white servants and an additional white servant for every twenty-five slaves.[63]

George M. Stroud, in his pamphlet entitled, "A Sketch of the Laws Relating to Slavery In the Several States of the United States of America" summarizes the laws in regard to the slaves as:

1. The master may determine the kind, degree, and time of labor to which the slave shall be subjected.

2. The master may supply the slave with such food and clothing as he may think proper or convenient.

---

[60] William Goodell, *The American Slave Code*, (New York, 1853), 321; Jay's *Inquiry*, 23.
[61] The ninth report of the association is found in the library of the University of Georgia.
[62] *The African Repository*, XVII, 117–122.
[63] *Colonial Acts of Georgia*, 95.

3. The master may, at his discretion, inflict punishment on the slave.

4. The master may place an agent or overseer over the slave.

5. Slaves have no legal right to property; such property as they may acquire belongs to the master.

6. The slave may be sold, mortgaged, or leased by the master.

7. The slave may be sold for debts of a living or deceased master.

8. A slave cannot be a party before a judicial tribunal.

9. Slaves cannot obtain, through themselves, a change of masters.

10. An owner may bring suit and recover damages for the injury of his slave.

11. Slaves can make no contract.

12. Slavery is hereditary and perpetual.

13. A slave cannot be a witness against a white person either in civil or criminal cases.

14. He cannot be a party to a civil suit.

15. The benefits of education are withheld from the slave.

16. The means for moral and religious instruction are not granted the slave.

17. Submission is required of the slave, not only to the will of the master, but to that of all other white persons.

18. The penal codes of the slave-holding states bear more severely upon slaves than upon white persons.

19. Slaves are prosecuted and tried by law upon criminal accusations.[64]

Such severe laws show a fear of the danger that might ensue because of the presence of slaves; the people realized that it might be unsafe to have too many negroes among them. It is this anxiety which explains the restrictions just mentioned, as well as the elaborate patrol system which was adopted. A lady in Georgia remarked that there was

[64] George M. Stroud, *A Sketch of the Laws Relating to Slavery in the Several States of the United States of America* (Philadelphia, 1856), 12–13, 44.

not a person on her plantation with whom she dared to
trust her life; and that she never retired at night without
an axe so near her pillow that she could lay her hands on it
immediately.[65] Such was the fear and distrust of the slaves.
There was constant fear in Georgia of slave insurrections,
although very few occurred, and a constant watch to prevent them. A letter from a Georgian to a friend in New
York, dated June 6, 1827, and printed in the New York
Enquirer, tells of an extensive and dangerous insurrection
of the blacks at Macon, Georgia. They had banded together to the number of three hundred, and were led by a
French immigrant from the Mississippi. Only one of the
rebels was arrested. All of the others, including the French-
man, made their escape.[66] The result of this insurrection
was to make the people of Georgia more prudent and more
careful in watching over the slaves.

Negroes were zealously watched and, if apprehended in
crime, were severely punished. In 1830 a great fire destroyed the largest hotel in Augusta. In investigating the
causes of the fire it was found to be the work of some of
the slaves belonging to the establishment. As a consequence
one slave woman was executed because of her supposed
complicity in a crime which involved the lives of so many
people.[67] This illustrates the fear the people had for the
negro. The harsh rules governing the slaves and the constant fear of an insurrection is plainly told by Charles Ball,
a negro, in narrating his adventures. He lived for forty
years in Maryland, South Carolina, and Georgia as a slave.
He gives an account of the manners and usages of the
planters and slaveholders of Georgia, a description of the
treatment of the slaves, observations upon the state of
morals among the cotton planters, and of the perils and
sufferings endured when he twice escaped from Georgia.[68]

---

[65] Emily P. Burke, *Reminiscences of Georgia*, (N. P. 1850), 156.
[66] *The African Repository*, III, 157.
[67] Albert Bushnell Hart, *Slavery and Abolition* (New York, 1906), 116; Buckingham, *The Slave States of America*, II, 47–50.
[68] Charles Ball, *Slavery in the United States: A Narrative of the Life and Adventures of Charles Ball, A Black Man* (Lewistown, Pa., 1836). Hereafter referred to as Ball's *Narrative*.

This condition of vague dread and unrest not only increased the severity of the laws and strengthened the patrol system, but it was one of the prime motives back of all the earlier efforts to check the further importation of slaves into Georgia.

The above mentioned laws, with certain modifications, were maintained not only during the existence of Georgia as a colony, but also until the failure of the Confederate struggle for independence brought about the liberation of the negroes from slavery. The negro population of Georgia has never been in excess of the white. Georgia became the native land of its dark as well as of its white inhabitants. The negro became a part of the master's family, priding himself upon its name and reputation. The slaves were Christianized. Most of them remained true and faithful to their masters. All through the Revolutionary war no records of any slave insurrections are found in Georgia. The negroes remained comparatively quiet and contented with their life on the plantations. The food raised by the negroes on the farm fed the soldiers in the armies and enabled them to win the war. Thus indirectly the negroes helped to overthrow the British government and to gain independence for the new nation. During the Revolution there was a tendency in all the states to enlist negroes in the armies and to grant them liberty in return for their service. In 1786 the legislature of Georgia emancipated two negroes because of their services in the Revolution.[69] Some leading patriots were in favor of more general enfranchisement for this purpose. In 1779 Congress recommended enlistments in South Carolina and Georgia and even offered compensation to the owners but it proved impossible to carry out the plan.[70]

When the pressure came for raising troops for the Revolution, negroes were freely enlisted, sometimes receiving freedom as their reward. Freedom was granted to the slave

---

[69] Watkins' *Digest*, 346.
[70] Mary Stoughton Locke, *Anti-Slavery in America*, (Boston, 1901), 83–84.

in case he would serve in his master's stead during the war. The most interesting case in this connection is that of Austin Dabney. Dabney, formerly a slave of a man named Aycock, was given his freedom in order that he might be his master's substitute in the Revolutionary war. The former slave was accordingly enrolled. In the Battle of Kettle Creek in Georgia, Austin Dabney was shot. He was found, carried home, and cared for by a man of the name of Harris. When Dabney recovered he worked for Harris and his children in gratitude to them. Dabney sent the oldest son to school, and afterwards to college, by the earnings of his own hands. When young Harris left college, Austin Dabney placed him in the office of Stephen Upson, then at the head of the legal profession in Upper Georgia. Through the influence of Stephen Upson, Dabney acquired land in Madison County. He received a pension from the United States government because of his services in the Revolution. When General James Jackson was governor of Georgia, Dabney was his guest at the Governor's mansion in Savannah.[71] We see in this instance how a slave was given his freedom and still maintained the highest respect of his white contemporaries because of his character and services.

The many laws in regard to the slaves seem unnecessarily harsh, but at that time they were deemed necessary in order to prevent the institution of slavery from becoming a menace. Laws were made for the control, protection, education, and regulation of the negroes. The harshness of the laws and the strict enforcement of them show the constant apprehension of the danger that might accrue to the whites because of the presence of the negroes among them.

---

[71] George R. Gilmer, *Sketches of Some of the First Settlers of Upper Georgia* (New York, 1855), 212–215.

CHAPTER VI

GEORGIA DURING THE PERIOD OF TRANSITION

During the period of the Revolution and the early years of the Republic, sentiment in the country in general was opposed to the institution of slavery. It was regarded as inconsistent with Christian civilization and with the principles of liberty for which the colonists had fought. Slavery was not a sectional issue during this period. On July 4, 1776, slavery existed in all of the American colonies that declared independence of Great Britain. The following table shows the slave population in 1776.[1]

1.	Massachusetts	3,500
2.	Rhode Island	4,373
3.	Connecticut	6,000
4.	New Hampshire	629
5.	New York	15,000
6.	Pennsylvania	10,000
7.	Delaware	9,000
8.	Maryland	80,000
9.	New Jersey	7,600
10.	Virginia	165,000
11.	North Carolina	75,000
12.	South Carolina	110,000
13.	Georgia	16,000
	Total	502,132

Such men as Washington, Jefferson, Monroe, Franklin, Hamilton, Madison, Jay, and Adams lamented the existence of slavery. There was a general regret that it had ever been planted in America, and it was hoped that it

---

[1] J. D. B. DeBow, *The Industrial Resources, etc., of the Southern and Western States* (New Orleans, 1853), III, 130.

would in time be abandoned. No effort was made to defend it as an ideal basis for the political and economic structure of society; at best it was considered a necessary evil.[2] The patriots of the Revolution made earnest efforts to carry out the principles of freedom and equality, but they thought it impracticable to do so at the time; they were induced to adjourn the question of emancipation to a future day. Southern patriots anxiously and hopefully looked forward to the period when they could remove what they denominated the "foul blot" of slavery.[3]

During the Revolution the new doctrine of "Freedom" and the "Rights of Man" made many slaveholders realize the inconsistency of the slave trade and the struggle for liberty. The struggle of the colonies for political freedom produced, North and South, a revulsion of feeling against slaves which was, in a political sense, the evil against which they fought.[4] The old fear of slave insurrections gained new impetus from the imminence of war and the well founded fear that the British might incite servile uprisings. During the revolution the slave trade languished because of the cessation of colonial intercourse with England. The First Continental Congress in 1774 adopted a nonimportation and nonexportation agreement as the most effectual means of securing a redress of grievances. It was resolved that: "We will neither import nor purchase, any slave imported after the first day of December next; after which time, we will wholly discontinue the slave trade, and will neither be concerned in it ourselves, nor will we hire our vessels, nor sell our commodities or manufactures to those who are concerned in it."[5] Later regulations of the Continental Congress continued the nonimportation until the end of the war.

[2] William Frederick Poole, *Anti-Slavery Opinions Before 1800* (Cincinnati, 1873); Stephen B. Weeks, "Anti Slavery Opinion in the South," *Publications of the Southern History Association* (Washington, 1898), II, 87–130.
[3] Daniel R. Goodloe, *The Southern Platform*, 2.
[4] W. D. Weatherford, *The Negro from Africa to America*, (New York, 1924), 125.
[5] W. C. Ford, *Journals of the Continental Congress* (Washington, 1904), I, 75, 77.

Although there were, in various places of Georgia, some evidences of disapproval, the state as a whole approved this resolution and the prohibition of the slave trade. An extract of a letter from Savannah to a gentleman in Philadelphia, dated December 9, 1774, shows the opinion of the people of that section.

> Yesterday the inhabitants of Savannah met and chose Deputies to meet in Provincial Congress; the Deputies of the several Parishes and Districts of this Province to be chosen before the eighteenth of next month, on which day they meet; and there is not the least doubt they will adopt every measure recommended by the Congress, and firmly enter into the Association. You may be assured they will on that day also elect Deputies to meet the Continental or General Congress, to be held in Philadelphia on or about the 10th day of May next. The spirit of opposition has subsided, and most of the Protestors against the former Resolves came to the poll and voted for Delegates. Two of our back Parishes which made the most noise, are now come over to us.[6]

On January 12, 1775, the people of Darien took action and declared their disapproval and abhorrence of the practice of slavery. In indorsing the proceedings of the first Continental Congress, among other resolutions, "the Representatives of the extensive District of Darien, in the Colony of Georgia" adopted the following:

> To show the world that we are not influenced by any contracted or interested motives, but a general philanthropy for all mankind, of whatever climate, language, or complexion, *we hereby declare our disapprobation and abhorrence of the unnatural practice of slavery in America,* (however the uncultivated state of our country, or other specious arguments may plead for it,) a practice founded in injustice and cruelty, and highly dangerous to our liberties, (as well as lives,) debasing part of our fellow creatures below men, and corrupting the virtue and morals of the rest; and is laying the basis of that liberty we contend for (and which we pray

---

[6] Peter Force, *American Archives* (Washington, 1837), 4th Series, I, 1033.

the Almighty to continue to the latest posterity,) upon a very wrong foundation. *We therefore resolve, at all times, to use our utmost endeavors for the manumission of our Slaves in this Colony, upon the most safe and equitable footing for the masters and themselves.*[7]

The Darien resolutions probably led to no practical results but they show the existence of a genuine anti-slavery sentiment. It should be remembered in this connection that when the slavery question was agitated in Georgia thirty-five years earlier, it was the Scottish immigrants of Darien who protested against the institution on the grounds of injustice and inhumanity.

So we see that whatever opposition in Georgia may have existed at first to the Association against the slave trade, it had practically subsided by 1774. The ratification convention already mentioned was duly held. On January 18, 1775, the first Provincial Congress of Georgia assembled at Savannah. Delegates from only five of the twelve parishes attended. Before this meeting could act Governor Wright adjourned it on the ground that it did not represent the province. However, it was not adjourned until forty-five of the delegates had signed an agreement, one article of which promised to stop the importation of slaves.[8] This of course was not binding on the province as a whole. It merely shows that the sentiment of the delegates present was against the slave trade. This Congress chose Noble Wymberley Jones, Archibald Bulloch, and John Houston as delegates to represent Georgia in the Second Continental Congress to be held in May, 1775. Forty-five of the deputies assembled at this Congress in Savannah entered into an association which adopted the Darien resolutions. They declared: "That we will neither import or purchase any Slaves imported from Africa, or elsewhere, after the 15th of March, next."[9] The foregoing Association having been determined upon it was ordered

[7] *Ibid,* 4th Series, I, 1136.
[8] *Ibid,* 4th Series, I, 1158, 1160; II, 280–281.
[9] *Ibid,* 4th Series, I, 1158.

that the several members should subscribe their names. Thereupon the following members added their names: John Glen, chairman, Noble W. Jones, Samuel Farley, Ambrose Wright, Peter Tondee, Thomas Lee, William Young, John McClure, Archibald Bulloch, John Houston, Joseph Habersham, George Houston, Edward Telfair, William Gibbons, Peter Bard, D. Zubly, Jr., James De Veaux, Joseph Clay, Philip Box, William Owen, George Walton, John Stirk, Isaac Young, Robert Rae, Robert Hamilton, Edmund Bugg, William Glascock, John Germany, L. Marbury, Hugh Middleton, Samuel Germany, John Wereat, Jonathan Cochran, George McIntosh, Raymond Demere, William Jones, James Cochran, Joseph Gibbons, Frances H. Harris, Samuel Elbert, Henry Jones, William Lord, John Mann, David Lewis, and George Wyche.[10]   These forty-five men of Georgia, assembled at Savannah, thus proclaimed to the world their agreement not to import slaves.

Since only five parishes out of twelve had been represented at the Provincial Congress at Savannah, the chosen delegates (Jones, Bulloch, and Houston) decided not to go to Philadelphia but to address a letter to John Hancock, the president of the Continental Congress. This letter expressed the embarrassment and humiliation of these patriots because of the unworthy part that Georgia had played. The other colonies could not understand the local troubles of Georgia, and South Carolina resolved to have no intercourse with her. South Carolina prohibited trade with Georgia because of the latter's failure to ratify the Association against the slave trade.[11]

The little parish of St. John in Georgia, which was strongly opposed to slavery and which resented the failure of the province to send delegates to the Continental Congress, appealed to South Carolina to be exempted from the boycott. But South Carolina refused any exemption since the

[10] *Ibid,* 4th Series, I, 1160.
[11] Force, *American Archives,* 4th Series, I, 1163.

parish was a part of the province of Georgia.[12] Then the parish of St. John appealed to the Continental Congress. At a separate meeting held in May, 1775, it was resolved to hold no commerce with Savannah or other places except under the supervision of a committee, and then only for the purpose of procuring the necessaries of life. Having avowed their entire sympathy with all the articles and declarations promulgated by the general Congress, the parish of St. John elected Lyman Hall to represent it in the Continental Congress. He went at once to Philadelphia, presented his credentials, and was unanimously admitted to a seat in the Congress as a delegate from the parish of St. John in the Colony of Georgia. Hall remained until the close of the session of Congress. Since he represented only one parish Dr. Hall declined to vote upon questions which were to be decided by a vote of the colonies, but he was there to represent the stand for liberty taken by the parish of St. John,[13] later known as Liberty County. He presented to the Congress "The Address of the Inhabitants of the Parish of St. John's in the Province of Georgia." This was an appeal to the Continental Congress to except the parish from the general boycott of the colony. The address contained a resolution that: "None of us shall directly or indirectly purchase any Slaves imported at Savannah, (large numbers of which we understand are there expected), till the Sense of the Congress shall be made known to us."[14] Accordingly, on May 17, 1775, Congress resolved unanimously that all exportations to Georgia, except to the parish of St. John, should immediately cease.[15]

In the meantime the province of Georgia had taken action. On July 6, 1775, the second Provincial Congress of Georgia, in which every parish was represented, resolved, among other things: "That we will neither import or purchase any slave imported from Africa or elsewhere, after this day."[16]

---

[12] *Ibid*, 4th Series, I, 1163.
[13] Jones and Dutcher, *History of Augusta*, 62–63.
[14] *Journals of the Continental Congress*, II, 47.
[15] *Ibid*, II, 54.
[16] Force, *American Archives*, 4th Series, II, 1545.

This Congress restored Georgia to the good favor of the other colonies.   It elected as delegates to the Continental Congress John Houston, Archibald Bulloch, The Reverend Mr. Zubly, Noble Wymberley Jones, and Lyman Hall. It placed the colony in active sympathy with the other twelve American colonies, it annulled within her limits the objectionable acts of parliament, questioned the supremacy of the realm, and inaugurated measures for the accomplishment of independence and the erection of Georgia into the dignity of a state.

The action of the first Continental Congress was supplemented by that of the second and third congresses.   The Continental Congress assumed the commercial powers previously vested in the crown.   In April, 1776, it was resolved that there should be no further importation of slaves into any of the thirteen united colonies.[17]   This measure was accepted without any opposition in Georgia.   One of the grievances which the colonies held against England during the Revolution was her attitude in regard to the slave trade. The Young Americans were opposed to the traffic in negroes, but England, for financial reasons, strongly supported it. Slavery had increased very rapidly in the colonies.   Act after act had been passed by the colonial assemblies restricting or prohibiting the importation of negroes, but they were all disallowed by the home government.   Mr. Robert Finley, agent of the American Colonization Society, in the course of an address made in Brooklyn, New York, in 1830, said: "Eleven times did the Colonial Assembly of Georgia pass acts to prohibit the importation of slaves into that colony, but as often, did the British king exercise the prerogative of his veto to annul and thereby defeat the provisions of those acts."[18]   This shows the opposition of Georgia to the slave trade but the inability of the colony to prevent it because of the continual interference of the mother country.   The legislation of all the Southern states

---

[17] *Ibid*, 4th Series, V, 1660; *Journals of the Continental Congress*, II, 122.
[18] *Southern Recorder* (Milledgeville) December 11, 1830.

(both as colonies and states) for more than 165 years was distinguished by constant efforts to embarass or entirely prohibit the African slave trade. It was a fruitless struggle against the policy of England, but they never abandoned their determination to exclude the importation of negroes.[19]

The vetoing of these non-importation bills was one of the indictments against England made by Jefferson in the original Declaration of Independence, but it was stricken out by the committee in the revision. The original draft of the Declaration contained a severe arraignment of Great Britain as the real promoter of slavery and the slave trade in America. In it the king was charged with waging cruel war against human nature, with violating the sacred rights of life and liberty in the persons of distant people who never offended him, with capturing and carrying the Africans into slavery in another hemisphere, some to incur miserable death in their transportation thither. Such was the warfare of the Christian king of Great Britain.

> Determined to keep open market where men should be bought and sold, he has prostituted his negative for suppressing every attempt to prohibit or restrain this execrable commerce; and that this assemblage of horrors might want no fact of distinguished die, he is now exciting those very people to rise in arms among us, and to purchase that liberty of which he has deprived them by murdering the people on whom he has also obtruded them: thus paying off former crimes committed against the liberties of one people, with crimes which he urges them to commit against the lives of another.[20]

The slave traffic was suspended during the revolution. Upon the conclusion of peace in 1783 it was resumed by Northern states for financial profit. Benjamin Franklin and other great leaders remonstrated against the evil, but all to no effect. At various times during this period an import duty was placed on negroes imported into Georgia

---

[19] George McHenry, *The Cotton Trade* (London, 1863), 199.
[20] Thomas Jefferson Randolph, *Memoirs, Correspondence, and Miscellanies, from the papers of Thomas Jefferson* (Charlottesville, 1829), I, 19.

in order to discourage the slave trade. At times this duty was so high as to practically prohibit their importation. A question arose as to whether this duty should be levied upon all negroes brought into the province or only upon those imported direct from Africa. The Georgia Assembly decided for the latter in 1751.[21] From that time until 1798, when the importation of negroes was forbidden by the state constitution, the duty upon them was consistently maintained. On April 20, 1761, a committee was appointed to draw up a bill equal to a prohibition to prevent the importation of negroes into Georgia.[22] In 1767 a duty was placed on all negroes who had been in any of the Islands or Colonies over six months.[23] This act was also designed to prevent negro convicts from being imported into and sold in the province. The act entitled "An Act to lay a duty upon negroes, etc.," was reenacted on December 24, 1768.[24] The duty was still further increased in 1770.[25] On September 29, 1773, was passed an act "To oblige masters of vessels and other transient persons importing negroes or other slaves, goods, wares, and merchandize, [sic] to pay tax for the same; and to compel the persons directed to receive the same, to give security for the due performance of their office, and for the monies that may be received by them, by virtue of any act of the province."[26]

On July 29, 1783, a tax was levied on all "goods, wares, and merchandize, and negro slaves sold at vendue." This act was repealed by an act of 1794.[27] On July 30, 1783, an act was passed to oblige masters of vessels and other transient persons importing negroes to pay a tax.[28] This was a renewal of the law of September 29, 1773. On February 26, 1784, further duties were levied on all negroes imported

---

[21] "Journal of the Trustees," *Colonial Records,* I, 560.
[22] "Journal of the Commons House of Assembly," *Colonial Records,* XIII, 524.
[23] *Ibid,* XIII, 358; *Ibid,* XIV, 452, 455; Watkins, *Digest,* 138.
[24] Watkins, *Digest,* 152.
[25] "Journal of the Commons House of Assembly," *Colonial Records,* XV, 141, 157–158.
[26] Watkins, *Digest,* 182.
[27] *Ibid,* 280, 539–540.
[28] *Ibid,* 281.

into the state.[29] This act was repealed by an act of 1787.[30]
Further duties were levied on negroes imported into Georgia in 1786 and 1787.[31] The act of 1787 repealed the act of
1784.[32] This same act was reenacted and amended in
1788.[33] The import duties were still further raised in 1789.[34]
Thus we see that these duties on the importation of negroes,
sometimes so high as to prevent the importation, were
continued from the time that the colonies won their independence until 1798, when the slave trade was finally
prohibited in Georgia.

Besides the duties levied upon negroes imported into
Georgia, there was a tax levied on the slaves already here.
In 1755 a tax of one shilling was laid on all "Negroes and
other Slaves."[35] In 1757 a tax of two shillings was laid on
every slave.[36] This act levying a duty on negroes and other
slaves was re-enacted and modified many times during the
Colonial period.[37] A law of 1768 levied a tax of "Two Shillings and Six Pence on every Negroe or other Slave whatsoever being within the limits of this province."[38] This act
was re-enacted in 1770,[39] and again in 1773.[40]

Immediately after the Declaration of Independence the
colonies began to realize the need of a strong central government. The Articles of Confederation were sufficient
as long as the colonies were united against a common enemy.
With the cessation of fighting a stronger union was necessary. As time passed the unsatisfactory nature of the Confederation became more evident and more distressing to
all citizens who hoped for prosperity and happiness under

[29] *Ibid*, 298.
[30] *Ibid*, 351–353.
[31] *Ibid*, 325, 351.
[32] *Ibid*, 351–353.
[33] *Ibid*, 380.
[34] *Ibid*, 384.
[35] "Statutes Enacted by the Royal Legislature of Georgia," *Colonial Records,* XVIII, 66.
[36] *Ibid*, XVIII, 241.
[37] *Ibid*, XVIII, 253, 338, 394.
[38] "Statutes, Colonial and Revolutionary, 1768–1773," *Colonial Records,* **XIX,** Part I, 31.
[39] *Ibid*, 162–163.
[40] *Ibid*, 451.

a strong, stable government. Yet there were many people in each colony who were firmly opposed to any sacrifice of authority by the members of the Confederation. Jealousies among the states increased the difficulties. Georgia was especially desirous of a stronger union. The proximity of the powerful Indian tribes, and the Spanish possession of Florida after 1783 made Georgia an outpost against two hostile powers. The citizens of Georgia looked to the citizens of the other states for mutual support against a common danger. So for several reasons Georgia was in favor of a strong central government in control of international affairs and matters of broad scope, while on the other hand she was not willing to make a complete surrender of her own political independence. A strong federal government was necessary.[41]

Georgia was well represented in the Constitutional Convention which met at Philadelphia in 1787. The Assembly of Georgia appointed as representatives to this convention William Few, Abraham Baldwin, William Pierce, George Walton, William Houston and Nathaniel Pendleton. Walton and Houston, although appointed, did not attend. Nothing was said concerning slavery in the credentials of these delegates.[42] In fact slavery occupied no prominent place in the convention for the reason that most of the delegates thought it inexpedient to touch upon a delicate subject which, if let alone, would very likely settle itself in a manner satisfactory to all.[43] It was decided that the delegates should vote by states, each state having one vote. Georgia used her vote constantly in advocating the policy of strengthening the central government. She favored the idea of depriving the state legislature of some of their powers without removing all authority from them.

The slavery question arose in the matter of the ratio of representation of slaves. It was finally decided to count

---

[41] Ulrich Bonnell Phillips, *Georgia and State Rights* (Washington, 1902), 16.
[42] Jonathan Elliot, *Debates on the Adoption of the Federal Constitution* (Philadelphia, 1888), I, 125, 138–139.
[43] DuBois, *The Suppression of the African Slave Trade*, 52.

three-fifths of the total negro population in apportioning representation. There was to be one representative for each 30,000 inhabitants. Under this apportionment Georgia was given three members in The House. In regard to the migration and importation of slaves it was at first decided that: "No tax or duty shall be laid by the legislature on articles exported from any state; nor on the migration or importation of such persons as the several states shall think proper to admit; nor shall such migration or importation be prohibited."[44] This clause precipitated a long and bitter debate. Georgia favored the article as it stood. It should be remembered that Georgia, the youngest colony, had had slaves only since 1750 and therefore was not yet ready for the slave trade to be cut off. Georgia assumed the State Rights attitude. Mr. Baldwin conceived national objects alone to be the objects before the convention— not those which were of a local nature. He looked upon it as a dangerous symptom of centralization. It seemed to him that the central states wished to be the "vortex for every thing," even matters of a local nature.[45] Mr. Baldwin spoke of the slave trade as an evil; he suggested that Georgia, if left to herself, would undoubtedly put a stop to the trade. "As one ground for this conjecture he took notice of the sect of —— which, he said, was a respectable class of people, who carried their ethics beyond the mere equality of men, extending their humanity to the claims of the whole animal creation.[46]

South Carolina took an extreme position which was approved by the representatives from Georgia. The delegates of these two states threatened that if the importation of slaves were not allowed, their states would refuse to ratify the constitution. Mr. Wilson of Pennsylvania observed that if South Carolina and Georgia were themselves disposed to get rid of the importation of slaves in a short time, as had been suggested, they would never refuse to unite because

---

[44] Elliot, *Debates*, I, 227.
[45] *Ibid*, V, 459.
[46] *Ibid*, V, 459.

the importation might be prohibited.[47] To him it seemed inconsistent that Southern men would denounce slavery in one breath and insist upon constitutional guarantees in the next. But it should be remembered that the whole question of State Rights was involved in that of Slavery, and to surrender the Sovereignty of the States was to open the way to consolidation. Allowing slavery to be an evil, the people of the South regarded themselves as better qualified to apply the remedy than the people of distant states who were not particularly interested in the matter.[48] Baldwin, the Pinckneys, Rutledge, and others asserted again and again that these states "can never receive the plan if it prohibits the slave trade;" that if the Convention thought that these States would consent to a stoppage of the slave trade, "the expectation is vain."[49] Finally a compromise was reached between the sections. The debate over the slave trade involved also the question of the power of the central government to control commerce. The Southern states were opposed to giving the federal government control over commerce; the Northern states favored the abolition of the slave trade. A compromise was effected by which control over foreign and interstate commerce was granted to the federal government, and Congress was expressly prohibited from interfering with the foreign slave trade for a period of twenty years. Thus the slave trade article of the constitution stood finally as follows: Article I. Section 9.

> The Migration or Importation of such persons as any of the States now existing shall think proper to admit, shall not be prohibited by the Congress prior to the Year one thousand eight hundred and eight, but a Tax or duty may be imposed on such Importation, not exceeding ten dollars for each Person.

Mr. Baldwin's prophecy that Georgia, if left to herself, would put a stop to the evil was fulfilled ten years later.

---

[47] Elliot, *Debates*, V, 459.
[48] Goodloe, *The Southern Platform*, 2.
[49] Elliot, *Debates*, V, 459 et sequitur.

Georgia prohibited the slave trade in 1798,[50] ten years before it was prohibited by the federal government. Thus we see that the sentiment of Georgia was decidedly against the slave trade in the years immediately following the ratification of the constitution. In regard to the rendition of fugitive slaves it was decided: "No person held to service or labour in one state under the laws thereof escaping into another shall in consequence of any law or regulation therein be discharged from such service or labour, but shall be delivered up on claim of the party to whom such service or labour may be due."

There was genuine anti-slavery feeling in the Constitutional Convention even though it did not occupy a prominent place. In this convention not a single voice (not even from Georgia and South Carolina—the extreme Southern States) was raised in unqualified defense and justification of slavery. The question of recognizing slavery was left to be dealt with by the individual states. The word "slave" was carefully avoided in the Constitution. Fugitive slaves were referred to as "persons held to service or labor;" the slave trade was spoken of as "the migration of such persons as the states might wish to admit." Representation was based on free whites and three-fifths "of all other persons." Even in 1789 the slavery question was a puzzle which was left to be solved by future generations. Instead of calling the whole moral energy of the people into action so as to gradually crush this evil, the Federal Convention attempted to settle it by a "bargain." "It left to the vacillating and unripe judgment of the States one of the most threatening of the social and political ills which they were so courageously seeking to remedy."[51]

The three-fifths compromise was generally accepted by all sections. However, a friend of Frederick Law Olmstead once said to a Georgian: "I confess, H., whenever I am reminded that your power in our Congress, by the reason

---

[50] Watkins, *Digest*, 673; Marbury and Crawford, *Digest*, 440.
[51] DuBois, *The Suppression of the Slave Trade*, 62.

of the hundred slaves you own, counts as sixty-one to my one, because I happen to live at the North, and chose to invest the results of my labor in railroads, instead of niggers, I have a very strong indisposition to submit to it."[52] To this the Georgian answered: "I declare, I should think that you would; I never thought of it in that light before; its wrong, and you ought not to submit to it and, if I were you, I would not."[53]

Georgia ratified the constitution unanimously. This prompt ratification was a true expression of the will of the people of Georgia. They had obtained practically all for which they had asked. They no longer feared lack of common support against possible attacks from Indians and Spaniards; the questions of slavery and the slave trade had been settled satisfactorily (at least for a time); and proportional representation in the lower house counting three-fifths of the number of slaves left nothing to be desired. Although the delegates from Georgia in the Federal Convention of 1787 insisted on legalizing the slave-trade, public opinion was decidedly against the traffic. The position maintained by the delegates was not upheld by the people in general as shown by the many acts passed by the legislature to prohibit the importation of Africans. We shall consider these acts in the succeeding chapter.

---

[52] Frederick Law Olmstead, *A Journey in the Seaboard Slave States* (New York, 1856), 530–531.

[53] Olmstead, *A Journey in the Seaboard Slave States*, 530–531.

CHAPTER VII

GEORGIA AND THE SLAVE TRADE

One of the best means of judging the extent to which the anti-slavery sentiment had made itself felt in Georgia is to examine the legislation during the period and to study the many laws that were passed to prohibit the slave trade. While legislatures do not always reflect popular sentiment, their action taken for a long period together, probably comes nearer to it than any other agent of public opinion. Although the delegates from Georgia in the Federal Convention of 1787 insisted on legalizing the slave trade, their position was not held by the people in general as shown by the many acts passed by the legislature to prohibit the importation of Africans. These enactments were in conformity with the Constitution, and with that clause of it which declares that the "migration or importation of such persons as any of the States now existing shall think proper to admit, shall not be prohibited by the Congress prior to the year one thousand eight hundred and eight, but a tax or duty may be imposed on such importation, not exceeding ten dollars for each person."

Under the Federal Constitution the slave trade was legalized until 1808, but Georgia destroyed it, as far as she was concerned, ten years earlier. This proves that public opinion in Georgia was definitely opposed to the slave trade. Indications of opposition to slavery in Georgia are found in every effort of the legislature to pass laws preventing the further introduction of Africans; this was intended indirectly to bring about the gradual abolition of slavery. No aspect of slavery was more objectionable to the majority of the people of Georgia than that of buying and selling negroes for profit. Justice James M. Wayne, in his charge to the Grand Jury in the Federal Court of Savannah in 1859, gave a severe indictment against the slave trade. Among other things, he said: "The colonial history of the States, in my judicial circuit, North and South Carolina and Georgia, exhibits the existence of a profound impression among the people, that the slave trade was not a legitimate commerce, but that it involved the perpetration of enormous crimes."[1]   Judge Berrien of Georgia said: "For myself, I abhor the slave trade. It is abhorred by my constituents. Even at the time when it was tolerated by our laws, it was not in the Southern portion of this Union that its practical advocates were found."[2]

Georgia, which had had legal slavery only since 1750 and had since passed no restrictive legislation, felt compelled in 1793 to stop the importation of negroes. An Act of Georgia, introduced in December, 1793, prohibited the importation of negroes.[3] This act was introduced into the House on December 17, 1793, when it was read for the first time.[4] After a second and third reading, it was then sent to the Senate where it was concurred in with another act, then returned to the House where it originated.[5] The slavery disturbances in Hayti and Santo Domingo prompted the legislature in this act to forbid the importation of slaves from the West Indies, the Bahamas, and Florida.[6] Any person found guilty of violation of this act was to forfeit to the state fifty pounds for each negro imported. This act also required all free negroes coming into the state to register at the clerk's office and to secure magisterial certificates of honesty and industriousness. This was to entitle them to the privileges of residence in the state.   Upon failure

---

[1] "Justice James M. Wayne's charge to the Grand Jury in 1859," *Georgia Historical Quarterly*, II, 101.

[2] *Ibid*, II, 111.

[3] Prince, *Digest*, 455–456; Watkins, *Digest*, 530; *House Journal*, 1793, 30, 34, 65; *Executive Minutes*, Nov. 5, 1793–Sept. 23, 1796, 34–35 (Manuscript in Georgia Department of Archives and History, Atlanta).

[4] *Executive Minutes*, Nov. 5, 1793–Sept. 23, 1796, 34; *House Journal*, 1793, 30.

[5] *Executive Minutes*, Nov. 5, 1793–Sept. 23, 1796, 35; *House Journal*, 1793, 34, 65.

[6] Ulrich Bonnell Phillips, *American Negro Slavery*, 133.

to secure such certificates the free negro could be committed to jail for a period not exceeding three months. The state was not to be held accountable for the value of slaves legally executed. Expenses and fees for prosecuting slaves convicted of crimes against the state were to be paid by the owners of the slaves. But in cases where slaves were convicted of crimes for which they might suffer death, the expenses attending the trial and execution were to be paid by the county where they were executed.[7] This Act prohibited importation of negroes from the West Indies, the Bahamas, and Florida; the African trade was left open until 1798 when it was closed both by legislative enactment and by constitutional provision.

In February, 1796, a bill was introduced to prevent the importation or emigration of negroes from certain places therein mentioned into the state.[8] Since debates arose on the bill it was ordered to be recommitted,[9] but was finally passed on February 17, 1796.[10] In that year 2,084 negroes were imported at Savannah including some who had been brought from the North for sale in Georgia.[11]

Governor Jackson of Georgia, on June 11, 1798, issued a proclamation in regard to the importation of slaves. Negroes were being imported into Savannah from the West Indies in violation of the law of 1796. In view of the recent uprisings of slaves in the islands, the governor considered their importation into the province of Georgia especially dangerous. The militia of the several counties were called upon to apprehend such slaves and to keep them in safe custody until they could be deported.[12] In accordance with the Governor's proclamation the legislature enacted a more stringent law forbidding the slave trade. The acts of 1793 and 1796 were reenacted in 1798 by legislative enactment and by constitutional provision. A bill was in-

---

[7] Prince, *Digest*, 455–456; Watkins, *Digest*, 530.
[8] *House Journal*, 1796, 96, 113.
[9] *Ibid*, 113.
[10] *Ibid*, 133.
[11] *American Historical Association Report* for 1903, 459–460.
[12] For the proclamation of Governor Jackson, see Appendix II.

troduced into the House on January 29, 1798, which forbade the further importation of slaves into the state.[13] The bill soon passed both houses.[14] This Act of 1798 prohibited the importation of Africans from abroad after July first of that year; the importation of slaves from other states was prohibited after three months from the date of passage.[15] Every offending person was to forfeit for the first offense the sum of $1,000 for every negro imported. For every subsequent offense the sum of $1,000 was to be paid, one-half for the use of the informer, and one-half for the use of the state. Persons bringing negroes into Georgia for the purpose of selling them into slavery were subject to the same penalties as if they actually sold them. This abolition of the slave trade was embodied in the new state constitution of Georgia adopted in 1798. Thus Georgia, of her own accord, prohibited the importation of slaves after October 1, 1798.[16] Article IV, Section 2, states:

> There shall be no future importation of slaves into this state from Africa, or any foreign place, after the first day of October next. The legislature shall have no power to pass laws for the emancipation of slaves, without the consent of each of their respective owners previous to such emancipation. They shall have no power to prevent emigrants, from either of the United States to this state, from bringing with them such persons as may be deemed slaves by the laws of any one of the United States.[17]

A bill was introduced into the House on November 16, 1803, which was entitled "An Act to prohibit more effectually the importation of slaves into this State."[18] The bill was referred to a committee; it was re-introduced the following

---

[13] *Executive Minutes*, Oct. 13, 1797–June 28, 1798, 101; *House Journal*, 1798, 20.

[14] *Executive Minutes*, Oct. 13, 1797–June 28, 1798, 104, 105; *House Journal*, 1798, 25, 47.

[15] *House Journal*, 1798, 20, 25, 47; Watkins, *Digest*, 673–674; Marbury and Crawford, *Digest*, 440–441; Also: *Executive Minutes*, Oct. 13, 1797–June 28, 1798, 101, 104, 105.

[16] Watkins, *Digest*, 31–43.

[17] Prince, *Digest*, 559; Watkins, *Digest*, 42; Marbury and Crawford, *Digest*, 30.

[18] *House Journal*, 1803, 25.

year,[19] and was passed on December 3, 1803.[20] The purpose of this act was to prohibit the importation of slaves into Georgia, or, "to prohibit, the more effectually, their introduction into this state." The case of Edmiston versus Wright was the result of an attempted violation of this act of 1803. The defendant had a gang of negroes let out in Jamaica. In 1803 he wished to transfer them to his estates in Georgia. A ship was dispatched to Jamaica to bring the negroes to Georgia. The negroes were put on board and carried to Port Antonio; "but as the captain had not got a permit to receiving them they were seized as forfeited, together with the ship and the rest of her cargo. To release them, the plaintiff paid as a composition 1200 pounds."[21]

In 1804 a bill was again introduced into the House to prohibit more effectually the importation of negroes into the state. This bill was introduced and read for the first time on November 9, 1804,[22] and was referred to a committee. Mention is not made of it again; evidently it was dropped.

The foreign slave trade was prohibited by the National government in 1808. It was Peter Early of Georgia who introduced the bill which passed making it a criminal offense to capture slaves in Africa and to bring them to this country.[23] The Constitution had made it impossible to forbid foreign importation of slaves prior to 1808. President Jefferson, in his annual message of December 2, 1806, congratulated his fellow-citizens that the time was approaching when they might interpose their authority constitutionally to withdraw the citizens of the United States from any further participation "in those violations of human rights which have been so long continued on the unoffending inhabitants of Africa, and which the morality, the reputation, and the best interests of our country have long been

[19] *Ibid*, 1803, 25, 74.
[20] *Ibid*, 1803, 82.
[21] Helen Tunnicliff Catterall, *Judicial Cases Concerning American Slavery and the Negro* (Washington, 1926), I, 26–27.
[22] *House Journal*, 1804, 42.
[23] *Annals of Congress*, 1806–1807, 167–168.

eager to proscribe. Although no law you can pass can take effect until the day of the year one thousand eight hundred and eight, yet the intervening period is not too long to prevent, by timely notice, expeditions which cannot be completed before that day."[24] Shortly afterward a bill was passed which provided that after the close of the year 1807 the importation of slaves was to be a felony punishable with death, and that the interstate coasting trade in slaves should be illegal.

This paragraph of the President's message was referred on December 3 to a committee of seven with Peter Early of Georgia as chairman. The committee's bill, reported on December 15, proposed to prohibit the importation of slavery and to penalize the fitting out of vessels for the trade by fine and forfeiture. It further provided that slaves illegally introduced into the United States should be forfeited, and persons engaged in buying and selling them should be fined; it provided that slaves forfeited should be sold at public outcry by federal officials.[25] During the debates on this act Early of Georgia pronounced slavery an evil that was regretted by every man in the country.[26] But he also opposed the granting of freedom to the forfeited slaves. He proposed that the captured slaves should be delivered to the several states in which the captures were made, to be disposed of as the states saw fit. The bill as finally passed made the importation of slaves from abroad a misdemeanor punishable with imprisonment; it prohibited the coasting trade by sea in vessels of less than forty tons; and it provided that smuggled slaves seized under the act should be subject to the laws of the state or territory in which the seizure was made.[27]

Two bills were introduced into the Georgia legislature in 1816 in respect to the importation of negroes. The first provided for the repeal of the second and third sections of the

---

[24] *Ibid,* 1806–1807, 14.
[25] *Ibid,* 1806–1807, 167–168.
[26] *Ibid,* 1806–1807, 174.
[27] *Ibid,* 1806–1807, 1266–1270.

act prohibiting the importation of negroes.[28] The other prohibited the importation of slaves into the state under certain restrictions.[29] However this bill was superseded by a
bill from the Senate. The laws against the foreign slave
trade were sometimes violated. These violations were
usually punished by state authorities. According to the
penal code of 1816:

> Any person except emigrants, bringing, importing or in-
> troducing into this state, by land or water, any slave or
> slaves, with intent to sell, transfer or barter such slave or
> slaves, such person shall be guilty of a high misdemeanor,
> and, on conviction, shall be sentenced to pay a fine not ex-
> ceeding five hundred dollars for each negro, and to undergo
> an imprisonment in the penitentiary, at hard labour, for
> any period of time not less than one year, nor longer than
> three years, as the jury may recommend; and the fact of
> offering for sale, transfer or barter, such slave or slaves within
> the term of one year after the bringing into this state, shall
> be sufficient evidence of the intent of such importation or
> introduction, (though no actual sale, barter or transfer be
> made); and every person so concerned or interested in bring-
> ing, importing or introducing such slave or slaves, shall be
> equally guilty as the principal, and, on conviction, shall
> suffer the same punishment as before prescribed.[30]

However, in spite of all precautions, slaves were illegally
brought into Georgia. The statement was made that 8,000
slaves were carried into Georgia in 1817 from the Northern
slave-holding states.[31] The number of importations must
have been great, for the Georgia legislature in that year
made another attempt to prevent the further introduction
of negroes. On December 20, 1817, the legislature passed
a law which provided that:

> It shall not be lawful, except in the cases herein authorized
> and allowed, for any person or persons whatsoever, to bring,

---

[28] *House Journal*, 1816, 20.
[29] *Ibid*, 1816, 56, 61.
[30] L. Q. C. Lamar, *Compilation of the Laws of Georgia*, (Augusta, 1821), 608.
Hereafter referred to as Lamar, *Compilation*.
[31] Winfield H. Collins, *The Domestic Slave Trade of the Southern States*, (New
York, 1904), 42.

import or introduce into this state, to aid or assist, or knowingly to become concerned or interested, in bringing, importing, or introducing into this state, either by land or by water, or in any manner whatsoever, any slave or slaves.[32] Persons guilty of violating this act were to pay a fine of five hundred dollars for every slave imported and to undergo imprisonment in the penitentiary for not less than one year nor more than three. Citizens of Georgia and those of other states coming to Georgia to live were permitted to bring in slaves for their own use. Before importing them they were required to make an oath before the authorities that the said negroes were not imported for sale, or hire, lend, or mortgage. The act was not to apply to travellers. Slaves imported from abroad might be confiscated. The law was distinctly not to apply to slaves brought by emigrants, or by residents for their own use. Persons concealing or harboring any slaves to the injury of the owners were to be sentenced to the penitentiary for a period not exceeding two years. Any person who should "remove or carry, or cause to be removed and carried away out of this state" any slave or slaves was to be sentenced to imprisonment in the penitentiary for a period of not less than seven years. Persons found guilty of beating, whipping or wounding a slave without cause were to be fined or imprisoned or both.[33] Persons purchasing or hiring slaves, knowing them to have been illegally introduced, were to be subject to a fine.

Another act of 1817 provided for the disposal of slaves illegally imported into the state. By this act the governor was authorized to appoint an agent who was to go to ports where negroes might be illegally introduced and to demand and receive such negroes and turn them over to the executive of the state in Milledgeville. The slaves, if captured, were to be considered the property of the state. Such negroes were to be sold at auction or given over to the Colonization Society for transportation, providing the Society would

---

[32] *Acts of the General Assembly of the State of Georgia*, 1817, 139. Hereafter referred to as *Acts of Georgia*.
[33] *Acts of Georgia*, 1817, 139–143.

reimburse the state for all expenses incurred and pay for the transportation.[34] In this way state statutes were to come to the aid of federal statutes in enforcing the federal enactment of 1817.

This act provided:

1. That the governor shall receive such negroes and
2. sell them or
3. give them to the Colonization Society to be transported, on condition that the Society reimburse the state for all expense, and transport them at their own cost.[35]

On November 3, 1818, Governor Rabun, in his address to the legislature of Georgia, expressed his desire for a more stringent enforcement of the non-importation act. In his message he declared that the law to prohibit the importation of slaves was not being upheld, and he expressed concern over the "abominable traffic." He called attention to the many violations of that act and to the difficulties of enforcement. He said:

> I beg leave to direct your early attention to that part of our Penal Code which was intended to prohibit the introduction of slaves into this State, except on certain conditions. The violation of that act becomes every day more common, and it is a lamentable fact, that this abominable traffic has so many advocates among us, that an informer, or even an officer, who would perform his duty by attempting to enforce the law, is by many considered an officious meddler and treated with derision and contempt. I hope the Legislature will make another effort to maintain the supremacy of the laws, by adopting such measures as will effectually prevent this species of speculation.[36]

In accordance with the Governor's suggestion several bills were introduced and the debates on the importation of slaves began. On November 16, 1818, W. T. J. Moors from the committee appointed reported a bill to repeal that

---

[34] Oliver H. Prince, *Digest of the Laws of Georgia to 1837* (Athens, 1837) 793–794; Lamar, *Compilation*, 808; Cobb's *Digest*, 989.

[35] Prince, *Digest* to 1837, 793–794; Lamar, *Compilation*, 808.

[36] "Message of Governor William Rabun," Nov. 3, 1818, *Journal of the Senate*, 1818, 8. Hereafter referred to as *Senate Journal*.

part of an act passed December 20, 1817, relative to the introduction of slaves.[37] On November 18, 1818, it was read a second time and ordered to be committed to a committee of the whole on the following Friday.[38] On December 9, 1818, a substitute bill was introduced. The bill was to alter the provisions of the act passed on December 20, 1817, entitled "An Act to amend the penal Code of this State."[39] This bill was passed on December 10, 1818.[40] Certain restrictions were placed on the importation of negroes, and violations of the law were to be severely punished. Thus the acts of 1817 were reinforced by this act of December 19, 1818. Persons seizing illegally imported negroes were to be entitled to one-tenth of the net proceeds of the sale, provided, that nothing should be so construed as to extend farther back than the year 1817.[41] The following extract is taken from the Act of 1818.

> From and after the passing of this act, it shall not be lawful for any free person of color, (Indians in amity with the State, and regularly articled seamen or apprentices, arriving in any ship or vessel excepted), to come into this State; and each and every person or persons offending herein, shall be liable to be arrested by warrant, under the hand and seal of any magistrate in this State, and being thereof convicted in the manner hereinafter pointed out, shall be liable to a penalty not exceeding one hundred dollars, and upon failure to pay the same within the time prescribed in the sentence awarded against such person or persons, he, she, or they shall be liable to be SOLD by public outcry, as a slave or slaves, in such manner as may be prescribed by the court awarding such sentence, and the proceeds of such sales shall be appropriated in the manner provided for the appropriation of penalties recovered under this act.[42]

In December, 1823, a resolution, introduced into the Senate by Mr. Berrien of Chatham County, provided:

---

[37] *House Journal*, 1818, 61.
[38] *Ibid*, 74.
[39] *Ibid*, 166–168.
[40] *Ibid*, 172.
[41] Lamar, *Compilation*, 817; Prince, *Digest*, 799.
[42] Prince, *Digest*, 794.

That the following shall be proposed as an amendment to the Constitution of the United States: That no part of the Constitution of the United States ought to be construed to authorize the importation or ingress of any person of color into any one of the United States contrary to the laws of such state. And that his excellency the Governor be and he is hereby requested to communicate this resolution to the Governors of the different states, with a request that the same may be submitted to their respective legislatures, and that he do also communicate the same to our senators and representatives in Congress.[43]

In 1823 the Common Council of Savannah refused to receive into the city treasury any money from the proceeds of the sale of free blacks.[44] Yet, after the great fire in Savannah of 1820, the mayor and council of the city refused a gift of money from New York to the sufferers of Savannah because it was given on condition that it be divided equally between the black and white sufferers.[45] However, the whites were not unwilling to divide the money with the blacks; they refused the money because to accept the condition would have implied that they were paupers accepting a gift of charity. It was also feared that the acceptance would create discord. The mayor wrote a polite letter of refusal and resolutions were drawn explaining the refusal.[46]

In December, 1824, an act was passed to repeal the statute forbidding the importation of negroes.[47] Slaves then were imported and disposed of without restriction. This legislature of 1824–25 also repealed all laws and parts of laws authorizing the sale into slavery of free blacks.[48] The Act of 1824 was repealed in 1829 and the act of 1798 which

[43] *Senate Journal*, 1823, 182.
[44] Alice Dana Adams, *The Neglected Period of Anti-Slavery in America*, 1808–1831 (Boston, 1908), 51.
[45] *Niles Weekly Register* (Baltimore), XVIII, 88.
[46] *Ibid.*
[47] *Acts of Georgia*, 1824, 124; *Senate Journal*, 1824, 107, 119, 287; W. C. Dawson, *Compilation of the Laws of Georgia* (Milledgeville, 1831), 411. Hereafter referred to as Dawson, *Compilation*.
[48] *Senate Journal*, 1824, 107, 119, 287.

prohibited the introduction of negroes was reenacted.[49]
In 1839 an effort was made to repeal the law of 1829. "Mr.
Ingram introduced a bill to repeal so much of the law that
was assented to Dec. 22, 1829, prohibiting the introduction of slaves into this state on certain conditions; which
was read for the first time."[50]   The bill was read a second
time, voted on, and lost.[51]

The law of 1817 and later acts forbidding the importation of negroes proved ineffective.   It was illegal to import
negroes for purposes of buying and selling them; however
immigrants coming to Georgia to reside were allowed to
bring in slaves for their own use.   The act did not apply
to travellers.   It was difficult to distinguish the trader for
profit from the citizen buying for his own use.   Many of the
regular traders posed as purchases of slaves for domestic
use.   Consequently, in his message to the Legislature of
October 19, 1930, Governor Gilmer advocated more stringent legislation on the subject.   He suggested that it should
be made a crime to introduce slaves into the state, either
for use or sale, and that slaves so introduced should be forfeited.   He believed that such a law could be enforced and
he recommended it for their consideration.   He said:

> The prejudices against slavery in many of the States, the
> increase of similar feelings in some of the slave holding
> states, attendant upon the decrease of the slave, and in-
> crease of their white population, the danger of having the
> slave population in the state dis-proportionately great to the
> free, without the possibility hereafter of throwing off that
> population when it becomes burdensome, and the unjust
> revenue system of the Federal Government, by which per-
> manent bounties are given to the manufacturing and me-
> chanical, at the expense of agricultural labor, (slaves being
> in general incapable of any except agricultural) indicate very
> clearly the policy for us to pursue.   It is believed that no
> benefit will result from the re-enactment of the law of 1817—

---

[49] *Acts of Georgia,* 1829, 171.
[50] *House Journal,* 1839, 94.
[51] *Ibid,* 1839, 115.

that law prohibits the introduction of slaves by negro traders, but permits every citizen to bring them into the State for his own use; the only consequence of which will be, that a much greater number of persons will become engaged in a traffic which, from its nature, the interest of society requires should be confined to as few as possible. The enforcement too of the law will be extremely difficult, because of the impossibility of distinguishing the trader for profit, from the citizen buying for his own use. If the law were so altered as to make it a crime to introduce slaves into the State, either for use or sale, (with the exception already mentioned) and forfeiting all slaves so introduced, in whatever hands they might be found, such law, it is believed, could be enforced without difficulty. This subject is recommended to your consideration, from the conviction that the future prosperity of the State may be deeply affected by the policy which you may pursue. . . .[52]

Not only was Georgia opposed to the foreign slave trade, but she was also opposed to the domestic trade. It was considered inexpedient to increase an acknowledged evil; it was feared that the "dregs" of the other states would be introduced into Georgia; it was prophesied that free negroes might be kidnapped and resold into slavery; it was considered best to refuse to receive slaves from other states who might, at a later period, join in a crusade against the South.[53] Georgia thus enacted laws prohibiting the admission of negroes from the North. On December 23, 1833, an act was passed to reform, amend, and consolidate the penal laws of Georgia. The thirteenth provision of this act related to slaves.

If any person or persons shall bring, import, or introduce into this State, or aid, or assist, or knowingly become concerned or interested in bringing, importing or introducing into this State, either by land or by water, or in any manner whatever, any slave or slaves, each and every such person or persons so offending shall be deemed principals in law and guilty of a

---

[52] *House Journal*, 1830, 25, (Governor Gilmer's Message of October 19, 1830).
[53] Letter from a citizen to the editors of the "Georgia Journal" (Milledgeville), December 4, 1821. Quoted by Ulrich Bonnell Phillips, *Plantation and Frontier Documents*, II, 67–70.

high misdemeanor, and may be arrested and tried in any country in this State in which he, she, or they may be found, and, on conviction, shall be punished by a fine not exceeding $500 each, for each and every slave so brought, imported, or introduced, and imprisonment and labour in the penitentiary for any term not less than one year, not longer than four years; provided, however, this Act shall not prohibit actual settlers from coming into this State with their slaves from any of the other States of the Union.[54]

However, according to this law of 1833, residents were allowed to bring in slaves for their own use, but they must make oath of their intentions; they must register and swear that they were not for sale, hire, or mortgage. Incoming residents had to make an affidavit that they had "not introduced such slave or slaves with a view to speculation, but with the intent solely of being held to service by themselves personally or their legal heirs and representatives."[55] This act was amended December 23, 1836, so that immigrants were allowed to hire out their slaves. It was again amended in 1849 so as to allow the importation of slaves from any other of the slave-holding states of the Union.

In 1835 a law was enacted making anyone subject to fine and imprisonment who should bring into Georgia any male slave who had been to a non-slaveholding state or to any foreign country.[56] The law of 1829 which prohibited the introduction of negroes was modified in 1836.[57] The law against the slave trade was repealed in 1841.[58] It was reenacted in 1842.[59]

Thus the non-importation act was passed, repealed, revived, modified, repealed, and again revived—showing how unstable public opinion was in Georgia in regard to the slave trade. It seems to have been the general opinion in Georgia that a citizen should be allowed to introduce

---

[54] Cobb's *Digest*, II, 1018.
[55] Prince, *Digest* to 1837, 812; Cobb's *Digest*, II, 1018.
[56] *Acts of Georgia*, 1835, 267.
[57] *Ibid*, 1836, 254.
[58] *Ibid*, 1841, 151.
[59] *Ibid*, 1842, 165.

slaves into the state for his own use, or an immigrant might bring his slave property when settling in Georgia; but no one should bring in slaves for the speculative purposes of selling and hiring them. These statutes were not always enforced and were sometimes openly violated. From 1810 to 1820 slaves increased in Georgia about 44,000 or 43 percent;[60] The illicit foreign trade was great during that time. However, there was a sincere attempt on the part of the authorities to enforce the law. In 1849 the law against the slave trade was again repealed. Cities and towns were given the right to regulate the sale of slaves by traders, and to prescribe the places in their jurisdiction where slaves might be kept and sold.[61]

In 1852 that part of the law which referred to the importation of slaves was repealed and the act of 1817 was revived. This Act of 1852 prohibited the importation of slaves into the state for the purpose of hire, sale, or traffic.[62] However, the penitentiary imprisonment clause was eliminated.[63] The law of 1852 was repealed by the legislature of 1855–56, and the Act of 1849 was revived, thus again opening the state to the unrestricted importation of slaves.[64]

The opposition to the slave trade was attributed to various motives. The humanitarian motive was obvious but not isolated. Other considerations were that the continuance of the slave trade would lower the prices of slaves already on hand, or at least prevent those prices from rising; that it would increase the staple exports and therefore lower the price; that it would drain out money and keep the community in debt; that it would retard the civilization of the negroes already on hand; and that by raising the proportion of blacks it would intensify the danger of slave insurrections.[65] By 1850 public opinion in Georgia had begun to favor the slave trade. However there was considerable

---

[60] Collins, *The Domestic Slave Trade of the Southern States*, 42.
[61] *Acts of Georgia*, 1849–50, 374.
[62] *House Journal*, 1851–52, 801, 806.
[63] *Acts of Georgia*, 1851–52, 263.
[64] *Ibid*, 1855–56, 271.
[65] Phillips, *American Negro Slavery*, 133–134.

opposition. Because of the general prosperity, the spread of cotton culture, and the rise of prices in cotton there was a general demand for more slaves, but this demand was defeated in Georgia. At a Southern Commercial convention held in Savannah in 1856, W. B. Goulden of Georgia moved that the members of Congress make attempts to have repealed all laws forbidding the slave trade. However, by a vote of 67 to 18 the convention even refused to debate the motion. Another attempt to have the subject discussed resulted in a gain of six votes for the negative.[66]

The firm of E. LaFitte and Company in South Carolina applied to the collector of the port at Charleston for a clearance to Africa for the purpose of importing African "emigrants." The collector then appealed to the Secretary of the United States Treasury, Howell Cobb of Georgia, who flatly refused. Cobb replied that if the emigrants were brought in as slaves it would be contrary to the laws of the United States; if they were brought in as free men it would be contrary to the laws of the state.[67] In Georgia about this time an attempt was made to expunge the slave trade prohibition from the state constitution, but the majority was still in favor of the prohibition; the expunging resolution failed by the close vote of 47 to 46.[68] In regard to the revival of the slave trade a gentleman of Georgia wrote, "The African slave trade was a great error, and productive of much evil; and its attempted revival indicates the insanity of the designers."[69]

On June 20, 1857, a Georgian wrote in regard to the slave trade: "The slave trade is one of the most abominable evils with which Africa and America are scourged."[70] He suggested that if England and the United States really desired

---

[66] *DeBow's Review*, XXII, 217, 221–222; Herbert Wender, "The Southern Commercial Convention at Savannah, 1856," *Georgia Historical Quarterly*, XV, 181.

[67] *House Executive Documents*, 36th Congress, 2nd Session, IV, No. 7, 632–636.

[68] Dubois, *The Suppression of the African Slave Trade to the United States of America*, 177.

[69] *The African Repository*, XXXIII, 377.

[70] *Ibid*, XXXIII, 249.

its abolition or effectual prevention, they would have to do
better than they were doing in the premises, at less cost,
and with more certainty. He believed that a law should
be enacted making the slave trade piracy, that the penalty
should be imprisonment for life, and that government
premiums should be given to American and British ships
which should succeed in capturing a slaver and in bringing it safely to port. He believed that there would be no opposition to such a law and that the president should insist
upon it.[71] From 1776 to 1860 only one attempt was made
by a Southern man to introduce African slaves into a
Southern port, and that attempt was a failure. A small
yacht called *The Wanderer*, was seized and condemned
and her officers were pursued with unrelenting vigor by a
Southern man, General Henry R. Jackson, of Savannah,
who was then Assistant Attorney General of the United
States.[72] In the speech of General Jackson on the Wanderer
Case he exposes the guilt of New England in carrying on the
slave trade.[73] General D. B. Mitchell, who had resigned
the office of governor of Georgia to become United States
agent to the Creeks, was concerned in the illegal introduction of Africans in 1819. Governor Clarke of Georgia
charged Mitchell with the offense and he was dismissed
from the agency.[74]

Thus we see that Georgia opposed the slave trade from the
beginning. Mr. Baldwin's prediction in the Federal Convention of 1787 was carried out—that Georgia, if left alone,
would do away with the slave trade. As we have seen the
Constitution of 1798 forbade the importation of negroes
into Georgia, and after that time more stringent laws were
enacted to carry out the constitutional provision and to
exclude the slave traffic.

---

[71] *Ibid*, XXXIII, 249–250.
[72] Charles H. Smith, *History of Georgia* (Boston, 1896), 121.
[73] *The Wanderer Case*: the Speech of Henry R. Jackson of Savannah (pamphlet, Atlanta, N. D.)
[74] Phillips, *Georgia and State Rights*, 157.

CHAPTER VIII

MANUMISSION OF SLAVES IN GEORGIA DURING THE COLONIAL PERIOD

Another means of judging the extent to which the anti-slavery sentiment had made itself felt in Georgia is to notice the number of instances where slaves were voluntarily manumitted and the laws that were passed prohibiting manumission. Laws on this subject were not passed until there was thought to be a need for them. Laws were then enacted fobidding the freeing of slaves. If such laws existed they are proofs in themselves that slaves were being given their freedom at least in small numbers. If some people had not been freeing their slaves, then these laws would not have been necessary. Records of emancipations or manumissions are so incomplete and unsatisfactory that no complete or exhaustive summary can be made. These records are found in wills which have been preserved, in certain testimonials granted to negroes, in bonds, bills of sale and deeds of gift, in the executive minutes, and in the Journals of the House and Senate. Another difficulty is found in the fact that sometimes several notices appear in either the official minutes or the official journals, and it is difficult to tell whether these are notices of the same or of different cases of emancipation. The result is likely to be a confusion of estimates. It is also difficult to discover the motives of the slaveholder in emancipating his slaves. If each slaveholder who emancipated his blacks explained the motives for his action, the problem would be much simplified. Frequently the emancipater expressed but briefly the reasons which led to the manumission of his slaves; these are usually stated in the last wills of the Masters. In many cases the negroes were given their freedom because of special services, or because of long continued and faithful service to the Master or Mistress. In some cases manumission was granted in return for money. Sometimes mulattoes were freed by masters who were also their fathers. Many men repented of the sin involved in that relation and were unwilling for their offspring to remain in slavery. Sometimes a negro was given his freedom because of military or other public service. In some cases the negro purchased his freedom; in some cases he purchased not only his own freedom but also that of his family.

Many slaves were manumitted in Georgia during the Colonial Period. The many wills recorded, in which slaves were given their freedom, show a sentiment in favor of the emancipation of slaves and that voluntary emancipations were being made. In 1741 Robert Thorpe of South Carolina manumitted two negroes, a negro woman Tula and her son Bob. After stating the identity of the two negroes and their condition of servitude their freedom was granted "for diverse good causes and considerations." The master stated that his intention was to "manumise enfranchise and set at liberty the said Negroe Woman named Tula and her said Child named Bob otherwise Robert with all their sequel issue or progeny gotten or to be begotton . . . ."[1] Evidently these negroes or their progeny later emigrated to Georgia, for a question arose as to their freedom and the same will was recorded in Georgia in 1779.

In the following will of 1755 Joseph Butler freed five of his negroes in return for five shillings paid by them to him, and in consideration of "Divers other good Causes."

> Whereas I the said Joseph Butler am presently possessed of one Negroe woman named Phillis and one Negroe girl named Mary and Negroe Boy named Doo and Negroe Girl named Sally and one Negroe Boy named Jack the Children of the said Negroe woman named Phillis—know ye That I the said Joseph Butler for and in Consideration of five shillings to me in hand paid at and before the Sealing and delivery of

---

[1] *Bonds, Bills of Sale, Deeds of Gift, Powers of Attorney,* 1779–80, 193 (Manuscript in the State Department of Archives and History, Atlanta).

those presents and for Divers other good Causes and Consideration me hereunto especially moving Have Given and Granted unto the said Negroe Woman named Phillis and to her said Children—Mary Doo Sally and Jack and to each and every of them their full and absolute freedom from all and all manner of Slavery and Servitude whatsoever from and Immediately after the date of these presents And I the said Joseph Butler do hereby for myself my EXtors and ADMtors fully and Absolutely to all Constructions and purposes whatsoever Infranchise Manumit and Set free the said—Negroe woman named Phillis and her said Children and every of them of and from all manner of Slavery and Servitude and Do for myself my EXtors and ADMtors fully and Absolutely Release and Quit all manner of Right To the Interest property Claim and Demand of in and to the same Negroe woman named Phillis and her said Children and each and every of them as Servants or Slaves in any ways howsoever. In Witness whereof I the said Joseph Butler have hereunto set my hand and Seal this third day of June in the year of our Lord One Thousand Seven Hundred and fifty-five.[2]

Sealed and   Joseph Butler   (L. S.)
Delivered in the
Presence of Will
Ben. Williamson
Jo: Menzies

In the following will John Smith gave freedom to Carolina, a negro formerly belonging to Elizabeth Bush of Port Royal. The latter had provided for the freedom of the negro after seven years of servitude. John Smith purchased the time of the negro and freed him at the end of the seven year period according to the previous will.

TO ALL whom it may concern, The Bearer Carolina a Negroe formerly belonging to Elizabeth Bush of Port Royal, who by her last Will and Testament appointing Robert William and Andrew Bell her Executors left the said Negroe Carolina his freedom after Seven Years Servitude which said time was to be sold and the money laid out as she Ordered in the said

---

[2] *Bonds, Bills of Sale, Deeds of Gift, Powers of Attorney*, 1755–1762, 2–3.

Will, now KNOW YE that I purchased the remaining part of the said time of seven year Servitude of the said Negroe Carolina from the said Robert Williams & Andrew Bell and for myself and Assigns have clothed and paid Tax for the said Negroe Carolina the said term of five say Seven years which time he has faithfully Served and now being expired in consequence of the said Will is intitled to his freedom.[3]

Given under my hand this 24th
August 1756
John Smith

According to the will of Isaac Barksdale, an Indian trader of Augusta, his negro wench Nancy, and her two children, Johney and Salley, were to be given their freedom. It also provided for the freedom of another negro woman Nanney, whom he had partly freed before. This will was recorded in November, 1757. It stated: "Item I give unto my Negro Wench Nancy and her two Mulatto children named Johney and Salley their freedom. Item I give unto my negro Wench named Nanney, whom I partly freed before, her freedom to all Intents and purposes."[4] In the following year the will of Margaret Pages, a widow of Savannah, provided for the manumission, maintenance, and education of a mulatto slave, Peter, who was to be taught a beneficial trade until he attained the age of twenty-one. At that time Peter was to be given his freedom.[5]

In 1760 Richard Hazzard gave freedom to a negro woman, Judy, as a reward of her faithful services. The negro was assured of her freedom and permission "to pass and Repass" in any of the colonies without molestation.[6] In 1762 John Hearn, a planter of Great Ogeechee, gave freedom to two mulattoes, a boy and a girl named Addin and Rachel respectively, children of a slave named Diana. At the time of the making of the will the boy Addin was hired out to William Patterson of Savannah and the Girl to Isabella

---

[3] *Ibid*, 1755–1762, 121.
[4] *Colonial Wills of Georgia*, Book A, 30 (Manuscript in State Department of Archives and History, Atlanta).
[5] *Ibid*, Book A, 271–272.
[6] *Bonds, Bills of Sale, Deeds of Gift, Powers of Attorney*, 1761–1765, 153.

Stanley of Savannah, wife of Joseph Stanley. Freedom was voluntarily granted to these two children "for divers good Causes and Considerations." They were given their perfect freedom "from all manner of Slavery and Servitude whatsoever" at the expiration of the term for which they were hired out to their master and mistress.[7]

James Habersham was a great landowner and planter of Georgia. He owned many slaves and was a very humane master. He even sent to London for clothes for his slaves.[8] In the following will he granted freedom to his negro Susannah.

> Whereas I the said James Habersham at the time of the sealing and delivery of these presents am possessed of a Negroe named Susannah commonly called Sue. Now know ye that I the said James Habersham for and in Consideration of the faithfull Service of the said Negroe Woman named Susannah have given and Granted and by these presents do for myself my Executors and Administrators give and grant unto the said Susannah Commonly Called Sue her full, absolute and perfect freedom from all and all Manner of Slavery and Servitude whatever forever from and immediately after my decease—and I the said James Habersham do also for myself, my heirs, Executors and Administrators hereby fully and absolutely and to all Intents and purposes whatever infranchise Manumit and set free forever after my decease the said Susannah—And I do moreover release and quit all my right, Title, Interest, property, Claims and demand whatever of in and to the said Susannah in any wise howsoever after my decease In Witness whereof I the same James Habersham have hereunto Set my hand and Seal at Savannah in the province aforesaid the twenty-first day of August 1767 and in the Seventh year of his Majesty's Reign.
>
> Sealed and Delivered   James Habersham (L. S.)
> in the presence of
> Joseph Clay
> James Habersham Junior[9]

[7] *Bonds, Bills of Sale, Deeds of Gift, Powers of Attorney,* 1755–1762, 509.
[8] Letters of the Honorable James Habersham, *Georgia Historical Collections,* VI, 15–17.
[9] *Bonds, Bills of Sale, Deeds of Gift, Powers of Attorney,* 1772–1777, 466–467.

John Rouviere of Savannah, in his last will which was recorded on August 4, 1767, liberated four of his negroes, viz., Tom, Judith, and the two children of Tom. "And in Consideration of the faithfull Services of my two Negroes named Tom and Judith I do hereby manumit and make free from all Slavery and Servitude Immediately from and after my Decease the Said Negroe named Tom with his two children named Billy and March and the said Negroe Woman named Judith." [10]

In 1767 J. Prunieres of Savannah manumitted Tommy, the son of a negro woman slave named Mary. Tommy was given his freedom "for divers good Causes and Considerations." He was to be given his "full absolute and perfect freedom from all and all Manner of Slavery and Servitude whatever from and immediately after the Execution of these presents." Thereupon the said J. Prunieres gave up all claim that he or his heirs might have over the said Tommy. "I do moreover release and Quit all my right Title Interest property Claim or demand whatever of in or to the said Child named Tommy as Servant or Slave in any wise howsoever." [11] The will was dated August 13, 1767.

The will of Daniel Ross, 1770, provided that a mulatto girl, Sally, daughter of a negro woman Phillis, was to have her freedom, but she was to live until she was fifteen years of age with a friend of the master, a certain Thomas Ross. It provided that the girl should be taught to read English and should be brought up in a decent and industrious manner. The very first provision of the will (following a general introduction) was in regard to the emancipation of his slave. It stated that it was the will of the Master "that the Mulatto girl named Sally, daughter to my Negroe Woman Phillis, shall receive her freedom, after my decease but that she shall live with my Friend Mr. Thomas Ross of the Province and Parish aforesaid, Vendue Master, until the age of Fifteen years, to whom I recommend that

---

[10] *Colonial Wills of Georgia*, Book A, 214–215.
[11] *Bonds, Bills of Sale, Deeds of Gift, Powers of Attorney*, 1765–72, 142, 143.

she be taught to read English and be brought up in a decent
and industrious manner."[12]

A will dated February 4, 1771, and signed by Josiah
Tattnell, gave freedom to his negro slave, Maria. In this
will the master ordered that: "from and immediately
after the Sealing and Delivery of these my said Negro
Slave named Maria shall be Emancipated and set Free and I
do hereby accordingly, manumise set free and dismiss from
Slavery forever my said negro Woman named Maria Immediately upon the Sealing and delivery of these presents."[13]
On the same date the same Josiah Tattnell, by will, granted
manumission to another negro woman named Hagar.
The said negro slave was given her freedom in consideration
of her long and faithful service to her master. "I do hereby
accordingly manumise set free and dismiss from Slavery
forever my said Negro Woman named Hagar Immediately
upon the Sealing and delivery of these presents."[14]

In the same year, 1771, Samuel Savery of Savannah
granted freedom to George Reeves Savery, a mulatto.
"Know ye that the said Samuel Savery for and in Consideration of the regard I have and bear for my Mulatto Boy . . .
have ordained and ordered . . . that . . .the said George
Reeves Savery shall be Emancipated and Set free and Do
hereby accordingly Manumit set free and Dismiss from any
kind of Slavery or Servitude whatsoever the said George
Reeves Savery." Thereupon Samuel Savery directed that
the deed of manumission should be recorded in the Secretary's office or other proper office "that this my Deed of
Manumission be publicly known, and that the Said George
Reeves Savery is thereby made free."[15]

In the following will of 1772 manumission was granted to
a negro woman, Diner:

> Whereas the said Charles Maran in his life time and at the
> time of his decease was owner and proprietor of a Certain

---

[12] *Colonial Wills of Georgia*, Book A, 329–330.
[13] *Bonds, Bills of Sale, Deeds of Gift, Powers of Attorney*, 1765–72, 451.
[14] *Ibid*, 1765–72, 450.
[15] *Bonds, Bills of Sale, Deeds of Gift, Powers of Attorney*, 1765–72, 523–524.

Negroe Female Slave named Diner and in and by his Last Will and Testament published made and executed bearing date the thirteenth day of March in the present year of our Lord one thousand Seven hundred and seventy-two proved and now remaining of Record in the Secretarys office of the said province in Book A folio 438 & 439 did therein and thereby Give her the said Negroe Female Slave named Diner her Freedom and directed the said John Couper to be her security if any was required   Now know that we the said James Butler and Couper Executors as aforesaid in Complyance with the will of the Charles Maran deceased as above Declared and also in pursuance of the power and authority devolved on us by the said Last Will and Testament also for Divers other good Causes and Considerations moving us thereto Have declared Confirmed given and granted, and by these presents Do declare Confirm give and grant unto the said Female Slave named Diner her full absolute and perfect freedom from all and all manner of Slavery and Servitude whatsoever from and immediately after the Executor of these presents to Have and to hold unto the said Female Slave named Diner her full and absolute freedom from all manner of Slavery and Servitude whatsoever as aforesaid from henceforth forever and by the said James Butler and John Couper do hereby for ourselves our and every of our Heirs Executors and Administrators fully and absolutely and to all intents and purposes whatsoever Infranchize— Manumit and set free the said Female Slave named Diner and do moreoever Release discharge and Quit all our and Either of our Rights Title Interest property Claim and Demand whatsoever of in or to the Female Slave named Diner in anywise howsoever in Witness whereof the said James Butler and John Couper have hereunto set our hands and Seals the fifth day of October in the year of our Lord one Thousand seven hundred and seventy-two and in the Twelfth year of the Reign of his Majesty King George the Third.

Sealed and delivered   James Butler (L. S.)
in presence of   John Couper (L. S.)
Israel Bird
John Dicks   Recorded 23 December 1772.[16]

---

[16] *Bonds, Bills of Sale, Deeds of Gift, Powers of Attorney,* 1772–1777, 80.

A will recorded March 10, 1772, and signed by Daniel and Moses Nunes of Savannah, gave freedom to a negro man by name of Peter Fleming. Daniel and Moses Nunes were joint owners of the negro Peter. Freedom was granted in consideration of the former good and faithful services rendered by the negro slave named Peter Fleming, "and also for and in Consideration of the sum of five Shillings Lawfull money of the province of Georgia aforesaid to us in hand paid by the Said Peter Fleming . . . & for divers other good Causes and Considerations . . . do give & Grant unto the said negroe man Slave named Peter Fleming his full absolute and perfect freedom from all and all manner of Slavery and Servitude whatsoever. . . . "[17]

Joseph Bryan of the Parish of Christ Church, in consideration of the many faithful services of his negro slave Peter, gave freedom to his said slave which manumission was to take place upon the death of the master. This will was recorded in 1774. In regard to the manumission of Peter it stated: "I do also in Consideration of the many faithful Services performed me by my negro Slave Peter hereby Manumit and get him free of & from all manner of Slavery and Servitude whatsoever immediately from & after my decease forever."[18] According to another will of 1774, William Wylly of Chatham County granted freedom to his mulatto boy named Ben.[19]

The will of John Forbes, 1775, provided that the mulatto girl, Dina, Babet's daughter in Charlestown, should be given her freedom and one hundred and sixty pounds sterling to be held in trust for her by executors. The same will provided that two hundred pounds sterling should be given to Janet, a free negro girl who was residing at his house. "Item I give & Bequeath to Janet a free Girl now at my house two hundred pounds Sterling—Item I

---

[17] *Bonds, Bills of Sale, Deeds of Gift, Powers of Attorney,* 1765–72, 527–528.
[18] *Colonial Wills of Georgia,* Book AA, (Georgia State Department of Archives and History, Atlanta), 112.
[19] *Will of William Wylly,* 1774, on file in Chatham County Court House, Savannah.

give to a Mulato Girl (Babet's daughter in Charles Town named Dina her freedom, and I give to my Executors hereafter named In trust for the said Girl Dina the Sum of one hundred pounds Sterling."[20]

Another case of manumission in 1775 was that of the negro Lucy.   Mrs. Ann Hopkins, a widow of Augusta, provided that freedom should be granted to her negro slave Lucy.   Manumission was to be granted after the death of Mrs. Hopkins.   Lucy was to be given her freedom "in consideration of her faithfullness and tender and affectionate care, manifested toward me, during a long course of years."[21]   This will was signed and sealed on March 14, 1775.

There was a certain Stephen, a free man of color, who had been kidnapped and sold into slavery in Georgia.   The negro complained of this injustice.   Letters were written to Northern friends of Stephen who confirmed the assertion of his freedom.   A Quaker meeting was held; money was freely donated; and men were sent to recover the negro. Stephen was found and after six months was liberated in the state of Georgia.[22]

Wilkes Flagg, who was owned by Dr. Tomlinson Fort of Baldwin County, was given his freedom by his master because of his long and valuable services on the plantation. He had learned the trade of a blacksmith and followed that occupation as a free man.   Today Flagg's chapel stands as a monument to his Christian faith and his love and interest in his race.[23]

A humanitarian motive may be detected in the following will: "To all Whom it may concern and especially to all Christian well disposed people know ye I hereby give unto my Negroe man George free liberty all his life time from me to go where ever he will and follow anything he thinks

[20] *Colonial Wills of Georgia*, Book AA, 148–149.
[21] *Bonds, Bills of Sale, Deeds of Gift, Powers of Attorney*, 1772–1777, 507.
[22] Jesse Macy, *The Anti-Slavery Crusade* (New Haven, 1919), 115.
[23] Anna Maria Green Cook, *History of Baldwin County*, (Anderson, S. C., 1925), 147.

proper for him in honest way—Blamless given under my hand this 12 Day August 1777."[24] The will was signed by Henry Sharpe.

In the will of George Galphin, made in 1780, freedom was granted to Dick and Juno Kelly and their eight children. The negro Dick, his wife, and their eight children, including any further increase they might have, were to be given their freedom after the death of the Master.[25] In 1782 John Galphin granted freedom to his negro wench Sapho and her five children in reward for her services plus a small amount of money paid to him.[26]

In the following will of April 3, 1782, David Brydie of Savannah granted manumission to his slave Celia in return for the sum of ten shillings sterling.

> I David Brydie of the town of Savannah in the province of Georgia Practitioner in Physic for and in consideration of the Sum of Ten Shillings Sterling Money of Great Britain to me in hand paid at and before the Sealing hereof by my Negroe Woman Slave named Celia, Have Manumitted Enfranchised and set free the above named Celia and for myself my heirs Executors and administrators do hereby forever renounce release and quit Claim to any right Title Interest or property in the Servitude of the said Negroe Woman Slave named Celia on which any person or persons Claiming or to Claim by from or under me the said David Brydie my Executors Administrators or Assigns hereafter may demand or require of in or to the same In Witness whereof I the said David Brydie have hereunto set my hand and Seal this Twenty-third day of April in the year of our Lord One thousand seven hundred and Eighty-two and in the twenty-second year of his Majesty's Reign before these witnesses.
>
> David Montaigut J. P.   David Brydie (L. S.)
> Chas. F. Chevalier
>
>   Recorded 5th May 1783[27]

---

[24] *Bonds, Bills of Sale, Deeds of Gift, Powers of Attorney*, 1779–1780, 267.
[25] *Ibid*, 1792–1813, 86–87.
[26] *Bonds, Bills of Sale, Deeds of Gift, Powers of Attorney*, 1783–1892, 3–4.
[27] *Ibid*, 1783–1792, 18.

In 1796 Absolom Davis of Elbert County, Georgia, gave freedom to his servant, Solvanah Randall. "A clear discharge for Solvanah Randall she being free into this world, a yellow woman being a servant to me hath bought the remainder of her time to my great satisfaction, and I hereby give her her freedom from me and all other persons forever. N. B. She being the daughter of Nancy Randall as witness my hand the 2 day of July 1796."[28]

In 1785 Samuel Stirk of Savannah granted freedom to his negro wench, Fanny, "for good causes and Considerations."[29] In 1786 Austin, a mulatto, was emancipated because of his services in the late war. Another negro, Harry, was also emancipated because of his services in the war. On August 14, 1786, a bill was passed by the Legislature of Georgia which provided: "An Act to emancipate and set free Austin, a mulatto, and Harry a negro fellow.[30] In 1789 William Wallace gave freedom to Tab, wife of old Luke. In this will we find the case of a slave who was given her freedom because of her attention to her mistress during the mistress' last illness.[31] In 1792 Patrick Hayes of Richmond county emancipated a slave, Violet, in his last will.[32]

In the following will, dated February 8, 1792, James M. Simmons, citizen of Georgia, left money for the buying and freedom of his slave, Suckey.

State of Georgia.
Richmond County.

To all to whom these presents shall come, Greeting: Know ye that I James M. Simmons of the County and State aforesaid for and in consideration of the Sum of Sixty-five pounds Sterling to me in hand paid in conformity to the last Will and Testament of John Meals deceased by Robert Forsyth his Executor at or before the Sealing and delivery of these presents the receipt whereof I do hereby acknowledge, and

---

[28] *Deed Book "D,"* 7. Will on file in office of the Clerk of the Superior Court of Elbert County, Georgia.
[29] *Bonds, Bills of Sale, Deeds of Gift, Powers of Attorney,* 1783–1792, 193.
[30] Watkins, *Digest,* 346.
[31] *Bonds, Bills of Sale, Deeds of Gift, Powers of Attorney,* 1792–1813, 81–82.
[32] *Ibid,* 1783–1792, 317–319.

for and in consideration of divers other good causes and considerations we thereunto Specially Moving Have granted bargained Sold aliened released relinquished and confirmed and by these doth grant bargain Sell alien release relinquish and confirm unto a certain Mulatto Woman called and known by the name of Suckey all right title interest claim or demand of property which I have or could have to the person or Service of her the said Suckey and which by the laws of the land might in any wise appertain unto me, and I do hereby for myself my heirs Executors administrators or assigns and for all and every other person or persons claiming in, by, through or under me *totally exonerate and freely Emancipate the aforesaid Mulatto Woman* Suckey from all right title interest claim or demand which I otherwise might have in the person or to the Service of her the said Suckey and Do hereby forever quit claim to her and her increase as fully freely utterly and entirely as if she the said Suckey had been born free. TO HAVE AND TO HOLD to possess and enjoy all the rights privileges and immunities incident to freedom as fully perfectly and Entirely to her and her increase forever as if she had been born free and I myself or any other person never had had any right title interest claim or demand to the person or service of her the said Suckey. And I do hereby from myself my heir Executor Administrators and assigns and from all and every person claiming in, by through or under me the free enjoyment and interrupted possession of Liberty freedom and perfect emancipation and every privilege and immunity incident thereto to her the said Suckey and her increase by these presents forever Warrant and Defend:—

IN TESTIMONY whereof I have hereunto signed my hand and Seal this eighth day of February in the year of our Lord one thousand seven hundred and ninety-two; and in the Sixteenth year of the Independence of the United States of America.[33]

In presence of us   Jas. M. Simmons
Geo. W. Walker
W Mead

---

[33] *Ibid*, 1792–1813, 1–4.

In February, 1795, Joseph Watts of Burke County manumitted by will his waiting boy Jim. He also added, "I desire that all my negroes may be humanely used and none of their families separated, but when divided or sold to be parted in families only."[34] The author of the following will foresaw and predicted the prohibition of the importation of negroes into Georgia. "But it is my will that in every instance where opportunities shall offer, the negro property of my Estate shall be increased for this intent, that I contemplate a Prohibition of the Importation of negroes in a Short time, and Georgia being the only State which now admits the Importation of them, the value of that Species of Property will be very much enhanced immediately after such Prohibition."[35]

Daniel Grant of Wilkes County, in his last will in 1796, provided for the freedom of his slaves. The negroes were accordingly emancipated by Act Number 544 of the state legislature of 1796.[36] By the terms of the will the executors were directed to apply to the legislature for the usual enabling act to carry the will into effect. The act stated that "the said Daniel Grant, deceased, hath by his last will and testament declared certain negro slaves therein named free at certain times, and under certain conditions and restrictions therein contained. . . . " The terms of the will in regard to the negroes, were then made valid by legislative act.[37]

In the same year Anthony Hayns of Columbia County liberated ten of his slaves. Hayns had provided for the manumission of his slaves in the preceding year by means of "a certain instrument in writing" which was recorded in the clerk's office of Columbia County. An enabling act was passed by the state legislature to put that "certain instrument" into effect. Thus the ten slaves of Anthony

---

[34] *Will Book A, April, 1775–July, 1801*, 245. Found in Chatham County Court House, Savannah, Georgia.
[35] *Ibid*, 266–267.
[36] Watkins, *Digest*, 585.
[37] *Ibid*, 585.

Hayns were freed by action of the state legislature. They were declared to be "forever manumitted, emancipated and freed, and capable of enjoying all the rights and privileges of citizenship."[38]   In the same year two other negroes, Reubin Going and John Going, of Greene County were given their freedom and authorized to hold property under the laws of the state.[39]

Joseph Gabriel Posner of Jefferson County sought to manumit his slave, Sylvia Posner, and her son David. One of the first acts of the Georgia legislature was passed giving the said Sylvia Posner her freedom. The first Digest of Georgia, published while Louisville (Jefferson County) was the capitol, contains the act of manumission.[40] The will of Joseph Gabriel Posner is on file at the Ordinary's office in Jefferson County. Posner was a Polish Jew. He lived and owned property in Louisville. In his will, dated November 18, 1812, he willed and bequeathed all his estate to the above-mentioned Sylvia Posner. He provided that the estate should be used for the sole benefit of his beloved wife, Sylvia Sigmond Posner, during her life; at her death the remainder was to be divided among nieces and nephews in England.[41]

In a will of June 4, 1801, Herman Herson, a shipwright of Savannah, provided for the manumission of two of his slaves named Fortune and Chance in return for money to be paid to his wife after his decease.[42]   On August 9, 1801, Valeria Gibbons of Savannah, widow of William Gibbons of revolutionary fame, provided in her will for the manumission of her negro slave Kingston.[43]   William Gibbons of Chatham County, in his will of September 21, 1803, provided for the manumission of some of his slaves.

---

[38] Watkins, *Digest*, 585.
[39] *Ibid*, 586.
[40] Marbury and Crawford, *Digest*, 206.
[41] *Will of Joseph Gabriel Posner*, original in Jefferson County Court House, Louisville, Georgia.
[42] *Record of Wills*, Aug. 3, 1801–April 1, 1807, 3.   (On file in Chatham County Court House, Savannah).
[43] *Ibid*, 5.

"I do hereby manumit and set free my negro man Bing and his wife Peg if it is their choice, and they are to have as much land free of any charge on my beech Forest tract as they themselves can."[44] And another item: "I do hereby manumit and set free my mulatto girl named Harriet and I desire that my Executors do take the necessary measures to have her freedom complicated agreeably to the law of the state."[45]

The will of Howell Cobb of Jefferson County (uncle of the more famous Howell Cobb—the Confederate statesman) expresses his desire to emancipate all of his slaves, but he also states his belief that such an act would be inexpedient. However, he did provide for the manumission of one of his slaves. He said that the liberation of the remainder of his slaves was prevented by a belief that the care of generous and humane masters would be much better for them than a state of freedom. In regard to the famous nephew, the will stated: "Whenever my said Brother's Son named Howell Cobb arrives at the age of twenty-one years, and discovers a humane and benevolent disposition towards my negroes my said brother John A. Cobb after his death and not before may give to my said nephew Howell Cobb all my above mentioned Estate, if he the said John A. Cobb think him truly worthy of it." In regard to his wife and her treatment of the slaves the will stated: "I think I have sufficient evidence of the goodness of my wife's temper and disposition, as to be under no apprehension whatever relative to the treatment of my Negroes but that she will use her best endeavours to treat them with all that kindness with which I used toward them." He again expresses his concern for the negroes in the following: "It is my most ardent desire that in whomsoevers hands fortune may place said Negroes that all the Justice and indulgence may be shown toward them as is consistent with the hope, that none of my relations, or connections, will be so ungrateful to my mem-

---

[44] *Will of William Gibbons.* Recorded April 20, 1804. On file in Chatham County Court House, Savannah, Georgia.
[45] *Ibid.*

ory to treat or use them otherwise." The will provided for the manumission of the negro, William Hill "for his long and faithful service and his kind attentions to me, and for whom I have a respect; I therefore entirely emancipate him from a state of slavery, and to be what he is really deserving—a Freeman." Cobb then expressed his desire to emancipate all of his slaves. "It would afford me the greatest pleasure and satisfaction, to liberate all my slaves; but such is the present existing state of Society, that by so doing I may act improperly; and it is by no means impossible that it would be no real lasting advantage to them; and I presume that their present condition, under the care & protection of generous & human masters, will be much better for them than a state of freedom."[46] This will is dated April 15, 1817. Since Cobb could not free his slaves he bequeathed them to his wife who he knew would treat them with kindness. But if his wife should marry again, thus putting her property under the control of a stranger, the slaves and the plantation were at once to revert to the testator's brother who was recommended to bequeath them in turn to his son Howell if he were deemed worthy of the trust. This incident shows the kindness of the master to the slaves and his conscious responsibility for their welfare.

The following is copied from the last will and testament of Raymond Demere of Glynn County, who died in 1829:

> Whereas, from the fidelity of my negro man Ivy and my negro woman, Rose, who not only saved and protected a great part of my property during the time the British occupied St. Simons, but actually buried and saved a large sum of specie with and which they might have absconded and obtained their freedom; it is therefore my will and I direct my executors to petition the legislature to pass an act for the manumission of my said negro man Ivy and my woman Rose with her two children, Jim and John, and any other children said Rose may have setting their meritorious behavior and faithful conduct during a period of invasion when nearly

---

[46] *Will of Howell Cobb* (Manuscript in Jefferson County Court House, Louisville, Georgia.)

all the negroes on St. Simons deserted and joined the British, but in case the legislature should refuse to pass an act for the manumission of said slaves it is my will that said Ivy Rose and her children shall be sent to any other State where the freedom of such people can be secured and permitted; said negroes to be transferred and freed at the expense of my estate. It is my will and I direct that if the said Ivy and Rose and her children are freed by law or remain in Georgia that the said Ivy, Rose and her sons, Jim and John shall each receive four cows and four calves from my stock on St. Simons and that Rose's son John shall receive four cows and calves from said stock, and it is further my will and I direct my executors to lay off separate lots of my land on St. Simons for the said Ivy, Rose and her children, sufficient for them to cultivate and be comfortable, with permission to build, live and reside thereon during their lives and it is my will that said lots of land should be laid off and the parties put in possession within one year after my decease, and that also said Ivy, Rose and her Children shall receive from my estate one year's provision from the time they take possession of their lots, and also that my Executors shall pay annually from my estate or have payment of the same secured viz—to my negro woman Rose during her life an annuity of seventy-five dollars, and also the further sum of five dollars for the support of her son John until he arrives at the age of twenty-one and then my said executors are directed to pay unto the said John from my estate the sum of one thousand dollars lawful money of the United States and it is further my will and I direct that the said John shall be taught reading, writing and arithmetic and to be brought up to and taught some mechanical profession."[47]

Thus we see that from the time that slavery was introduced into Georgia in 1750 slaves were being continually manumitted. Many manumissions took place during the Colonial period, during the revolution, and before and after Georgia arrived at statehood. In the following chapter we shall see that negroes continued to be freed by wills, deeds, certificates of freedom, special legislative enactment,

---

[47] *Will Book "D,"* 158, Glynn County, Georgia records.

and that some negroes were refused their freedom by the legislative assembly.   However, the sentiment in favor of voluntary manumission prevailed during this period.

CHAPTER IX

MANUMISSION OF SLAVES—Continued.

Many slaves were manumitted during the colonial period; this voluntary manumission continued until the civil war and the consequent emancipation of the slaves. Slaves were freed; laws were passed describing the mode of manumission; and in many cases manumission was prohibited by the state legislature. But in spite of this voluntary emancipation was taking place.

In 1811 a bill was passed by the state legislature to emancipate a certain negro woman named Hannah.[1] In 1818 a bill was passed to manumit a "certain person of colour therein named." The yeas were 43 and the nays 41.[2]

In addition to the wills of the masters which granted manumission to slaves, sometimes testimonials were granted which certified the freedom of the negro. In the following Henry Ellis declares the bearer of the testimonial, Harry, to be a freeman.

> To whomsoever this may come
> These are to certify, that the Bearer, who calls himself Harry, is, and ought to be considered, a free man, untill sufficient appears in a legal way, to the contrary Given under my hand at Savannah the 23rd day of May 1758
>
> Henry Ellis
>
> Recorded the 25th day of May 1758.[3]

In another testimonial Bob, a mulatto, was given his freedom by C. Pryce. Bob had already been given his freedom by his former Master, John Palmer; John Street of Savannah was appointed as his guardian. Bob's posi-

---

[1] *House Journal*, 1811, 92, 132.
[2] *Ibid*, 1818, 31, 36, 132.
[3] *Bonds, Bills of Sale, Deeds of Gift, Powers of Attorney*, 1755–1762, 192.

tion as a free man was contested by Benjamin Smith. The case was brought before the General Court of Pleas held in Savannah. The verdict of the jury was that Bob was a free man.[4]

In 1770 John Riely testified as to the freedom of William Dawkins, a negro and former slave. Riely swore that the formal deed of manumission had been in his possession but that he had left the paper at Kingston in Jamaica "with Messieurs McLean and Moore Merchants at Kingston to get the said Paper recorded."[5] Consequently the freedom of William Dawkins was left unmolested.

At the request of a slaver's captain the government of Georgia issued in 1772 a certificate to a certain Fenda Lawrence reciting that she, a free black woman from Africa, had voluntarily come to this province, and giving to her permission to pass unmolested within the said province. Thus it was that an African tourist was granted the freedom of the province of Georgia.[6]

The following are testimonials of free negroes in Georgia. "Permit the Bearer Ned his Wife and Family free Negroes to pass and repass Unmolested."[7] The permission was signed by B. Lane, town adjutant, and dated June 4, 1780. Another free pass was granted to the same Ned, free negro, and his wife and family by David Montaigut of Savannah.[8] A certificate of freedom was granted to Michael Thomas, his wife Sarah, and their children. The undersigned declared: "That we never knew any body lay or make good any lawful claim to them or any of them as their Right and property nor ever heard that any of them forfeited his her or their Title to their freedom and we do sincerely believe that said Michael Thomas his Wife Sarah, and their children are and should be free to all intents and purposes."[9] A man by the name of Smith testified that "The Bearer hereof Michael Thomas came with me from Pensacola

---

[4] *Ibid,* 1761–65, 246.
[5] *Ibid,* 1779–1780, 108.
[6] *Ibid,* 1772–1777, 14–15.
[7] *Ibid,* 1779–1780, 250.
[8] *Ibid,* 250.
[9] *Ibid,* 250–251.

into the Creek Nation and thence into Georgia between eight or nine years ago, and was then reputed with his family to be free negroes."[10] A free pass was also granted to Michael Thomas, Andrew Thomas, Thomas Thomas, Sarah Thomas, the mother, and to Philly Thomas. "The above free man and his family have liberty to pass and repass unmolested by order of Col. Clarke."[11] A free pass signed by Robert Lane, town adjutant, stated that "The Bearer Mich¹ Thomas has Lt. Col. Clarke's permission to pass and repass about his business."[12]

John Wright of Savannah rented his house, garden, and fields, situated two miles from Savannah near the Little Ogeechee river, to a certain free negro by the name of David George.[13] In 1780 a free pass was granted to the said negro by Edward Cooper, the town adjutant of Savannah.[14] Certificates of freedom were granted to the wife and family of David George. "The within mentioned David George has a wife named Phillis and three Children (who are also free) Jesse David and Ginney who are all recommended to the Protection of his Majestys Subjects."[15] This was signed by Edward Cooper, adjutant of Savannah. Another stated that "The bearer David George has my leave to pass and Repass on his business," and was signed by A. Clarke.[16] Certificates of freedom and free passes were granted to a negro by the name of George of Savannah in 1779. One testimonial was signed by order of the Lieutenant General, Prevost, and by Philip Moore, colonel in the Georgia militia.[17] Another was signed by Robert Barrow, major-general.[18] Another, dated 1780, was signed by Archibald McArthur, Major of the 71st regiment.[19]

---

[10] *Ibid*, 251.
[11] *Ibid*, 251.
[12] *Ibid*, 1779–1780, 251.
[13] *Ibid*, 1779–1780, 249.
[14] *Ibid*, 1779–1780, 249.
[15] *Ibid*, 1779–1780, 250.
[16] *Ibid*, 1779–1780, 250.
[17] *Ibid*, 1779–1780, 266.
[18] *Ibid*, 1779–1780, 266.
[19] *Ibid*, 1779–1780, 266–267.

The following is a certificate and testimonial of the status and character of Moses Handlen, a free black man.

> This is to satisfy to whom it may concern That this Black Man, Mr. Moses Handlen is Free Man leaft by his Master Mr. Champernown Handlen, deceased in the year of our Lord 1760. This very Black Moses Handlen is a very onnis Black Man. I knowed him from a boy. Witness my hand.
>
> George Smith[20]

In a testimonial made by a clergyman, Alexander Richardson in 1784, he attempted to aid the negro Marcus in gaining his freedom. Richardson had visited the Master of Marcus, Fenwick Bull, during the last illness of the latter. The clergyman heard Bull say that he intended to manumit his slave; but the master died before the legal deed was drawn up. Richardson testified that he commanded the attention of the Master to his slave Marcus and that Bull uttered these words: "That in case he the said Fenwick Bull died, he the said Marcus should return to his Friends in Carolina and be no longer to any person a Slave." The clergyman continued: "And I verily believe that had the said Fenwick Bull imagined that the time of his dissolution was so near as it proved to be, he would have Emancipated his said Negro Servant Marcus under, Fenwick Bulls, seal and Signature, but his hopes of recovery continued to the very last, and then he was not able to Execute any Instrument of Writing to that Effect." Consequently Richardson thought that it was only fair that the wishes of the late Master should be carried out and that Marcus should be given his freedom.[21]

The following certificates of freedom are evidences of negroes who were emancipated by the last will and testament of their Mistress, Mrs. Jane Somerville of Augusta. In the first one, Leo Marbury gives a certificate of freedom to Bob, emancipated by Mrs. Somerville.

---

[20] *Deed Book* (1780–1781), 236. Georgia Archives, Department of State, Atlanta. Quoted by U. B. Phillips, *Plantation and Frontier Documents*, II, 141.

[21] *Bonds, Bills of Sale, Deeds of Gift, Powers of Attorney*, 1783–1792, 168–169.

I do hereby Certify that the bearer hereof Bob a Mustee fellow formerly the property of Mrs. Jane Somerville deceased, was by her last will and Testament emancipated, and that he was set at liberty by her executors, viz. Col Robert Rae James Rae & Gen. Samuel Elbert immediately after her decease sometime in the fall 1779 since which time he has always been considered a free man. Given under my hand this 11th day of May 1789.

Leo Marbury[22]

In the following James Rae gives to negro Tom a certificate of freedom. Tom had formerly been freed by Mrs. Somerville.

I do certify that Tom is a freeman and that the record of Mrs. Jane Somervilles Will is a testimony of the same.
Recorded 28 July 1789

James Rae
Executor the Estat
Mrs Somerville[23]

Leo Marbury also testifies that Tom is a free man.

State of Georgia. Richmond County.
I do certify that Negro Tom was emancipated by the will of Mrs. Jane Somerville, since whose decease he has always been considered a free man given under my hand this 27th July 1789.
Recorded 28 July 1789.

Leo Marbury[24]

The following is a testimonial of the status of the negro, Sam Woodward, a free man who had lost his free pass. Thus Dalziel Hunter gave to the negro Sam a certificate of freedom.

State of Georgia.
Mr. Sebastian Blash of Augusta Informs me of a Negro Man named Sam Woodward at present in said place who he well knows to be a free man as he saw him in the year 1782 on board of a Ship of War of only four Guns, & Wrought on board of her as a hand & passed Generally as a free man. These are therefore to Certify & make known to all persons Whom it may concern that I have known the above mentioned

---

[22] *Ibid,* 1783–1792, 256.
[23] *Ibid,* 277.
[24] *Ibid,* 277.

Sam for these four or five years past & hired himself to different persons in Augusta & always passed for a free man behaving himself Soberly and honestly he the said Sam Woodward has therefore my permission to pass & live in the said place unmolested so long as he behaves himself well, and the reason of his applying to me now is that he lost the free pass he had from Captn Samuel Carns Who Commanded the Poris privateer, while he was on board of a Pelacre Ship Comanded by Captain Bailey at Savannah Light House about five years ago—

In testimony whereof I have hereunto subscribed my name as Justice of the peace in the County of Richmond in the state aforesaid & Caused my Seal of Office to be affisced— as also Subscribed by Mr. Sebastian Blash of Augusta this firs(t) Day of June Seventeen hundred and Ninety-one in the fifteenth year of the Independence of the United States of America.

Dalziel Hunter J. P. (L. S.)[25]

Blache

The manumission of slaves in Georgia was permitted by law. An act passed December 5, 1801, prescribed the mode of manumitting slaves in Georgia.[26] According to this act slaves were to be manumitted by the legislature. Thus we have the spectacle of slaves being freed in Georgia by action of the legislature of the state. It was only by authority of the legislature specifically granted that a valid emancipation could be made. It was unlawful for any person to manumit a slave or any person of color who might be deemed a slave. The attempt to set free a slave by any other mode than by application to the legislature was visited with severe penalties. According to the Act of 1801 it was made illegal for any clerk to enter on record any deed of manumission or other paper which had for its object the manumitting or setting free any slave or slaves. If any person should set free any slave or slaves in any other manner than by special legislative act, he was to forfeit for such

---

[25] *Ibid*, 1792–1813, 109–111.
[26] Prince, *Digest*, 456–457; Cobb's *Digest*, 982.

offense two hundred dollars, half to be applied to the use of the county in which the offense was committed, and the other half to be given to the informer; and the slave so manumitted was still as much in a state of slavery as he was before he was manumitted by the offending party.[27] By a subsequent act of 1818 the penalty for this offense was increased to five hundred dollars,[28] half to be given to the person suing or prosecuting under the act, and the other half to be applied to the use of the county in which the offense was committed.[29] It was prohibited that these deeds of manumission be recorded.[30] Therefore we have no complete and satisfactory records of the number of slaves who were given their freedom.

It is very probable that a great number of slaves were being emancipated and that this gave rise to the demand for more rigid rules concerning manumission. This law prescribing the mode of manumitting slaves was amended in December, 1815, so as to permit the recording of deeds of manumission.[31] This act permitted an owner to free his slaves by will and testament. It was again amended in 1818 in order to prevent the migration of free persons of color into Georgia, and to regulate free persons who already resided there.[32] Congressman Reid of Georgia said in the National House of Representatives that this act "was designed more completely to carry into effect the provisions of a law prescribing the manner of manumitting, and which had been enacted several years before . . . certain it is, that the statute book of that State [Georgia] contains no law by which it is declared that slaves cannot be made free."[33] This act of 1818 rendered void all subsequent manumission by testament. No slave was to be manumitted by will or by contract.[34] "All and every will and testament, deed, . . .

---

[27] Cobb's *Digest*, 982; Prince, *Digest*, 457, 787.
[28] Cobb's *Digest*, 990; Prince, *Digest*, 795.
[29] Prince, *Digest*, 795.
[30] *Ibid*, 457.
[31] *House Journal*, 1815, 72, 85, 141, 224; Lamar, *Compilation*, 801.
[32] Lamar, *Compilation*, 811–816.
[33] *Annals of Congress*, 16th Congress, 1st Session, 1024.
[34] Lamar, *Compilation*, 811–813; Prince, *Digest*, 466.

contract, agreement, or stipulation, or other instrument in writing, or by parol, made and executed for the purpose of effecting, or endeavoring to effect the manumission of any slave or slaves . . . shall be, and the same are hereby declared to be utterly null and void. . . . "[35]

All persons making or concerned with such wills or contracts were to be subject to a penalty of not more than $1,000, and the slaves attempted to be made free were to be sold.[36]   This section of the act was repealed later.[37] In spite of the punishment imposed for the crime of manumitting slaves, it is presumed that some Georgians were guilty of the offense or else the law of 1818 would not have been necessary. The terms of the law were:

> All and every will and testament, deed, whether by way of trust or otherwise, contract or agreement or stipulation, or other instrument in writing or by parole, made and executed for the purpose of effecting or endeavoring to effect the manumission of any slave or slaves, either directly by conferring or attempting to confer freedom on such slave or slaves, indirectly or virtually by allowing and securing or attempting to allow and secure to such slave or slaves the right or privilege of working for his, her or themselves, free from the control of the master or owner of such slave or slaves, or of enjoying the profits of his, her or their labour skill, shall be and the same are hereby declared to be utterly null and void; and the person or persons so making &c. any such deed &c. &c. and all and every person or persons concerned in giving or attempting to give effect thereto, whether by accepting the trust created or attempted to be created; or in any other way or manner whatsoever, shall be severally liable to a penalty not exceeding one thousand dollars to be recovered, &c. &c; and each and every slave or slaves in whose behalf such will or testament &c. &c. shall have been made shall be liable to be arrested by warrant under the hand and seal of any magistrate of this state, and, being thereof convicted, &c. shall be liable to be sold as a slave or

---

[35] Prince, *Digest*, 795.
[36] *Ibid*, 795.
[37] Lamar, *Compilation*, 801.

slaves, by public outcry, and the proceeds of such sales shall be appropriated, &c. &c.[38]

According to the constitution of Georgia of 1798, slaves were not to be emancipated without the consent of their owners.[39] In 1825 a bill was introduced into the legislature which prescribed the mode of manumission. After a second reading the bill was lost.[40] "The Senate took up the bill to be entitled an act to amend an act supplementary to an act more effectually to enforce an act prescribing the mode of manumitting slaves in this state, and also to prevent the inveigling and illegal carrying out of the state, persons of color. Which was on motion, ordered to be laid on the table the balance of the session."[41]

The mode of manumitting slaves in Georgia was still further amended in December, 1826. According to this act clerks were not to issue certificates of registry of freedom to any colored person, only upon the oath of his guardian. Clerks were to give notice before such certificates were issued. Section one read:

> From and after the passage of this act, it shall not be lawful for the clerk of the inferior court of any county of this State, to issue any certificate of registry of freedom to any colored person, but upon affidavit first made by the guardian of such person of colour, that he or she is a free person of colour duly manumitted agreeable to the laws of this State; and that he or she is about to remove into another county, or beyond the limits of this State, or about to depart in the capacity of a servant to some inhabitant of this State.[42]

This act shows that, although the people of the state supported manumission, they tried to prevent the presence of the free negro among them except in the capacity of a servant. Although the law forbade any man to give freedom to his slave unless he should be taken out of the state, it

---

[38] Prince, *Digest*, 466; Cobb's *Digest*, 991.
[39] Watkins, *Digest*, 42; Prince, *Digest*, 559.
[40] *Senate Journal*, 1825, 150, 227.
[41] *Ibid*, 1825, 227.
[42] Arthur Foster, *Digest of the Laws of Georgia*, 1820–1829 (Philadelphia, 1831), 311. Hereafter referred to as Foster, *Digest*. Dawson, *Compilation*, 411.

was evaded by some humane owners, who, though they could not give their slaves legal freedom within the state, gave them the entire command of their labor, and allowed them to work for themselves and to enjoy without deduction all the fruits of their industry.[43]

As late as 1859 a law was passed against the manumission of slaves. This law declared: "that from and after the passage of this Act any and every clause in a deed, will, or other instrument, made for the purpose of conferring freedom on slaves directly or indirectly, within or without the State, to take effect after the death of the owner, shall be absolutely void."[44] Thus it was sought to prevent the post-mortem manumission of slaves.

Another method of manumitting slaves in Georgia was by purchase. Negroes were allowed to buy their own freedom. In the case of Solomon Humphries of Macon, Georgia, we find the unique example of a slave who bought his own freedom, became a well known business man of the city, and was readily trusted by the white merchants. Humphries was originally a slave to a Georgia planter, but, since he was possessed of unusual intelligence and activity, he had special privileges granted to him. By these means he acquired small sums which he placed at interest, and by his perseverance he acquired enough money to buy his own freedom. He set up his own business and soon acquired enough money to buy the freedom of his family. Every year his accumulations increased. Although he was unable to read or write he obtained the services of two white clerks who kept books and carried on his correspondence. The merchants and traders of the North, with whom he dealt and corresponded, always visited him when they came South for business or pleasure. He kept an excellent house and entertained lavishly.[45] The case of this negro is evidence that negroes could manumit themselves, engage in business, and maintain the highest respect of their

[43] Buckingham, *The Slave States of America*, I, 168.
[44] *Acts of Georgia*, 1859, 68.
[45] Buckingham, *The Slave States of America*, I, 211–213.

fellow-citizens. Although much abusive language has been recorded concerning the free negro, it is evident that many of them were economic assets to their communities.

Another interesting case in Georgia, at a much later period was that of the Reverend G. H. Dwelle, a negro. He was born in Columbia County, Georgia, in January, 1833. After nearly thirty years in slavery he was able to purchase his own freedom and that of his mother with money he had made as a cabinet maker in Augusta. Dwelle was ordained to the ministry in 1866, and served for twenty-seven years as pastor of the Springfield Baptist Church, one of the oldest churches in the state. He was sent as a missionary to Southwest Georgia, the first missionary to be sent out by the church and the Ebenezer Association. He organized a number of churches in that section of the state including the Eureka Church at Albany and the Shady Grove Church at Americus, both of which he served as pastor for a number of years. Reverend Dwelle was the only living man of his race who took part in the organization of the Baptist state negro convention of Georgia, which took place in the Central Baptist Church at Augusta in June, 1870. He was the first recording secretary and when the convention split into two sections in Atlanta in 1893, he became first president of the Northern section. He was instrumental in combining the two sections in 1915. He was one of the oldest living negro Masons, being a charter member of the St. John Lodge F. & A. M. of Americus. He was one of the first men to raise money for Spelman Seminary, now Spelman College. Reverend Dwelle led one of the most successful and constructive lives of any man of his race in the history of Georgia. He began life as a slave and purchased his own freedom. This is another instance of a self manumitted slave who maintained the highest respect of the people because of his character and services. Dwelle died at the age of ninety-five at the home of his daughter, Dr. Georgia Dwelle of Atlanta. He was buried in Augusta.[46]

---

[46] *The Atlanta Journal,* March 30, 1928.

Although manumission was discouraged by law, special acts were passed every year to give freedom to certain slaves. A record is given of a certain slave by the name of Davy and a female slave by the name of Hannah who were manumitted by action of the state legislature in 1827.[47] The yeas and nays were required. The yeas were 35 and the nays 20. A clause was inserted in the last will and testament of Thomas W. Cobb of Greene County providing for the emancipation of certain negroes mentioned therein. At the same time it was decided to emancipate the wife and father of the above mentioned Solomon Humphries of Macon, Georgia.[48] Thomas W. Cobb was a prominent Georgian of his time. He was Congressman, United States senator, and judge. The bill was introduced "to manumit and set free certain negro slaves therein mentioned in pursuance with a request contained in the last will and testament of Thomas W. Cobb, late of Greene County, dec'd and to emancipate the wife and father of Solomon Humphries, free man of color, was read the third time and passed."[49] Solomon Humphries bought the freedom of his wife and father but this freedom could not be granted except by action of the state legislature. However both of these bills were rejected by the Senate.[50] The bill in regard to the wife and father of Solomon Humphries was again introduced in 1834 and passed. The yeas were 88 and the nays 46.[51] Thus it was that Patsey, the wife and Cyrus the father, were given their freedom in 1834 by action of the state legislature.

In 1833 a woman and child, the wife and child of a free man of color, were set free by action of the state legislature.[52] "The House took up the report on the bill, to manumit and make free, Mary, a woman of colour and her child Cordilia, now the property, wife and child of Lovewell C.

---

[47] *Senate Journal,* 1827, 117–118.
[48] *House Journal,* 1830, 255, 318, 333.
[49] *Ibid,* 1830, 333.
[50] *Senate Journal,* 1830, 349–350.
[51] *House Journal,* 1834, 378.
[52] *House Journal,* 1833, 377, 419.

Fluellin, a free man of colour, which was agreed to, the bill was read the third time, and passed under the title thereof."[53] In 1834 a bill was passed which provided for the manumission of certain persons.[54] In 1834 a negro named Edmund, slave of a certain Theophilus Rills, was set free.[55] In at least one case the legislature appropriated money to purchase a negro in order to set him free. This negro, by the name of Sam, was purchased from his owner for the sum of $1,800. Freedom was extended to him as a reward for his extraordinary services in extinguishing a fire on the State House. Sam received his freedom by action of the legislature in 1834.[56] In the same year a bill was passed by the legislature to manumit "certain persons."[57] In 1836 a negro slave by the name of Hannah Lanos was manumitted by the state legislature.[58] In that same year the legislature voted to extend freedom to Philip, Phillis and children, all slaves, property of Catherine Cates of Bibb County.[59] In 1839 the legislature voted manumission to Eliza, Charles, and Thomas, all slaves.[60] In 1850 there were nineteen manumitted slaves in Georgia and eighty-nine fugitive slaves.[61]

John Randolph of Virginia who died in 1833 provided in his will for the emancipation of his slaves. He also provided that lands should be purchased for them North of the Ohio. The complete text of the will was published in the Southern Recorder,[62] a Georgia paper, and no protest was made. The failure to carry out the will was due to sentiment at the North and their unwillingness to admit the emancipated slaves into the free states.

There were instances where a man sought to liberate his slaves but was prevented from doing so by the state legisla-

---

[53] *Ibid*, 1833, 419.
[54] *Ibid*, 1834, 258.
[55] *Senate Journal*, 1834, 370.
[56] *Senate Journal*, 1834, 147, 212, 330, 368; *The African Repository*, X, 313.
[57] *Senate Journal*, 1834, 294, 320, 336, 367, 377.
[58] *House Journal*, 1836, 199.
[59] *Ibid*, 1836, 166.
[60] *Ibid*, 1839, 77.
[61] J. B. D. DeBow, *Statistical View of the United States* (Washington, 1854), 64.
[62] *The Southern Recorder*, August 11, 1835.

ture. A certain Mark Cole of Georgia provided in his will for the liberation of ten of his negro slaves. The usual enabling act was introduced into the state legislature in November, 1824, but failed to pass.[63] In 1832 a bill was introduced to manumit certain mulattoes and to enable them to hold property.[64] This bill was defeated.[65] The yeas were 19 and the nays 121.[66]

On December 5, 1832, a bill was reported and read for the first time which provided for the manumission of certain persons of color therein named.[67] It was read a second time on December 12, was referred to a committee of the whole house and consequently lost.[68] In 1833 a bill was introduced into the House by Mr. King of Greene County providing for the manumission of certain slaves; after a second reading the bill was lost.[69]

In 1838 a bill to emancipate and set free a female slave named Peninah, the property of Alden McElberry of Butts County was introduced into the Senate and passed that body.[70] "The report of the committee of the whole on the bill to manumit and set free Peninah, a slave, the property of Alden McElberry, of the county of Butts, was taken up, amended and agreed to, the bill read the third time, and on the question, shall this bill now pass, was decided in the affirmative by yeas and nays; yeas 45, nays 20."[71] So the bill passed under the title thereof. During the same legislative session the bill to manumit Peninah was introduced into the House. After a first and second reading the bill was referred to a committee of the whole house.[72] Although the bill had already passed the Senate it was defeated in the House. "The House took up the report on the bill to manu-

---

[63] *Senate Journal,* 1824, 119.
[64] *House Journal,* 1832, 131.
[65] *Ibid,* 1832, 215, 229.
[66] *Ibid,* 1832, 229.
[67] *Ibid,* 1832, 226.
[68] *House Journal,* 1832, 275.
[69] *Ibid,* 1833, 128, 131.
[70] *Senate Journal,* 1838, 281.
[71] *Ibid,* 1838, 281.
[72] *House Journal,* 1838, 379, 406.

mit and set free Peninah, a slave, the property of Alden
Mickleberry, of the county of Butts. On motion of Mr.
Merriwether, the bill was laid upon the table for the balance of the session."[73] In the next year the same bill was
re-introduced into the House by Mr. Berry of Butts County.
It was read for the first time on December 5, 1839.[74] On
December 16, when the bill came up for the third reading
and was voted upon, it was rejected by the House. The
ayes and nays were recorded: the ayes were 60 and the nays
116.[75] So the position of the two houses was reversed over
the question of the emancipation of Peninah. Although
the bill passed the Senate in 1838, it failed in the House
in 1838 and again in 1839 and the said slave Peninah failed
to receive her freedom.

On November 15, 1839, a bill was introduced into the
House providing for the manumission of a woman and her
two children. After a second reading the bill was lost.[76]
A bill to emancipate Nancy and John, the property of
Peter Ray, failed in the Senate on November 21, 1842,
by a vote of 61 to 18.[77] John Stephenson of Union County
attempted to emancipate his slave, James, but was prevented from doing so by the legislature. The Senate
Journal of November 25, 1841, has the following item:
"The Committee to whom was referred the petition of
John Stephenson, praying for the emancipation of a certain
negro man Report, that they have had the same under
consideration, and they believe the prayer of the petitioner
unreasonable, and ought not to be granted."[78] In 1842 the
bill, providing for the manumission of James, the property
of John Stephenson of Union County, was again introduced
into the House.[79] On November 30, 1842, the House refused to reconsider the bill to emancipate the said negro

[73] *Ibid*, 1838, 426.
[74] *Ibid*, 1839, 207.
[75] *Ibid*, 1839, 302–303.
[76] *Ibid*, 1839, 63, 77.
[77] *Senate Journal*, 1842, 79–80.
[78] *Senate Journal*, 1841, 166–167.
[79] *House Journal*, 1842, 157.

slave named James, the property of the said John Stephenson of Union County.[80] In 1842 a bill was introduced into the House providing for the manumission of Joseph Clark, the property of a citizen of Columbus.[81] On December 2, 1842, the House refused to reconsider the bill to emancipate Joseph Clark, the property of David Hudson of Columbus.[82] In 1847 a bill was introduced to emancipate certain slaves therein named. It was read a third time and indefinitely postponed.[83]

Even as late as 1859 and 1860 there were attempts in Georgia to manumit slaves. William Satterwhite of Columbia County attempted to emancipate one of his slaves in that year (1859), but the bill was definitely postponed.[84] Mrs. Owen of Upson County attempted to emancipate a negro woman belonging to her.[85] That bill was definitely postponed. The act of 1859 prevented the conferring of freedom on slaves within or without the state after the death of the owner.[86] The passage of this act shows that emancipation of slaves was taking place in Georgia even as late as 1859. The necessity of such a law as this as late as 1859 shows that slaves were still being freed by the will of the owners. It was sought to prohibit this post-mortem manumission of slaves.

Many cases in regard to the manumission of negroes came before the Supreme Court of Georgia. Several wills which provided for the emancipation of slaves were declared illegal since they were contrary to the law of 1818 which forbade manumission. In many cases the testator provided that the negroes should be removed from the state and then set free. The manumission of slaves to be sent out of the state was not in conflict with the public policy of the laws of Georgia. From some of the decisions the

---

[80] *Ibid*, 1842, 164.
[81] *Ibid*, 1842, 182.
[82] *Ibid*, 1842, 190.
[83] *Ibid*, 1847, 465.
[84] *Ibid*, 1859, 68.
[85] *Ibid*, 1860, 297.
[86] *Acts of Georgia*, 1859, 68.

movement to remove the slaves to Liberia is clearly seen. In the case of Vance versus Crawford in 1848 it was decided that it was not against the policy of the state of Georgia for the owner of slaves to remove them out of the state for manumission.[87] Thus the acts of Georgia against manumission did not prohibit the removal of the slave beyond the limits of the state to be there liberated. There are numbers of wills which were passed upon by the Supreme Court of Georgia in which provisions for the liberation of slaves were held to be valid. These decisions held that slaves could be liberated under certain limited conditions, and there is no doubt that many wills made similar provisions. As before stated there could be no voluntary liberation of a slave within the state.

The will of Marshall Keith of Columbia County, 1839, provided that three of his negroes should be set free but that they should not live in or within three miles of any town or village in Georgia or Carolina. It was charged that this will was contrary to the laws of Georgia which prohibited manumission. But the Supreme Court of Georgia decided that it was not against the policy of the state for the owner of slaves to remove them out of the state for manumission.[88] This will showed the remarkable consideration of the planter for his slaves. He willed some of the negroes to his kins-folk; others he left to be sold with the estate. In regard to the three negroes the will provided that they should be given over to the Colonization Society "for the purpose of being sent to Liberia, and also five shares of the Mechanics' Bank of Augusta for each—the proceeds to be paid to them or the survivor, on their arrival in Liberia, and for no other use or purpose. And as I leave it optional with them to go or not, should they, or either of them refuse, I give him or them as follows . . . ." Then it was provided that in case of their refusal they should be held by the executors

[87] *Reports of the Supreme Court of Georgia*, IV, 446. Hereafter referred to as 4 *Ga.* 446.
[88] 4 *Ga.* 446.

of the estate for various uses.[89]   Another provision of the
will showed even more remarkable consideration.   "It is
my desire, that my servant Ishmael should be freed; but
if that cannot be accomplished, I give him to my Executors
hereinafter named, in trust, for his own use, to go wherever
he may please, and if it suits him to take with him, sell or
dispose of, the property hereinafter devised to my Executors in trust for said Ishmael."[90]   Thereupon Keith willed
to him one hundred fifty shares of stock of the Mechanics
Bank of Augusta and a tract of land for a home for him and
his two sisters, Minny and Elizabeth.   But Keith went
even further—he willed to those three negroes whom he had
set free, twelve of his slaves, together with tools, live-
stock, furniture, food, and other provisions.   He provided
that each of them should be given shares of bank stock.[91]
In discussing that part of the will referring to the transportation of the negroes to Liberia Judge Lumpkin said:

> As to so much and such parts of the will as authorize the
> emancipation of three of the testator's slaves in Liberia,
> we are clear that it was entirely competent for him to make
> ruch post mortem disposition of his negroes.   Owners can,
> in their lifetime, carry or send their slaves to the coast of
> Africa to be colonized, or elsewhere, for the purpose of
> freeing them.   And they can appropriate the whole, or any
> portion of the remainder of their property, if they so please,
> to their transportation and maintenance in their new homes.
> We hold it equally certain, that they can direct the same
> thing to be done by their Executors, after their death.   For-
> eign emancipation neither conflicts with the letter or spirit
> of our municipal regulations relative to this subject.[92]

It was the intention of the Georgia legislature, in the
Acts of 1801 and 1818, to prohibit manumission and to pro-

---

[89] *Ga.* 453.   (A copy of this will is on file in the Court House of Columbia
    County, at Appling.   The will was made, May 8, 1839, and was recorded,
    Jan. 6, 1842.)
[90] 4 *Ga.* 452.
[91] A discussion of this will is found in an article by E. Merton Coulter, "A
    Century of A Georgia Plantation," *Mississippi Valley Historical Review*,
    XVI, 338–341.
[92] 4 *Ga.* 458.

hibit owners from placing the slaves in a situation where, according to law, they would be pronounced slaves, and yet would be entitled to some of the rights and immunities of freemen. There were cases in Georgia where it was sought to avoid the manumission laws and to grant to the slaves the privileges of freemen even though such freedom could not legally be bestowed upon them. Elisha King stated in his will his desire that his old servant, Writ, and her five children, and her husband Jacob, "may be made to live comfortable, under the superintendance of my friends, Samuel Robinson and Henry Wood, into whose care, and under whose protection I do hereby give and place the negroes herein named, in view of their being treated with humanity and justice, subject to the laws made and provided in such cases." [93] Robinson and Wood admitted that the object and intention of the testator, in bequeathing the slaves to them, was to avoid the manumission laws of Georgia and to virtually set the slaves free. The will was interpreted by the court to mean that the testator did not intend to give the negroes to Robinson and Wood, but to make them agents or trustees over the negroes, to hold them in order that they might enjoy the privileges of manumission. The testator intended to create a trust which granted practical freedom to the negroes. [94] The will was declared to be illegal and void since it was in conflict with the laws of the state against manumission.

A will similar to that of Elisha King was that of Nathan Truitt of Troup County who died in 1858. Most of his property passed to his wife and daughter. But in the third item of the will he bequeathed certain negroes (described as old and faithful slaves) to his friend Samuel D. Ellis to be held in trust. "I give and bequeath unto my beloved and trusty friend, Samuel D. Ellis, my old and faithful slaves, to wit: Jim, Sam, George, the blacksmith, Cyrus, London, Isaac, Nancy, Fanny, Nelly, Jinny, and Harlow." [95]

[93] 6 *Ga.* 539–540.
[94] 6 *Ga.* 547.
[95] 42 *Ga.* 175.

Ellis was directed that the slaves should be allowed to cultivate, for their own support, a certain parcel of land, and to see to it that the negroes were well treated. The said negroes were given to him "for the purpose of providing for and taking care of them during their natural lives, with the right of using and cultivating the said land, and other property so given for the benefit, use and support of said slaves, the said slaves to be kindly treated by him and to work and cultivate said land for their support."[96] The testator provided that at Ellis' death the trust should pass to James Truitt, nephew of Nathan Truitt. In this way the slaveholder attempted to give his slaves the benefits and privileges of freedom even though he was forbidden by law to manumit them. The Court of Georgia declared that, since the intention of the testator was to make the slaves practically free and to permit them to enjoy the proceeds of their own labor, the will was illegal. The will was made in 1858 and recorded in 1859. The decision of the court was not rendered until after the negroes had already been given their freedom by the Emancipation Proclamation and the thirteenth amendment.

The will of Gwyn Allison of Greene County directs that his executors pay the sum of $100.00 to each of three negro men slaves whom he mentions by name. He also directs that each of his negro women be paid $20.00 each; and directs that it be paid in silver. He further directs that none of his negroes were to be sold. And that they should be allowed to choose their own masters, and if the master chosen proved to be unkind, that they should have the right to choose another. The women were to choose masters for their children up to twelve years of age, and after that they could choose their own master. But in no event, were they allowed to leave Greene County.[97]

Another will involving the same principle was that of Pierce Bailey of Warren County. The testator was accused

---

[96] *42 Ga.* 175.
[97] Will on file at Greene County Court House, Greensboro, Georgia.

of having made certain declarations, both before and after the execution of the will, that his intentions were to defeat the statute against the manumission of slaves. In the third item of the will Bailey provided that his house servant Adeline and her child Tolbert should go to his nephew, Lawrence Battle; he expressed his desire that the mother and child should never be separated. He also expressed his desire that his nephew, Lawrence Battle, should treat the negroes kindly, "and see that they are as comfortably provided for as their condition in life and their conduct and behavior will justify. I wish him to treat them just as he may at all times think I would treat them if I were in life. This confidence I repose in him with the full assurance that it is not misplaced, and that it will not be abused."[98] This item of the will was declared void since it was an attempted violation of the laws against manumission.

Reuben B. Patterson of Georgia wished to manumit his slave, Sophy. Since such action was contrary to the laws of Georgia the testator directed that the slave be removed to a state in which the laws would allow her manumission. The second clause of the will read as follows:

> It is my wish and desire, that Sophy, a colored girl, (now three years old since the 9th of June, 1848,) the daughter of my woman Margaret, be not considered as a part or parcel of my estate; and that my executor deliver the said girl Sophy, to my friend, George D. Blakey, of Rural Choice, Logan County, State of Kentucky, who I hereby nominate and appoint guardian of the said girl Sophy; and it is my wish and desire that the said George D. Blakey shall take the girl Sophy to his residence in Kentucky, and as soon as she can be manumitted by the laws of the said State, to have it done; but should the laws of Kentucky be adverse to manumission of the said girl Sophy, that he take her to such a State where she may be manumitted and become free. I also wish and desire, that the said George D. Blakey shall superintend the education of said girl Sophy, and that she remain under his care and control until she is sixteen years of age, unless (with his consent) she marries.

[98] *34 Ga.* 459.

The Supreme Court of Georgia decided, in 1851, that the will did not violate the policy of the laws of the state which prohibited domestic emancipation of slaves; but that it was lawful for a testator to direct that his slaves should be taken into any other state where the law authorized it, and there emancipate them. So no impediment was placed in the way of the manumission of the slave, Sophy.[99]

Another testator provided in his will that, after the payment of his debts, his desire was that his negroes should be hired out until their hire should amount to $1,800. That when this sum was raised and in the hands of his executor, he willed to his executor certain slaves in trust to be conveyed by him to some of the free states and there left; but if the executor was prevented from executing this provision, then he bequeathed the negroes to the executor in trust to be delivered by him to the Colonization Society. And he said further that he gave to the executor $200 for his trouble in carrying out the above provisions; and that the surplus, if any, of the $1,800 was to be divided among the negroes after their removal. However the Supreme Court, in the Pinckard versus McCoy case, held that these provisions were void.[100]

On February 25, 1852, Owen Thomas of Muscogee County made and executed his last will, by one clause of which he desired that certain negro slaves therein named should be conveyed to Liberia, or to any other free state in which they might lawfully reside, and there to be forever manumitted and freed, they and their posterity. Item three read: "I desire that my negroes, Griffin and his wife Esther, and their children now born, and such as they may hereafter have, (and others with their children born or to be born, naming them,) to be conveyed to Liberia, or any other free State, foreign to Georgia, into which they severally elect to go, and in which they may lawfully reside, and there to be forever manumitted and freed, they and

---

[99] 10 *Ga.* 263–264.
[100] 22 *Ga.* 28, 31.

their posterity."[101]   The testator also desired that his other property should be sold, part of it was to pay the expenses of transportation of the negroes who were to be manumitted, and that a part should be divided among the negroes, to be paid to each person eighteen years of age, on his or her arrival in his or her new home.   This will was made in 1852 before the passage of the prohibitory act of 1859 and before the emancipation of the slaves as a result of the war. Owen Thomas died in 1868.   Therefore the portion of the will in regard to the manumission of the negroes was held void.[102]   In this instance we have the case of a testator who made his will prior to the emancipation of the slaves, who provided for the removal of his negroes to a free state there to be manumitted, who bequeathed to them certain legacies, but his will was thwarted by the emancipation of the slaves as a result of the war.

Augustus H. Anderson of Burke County, who died in 1853, directed that his executors should cause to be removed to a free state, and there emancipated, his negro boy John, and that the executors should pay the expense of his removal, and for his reasonable support and schooling until he should be put to a trade, and that when he should reach the age of twenty-one years, they should invest and secure for his benefit the sum of $3,000 to be raised out of the estate.   The same will provided that the slave Louisa, mother of the above-mentioned John, should be kept on the owner's plantation until 1875, after which time she was to go (if she chose) to a free state and be emancipated. It was declared by the court that the provision in the will directing that the slave should be sent to a free state and there manumitted and provided for was not in violation of the laws of Georgia.[103]

A lengthy discussion of the legislative policy of the laws of Georgia with reference to the manumission of slavery and with the regulation of free persons of color is

---

[101] 40 *Ga.* 20; 50 *Ga.* 184.
[102] 40 *Ga.* 19.
[103] 38 *Ga.* 655.

set forth in the case of Cleland versus Waters, decided at the
October term, 1854, of the Supreme Court of Georgia.
In this case it was decided that the manumission of slaves
to be sent out of the state was not in conflict with the public
policy of the laws of Georgia; that extra-territorial emancipation was not forbidden by the laws of 1801 and 1818.[104]
This case arose from the will of George M. Waters which
specifically stated his desire for the manumission of his
slaves.   "On account of the faithful services of my body
servant, William, (the husband of Peggy), I will and desire
his emancipation or freedom, with the future issue and
increase of all the females mentioned in this item of my
will."   The testator then stated that if the manumission
of the slaves was considered contrary to the laws of Georgia,
he then desired that the negroes should be sent out of the
state to such place as his executors might select, and there
be manumitted.   The court held the will to be valid and
not repugnant to the acts of 1801 and 1818.[105]

In this will Major Waters, a wealthy planter of Gwinnett
County, manumitted thirty-seven slaves; his executor delivered them in Savannah to the Colonization Society.
They were well provided with clothing, $100 in gold was
presented to each, and they were sent to Liberia free of
charge.   Thirty of them died within twelve months.   The
remaining seven escaped from their exile and found passage
in a merchant vessel for Philadelphia.   Thence the negroes
returned to Georgia through the friendly aid of Howell
Cobb and Alexander H. Stephens, who furnished them the
means of getting home.[106]   In the decision of the Superior
Court in the Cleland case, prepared by the Honorable
Joseph H. Lumpkin, is found the following:

> The foregoing analysis will suffice, I might say, vindicate,
> the temper and tone of our legislation in regard to slavery.
> And notwithstanding the perservering efforts which have
> been made by the fanatics of the North to jeopard the safety

---

[104] 16 *Ga.* 496, 520; 19 *Ga.* 35.
[105] 19 *Ga.* 36.
[106] Charles H. Smith, *History of Georgia,* 122.

of our people—to rob them of their property—to desecrate and disregard their constitutional rights and violate and harass their domestic peace it is truly gratifying to contemplate the justice, wisdom, and moderation of our Legislature respecting slaves, and free persons of color. All the cruel attempts of these infuriated incendiaries have hitherto utterly failed to influence our people to forget their duty to themselves and this dependent race. Every act upon our Statute Book, in reference to them, is replete, upon its face, with undeniable proof of that dispassionate deliberation which is the true characteristic of a great and magnanimous people. Humanity to all slaves and free persons of color and a just regard to their rights and welfare have never in a single instance been overlooked or unheeded.[107]

Isaac Thornton of Muscogee County provided for the manumission of his slaves in 1855.

State of Georgia,
Muscogee County:

Know all men by these presents, that I, Isaac Thornton, from motives of benevolence and humanity, have manumitted and set free, and by these presents do hereby manumit and set free from bondage or slavery, Jane, a woman about twenty-seven years, of dark complexion and small stature, and Sarah Frances, her daughter, about thirteen years of age, of yellow complexion; and John, a boy, son of Jane, about one year and six months old, and Amanda, a woman about nineteen years old, of yellow complexion; and her daughter, Josephine, about five years old, of yellow complexion; and her son Jacob, about three and a half years old; and her daughter, Mary Elizabeth, very white complexion, about one year and six months old; all of said named slaves now in my possession, and to remain, during my natural life, subject to my control and direction; after which I do hereby grant and release unto my trusty friends, Edwin G. Thornton and William A. Chisholm, my chosen trustees, for the following purposes: All of said slaves, with each and all their natural increase, born of their bodies or that of their children, after this date and hence-forward; that is to say, to remove said slaves to

---

[107] 16 *Ga.* 512.

some free State or to the State of Liberia, on the coast of Africa, according to their discretion; and that my trustees shall, immediately after my death, take possession of all my property, both real and personal, and choses in action, for the purpose of carrying out the trust herein created; that is to say, to pay the expenses of transportation or passage to their destination; and all monies or effects of mine in the hands of my trustees, remaining after paying said expenses, to be given and appropriated by my said trustees to said named slaves, for their support, use and maintenance.

In testimony whereof, I have hereunto set my hand and seal, this the twenty-seventh day of March, 1855.

Isaac Thornton, (L. S.)

In presence of

Beverly A. Thornton,
Wiley Adams.[108]

Robert Bledsoe of Putnam County provided in his will that a sufficiency of good and arable land should be purchased for his negroes in Indiana or Illinois, that the said negroes should be removed to one of these states and there emancipated. However the court held that the will could not be fulfilled, (the state of Indiana prohibiting, by her Constitution and Laws, and the state of Illinois by statute, the introduction of negroes into these states.)[109] Another testator bequeathed his slaves to his widow, with directions to his executors, to remove them at her death to a free country. If funds could not be raised from the sale of the other property, sufficient to cover the expenses of their transportation, the negroes were to be hired out until enough money could be raised for that purpose. However, the will was declared void because of the anti-manumission acts of the state.[110]

In 1855 a case came before the Supreme Court of Georgia involving the manumission of two negroes. Mrs. Christina Hall wished to provide for the emancipation of her two

---

[108] 20 *Ga.* 338–339.
[109] 18 *Ga.* 131.
[110] 26 *Ga.* 225, 227.

slaves but was prevented from doing so by the law of 1818 which declared all acts providing for the manumission of slaves null and void. Consequently the terms of the will were indefinite. The fifth item of the will read as follows:

> As manumission is, by the laws of the State, forbidden, (which I could have wished otherwise,) I will and bequeath to Wiley E. Mangham my trusty and faithful servants, Charity and Starling, to have and to hold unto him and his executors forever, in fee, with the very urgent request that he and they will treat said negroes kindly and affectionately, and watch over and protect them—finding them a comfortable home, and allowing them as many privileges and liberties as the laws of the State will permit negro slaves to possess or enjoy.

It was charged that this item of the will was void and rendered the whole of the will illegal and in violation of the laws of the state. However, the court decided that the fifth item did not provide for the manumission of the slaves, that it recognized the impossibility of such action, and that it bequeathed the slaves to Mangham as property. It was decided that, although the will indicated a desire that the slaves should be set free, the terms of the will manifested an intention to convey the slaves, absolutely and in fee simple, to Mr. Mangham. Thus the decision prevented the two slaves, Charity and Starling, from receiving their freedom.[111]

Nathaniel T. Myrick of Monroe County executed his last will and testament on June 21, 1856. He directed his executors to remove his servants (Owen, Elizabeth, Joseph, Samuel, William, Flora, George, Harriette and Leonard) to some free state and there to manumit and set them free, to act for themselves and their heirs forever. The executors were also directed to purchase in the free state a parcel of land sufficient for the servants, with a supply of provisions, household and kitchen furniture, farming utensils horses, mules, cattle, hogs and sheep, "with money arising from my estate." Any surplus after paying for said property

---

[111] 18 *Ga.* 563.

and the expenses of removing the slaves, was to be paid to the slave Owen and he and the other named slaves were to share equally in the money, land and other property. The Supreme Court of Georgia held that this will was not contrary to law, and did not violate the Acts 1801 and 1818. Therefore this group of negroes received the property and their freedom.[112]

So we see that there was a desire among a minority of the people of Georgia to liberate the slaves, or at least to give freedom to individual slaves. From the time that slavery was first introduced into the province until the slave was finally given his freedom there was a difference of opinion in Georgia in regard to the institution. There was a large class of non-slaveholding whites who were opposed to slavery, but they had no effective organ for expression. The opposition to slavery was expressed by various acts: laws to control and regulate the slaves, attempts to prevent the introduction of negroes, the placing of import duties on them, abolition of the slave trade, the frequent manumission of individual slaves, and the laws passed to prevent manumission. These measures were designed to prevent slavery from acquiring a firmer hold on the state and to facilitate, in that way, the work of gradual emancipation. We shall now turn to the more heated side of the argument and the beginning of the slavery controversy.

------

[112] 25 *Ga.* 109.

CHAPTER X

THE BEGINNING OF THE SLAVERY CONTROVERSY

The purpose of this chapter is to show: (1) the status of slavery in Georgia, (2) the sentiment of the people regarding the institution, and (3) the progress of opinion in other parts of the country.

We have seen in former chapters that Georgia was established by Oglethorpe and the Trustees; that it was to be a refuge for people suffering from oppression, and a military outpost for the colonies; and that slavery was excluded from the province. We noticed the failure of Georgia under the Trustees' plan, the final admission of negroes into the province, and the success and prosperity which followed. We have seen how the introduction of negroes necessitated a great many new laws for the control, protection, education and regulation of the slaves. Many of these laws were not enforced except on very rare occasions. In most cases the master rendered informal justice on his own plantation; the protection as well as the punishment of the slave was in his hands. We have noticed the many laws passed against the slave trade and against manumission. Although manumission was discouraged by law it was by no means stopped. Cases of voluntary manumission were continually arising.

The anti-slavery cause in Georgia was advanced in 1855 by the publication of "Slave Life In Georgia" by L. A. Chamerovzow, who was secretary of the British and foreign anti-slavery society. It is a narrative of the life, sufferings and escape of a certain John Brown, a fugitive slave who made his way to England. John Brown shows the cruelty of the

masters and the effect on the slaves.[1]   Other writers, such
as Frances Kemble and Frederick Law Olmstead, also pictured the cruel side of the slave system.

Frances Anne Kemble, a celebrated English actress, came
to America in 1832.   In 1834 she married a Southern planter,
moved to Georgia, and decided to investigate the institution of slavery during her residence there.   She published
her "Journal of a Residence on a Georgia Plantation in
1838–1839," which is distinctly anti-slavery in sentiment.
The journal is written in the form of letters to a friend
abroad.   Frances Kemble found nothing good in the slavery
system.   Slavery, as she saw it, made life under those conditions intolerable to her; she felt an ever-present wrong
of living on the unpaid labor of servants.   She describes
the parting of a family of slaves and the husband's awful
distress.   She describes Frank, the head-driver and a negro
of superior intellect, who was left in sole charge of the
plantation, but his wife was taken from him and made the
mistress of the overseer.   There was engineer Ned, intelligent, capable, and well treated, whose wife was broken down
by being driven to the field too soon after the birth of a
child.   Half the women on the plantation suffered from the
same cause.   She believed gradual emancipation unwise;
in her opinion the system was too bad for slow measures.
Had she owned her husband's plantation, she would have
freed the slaves at once and hired them as a means of financial
salvation.[2]   In one of her letters to her friend back in England Frances Kemble said: "How is such a cruel sin of
injustice to be answered?   Mr. ——, of course, sees and
feels none of this as I do, and, I should think, must regret
that he ever brought me here, to have my abhorrence of
the theory of slavery deepened, and strengthened every
hour of my life, by what I see of its practice."[3]

---

[1] L. A. Chamerovzow, *Slave Life in Georgia* (London, 1855).

[2] Frances Anne Kemble, *A Journal of a Residence on a Georgian Plantation
in 1838–39.* (New York, 1863).

[3] *Ibid,* 115–116.

Frederick Law Olmstead, an American landscape architect from Connecticut, fond of making tours and writing his impressions of them, based his publications on extended journeys throughout the South.   His publications constitute a severe indictment against slavery.   A horseback trip through the Southern states was recorded in "A Journey In the Seaboard Slave States," (1856), "A Journey Through Texas," (1857), and "A Journey In the Back Country," (1860).   These were reprinted in England in two volumes called "The Cotton Kingdom."   These volumes give a picture of conditions surrounding American slavery and they were much quoted in the controversies at the time of the. Civil War.   Olmstead said that a man forced to labor under the slave system was driven to "indolence, carelessness, indifference to the results of skill, heedlessness, inconstancy of purpose, improvidence, and extravagance;" whereas precisely the opposite qualities were encouraged and inevitably developed in a man who had to make his living by his labor voluntarily directed.[4]   Olmstead studied the question from the point of view of a farmer and a practical man; he was a well equipped and keen observer.   He discusses the economics of the system, the frequent cruelties, the demoralization of both master and slave, and the need of its ultimate extinction.   Olmstead gave the darker side of slavery.   He showed the anti-slavery sentiment of the mountaineers, the poor people of the back country, and the small planters who could not afford slaves.   In speaking of the opposition of the Highlanders of New Inverness in Georgia to slavery, he said: "They considered perpetual Slavery as shocking to human nature, and deemed the *permission of it a grievance*, and which, in some future day, might also prove a scourge, and make many feel the smart of that oppression they the poor Englishmen, so earnestly desired to introduce."[5]

Hinton Rowan Helper, a native of North Carolina, in 1857, wrote "The Impending Crisis of the South: How to

[4] Frederick Law Olmstead, *A Journey In the Seaboard Slave States*, 147–148.
[5] *Ibid*, 527.

Meet It." He cited copious statistical facts showing the
extent to which the North had surpassed the South in
commerce, agriculture, manufacturers, arts, sciences, and
literature, and contended that this great difference in prosperity was due solely to slavery; he suggested methods by
means of which slavery might be abolished; he gave Southern and Northern testimony against slavery—also that of
other nations, the churches, and the Bible, as well as many
other arguments.[6] He said that Georgia was perhaps the
most thrifty of the Southern States. He attributed the
prosperity of the state to her hundred thousand free white
laborers most of whom were engaged in agricultural pur-
suits. "In few other slave states are the non-slaveholders
so little under the domination of the oligarchy."[7] The publication of this book had a far reaching effect on the anti-
slavery movement. It aroused much interest in the North
and South. In 1857, the year in which it was published,
thirteen thousand copies were put upon the market.[8]
Helper's book was a plea to the non slaveholding whites
for themselves. It presented an overwhelming series of
statistics and arguments on the economic evils of slavery.
His method was largely the comparison of the industrial
progress of the two sections; his chief source was the United
States census. He said that at the beginning of the government of the United States the advantages of soil, climate,
rivers, harbors, minerals, forests, etc., had been with the
South, but that in sixty years she had been completely
surpassed by the North. He compared Virginia and New
York, North Carolina and Massachusetts, South Carolina
and Pennsylvania, etc. Helper predicted that emancipation would be followed by general prosperity. Southerners
denounced the book, but the more it was denounced the
more it was read. It was a "best seller" of the time. Helper
was driven out of North Carolina and his book was used

---

[6] Hinton R. Helper, *The Impending Crisis of the South: How to Meet It,* (New
   York, 1857).
[7] *Ibid*, 230.
[8] Edward Channing, *A History of the United States* (New York, 1925), VI, 206.

as a campaign document in 1860. The hostility to slavery from an economic standpoint and in the white man's interest thus found passionate expression in Helper's "The Impending Crisis of the South: How to Meet It."

In 1847 Augustus Baldwin Longstreet, a Georgian, published in the Baltimore "Western Continent" a series of letters addressed from Georgia to her sister, Massachusetts. There were eleven of these letters—nine from Georgia to Massachusetts, and two addressed by Georgia to her sister states in the South. These letters were transcribed from the "Western Continent" and published in a pamphlet entitled "A Voice from the South." Longstreet reminds the Abolitionists of Massachusetts that Georgia at first would have nothing to do with slavery, that she adhered to her resolution until overpowered by the complaints of her own children who were influenced by their neighbors across the Savannah, and that Massachusetts and her neighboring sisters of the North became rich by bringing and selling the slaves to the South.[9]

Lewis W. Paine, who moved to Georgia from Massachusetts in 1841, was later convicted of violating the fugitive slave law. He suffered six years of imprisonment in Georgia for the crime of aiding the escape of a negro from that state after he had fled from slavery. After his release he wrote:

> We must correct this great national wrong, this great national hypocrisy, which have made us the scorn of the enlightened, and the taunt of the oppressor; we must take off all restrictions, and give the great principles of our institutions full scope and sway; we must not make war on tyrants abroad, and protect far more monstrous tyranny at home! We must not claim for ourselves the largest liberty, and impose upon the very members of our household the most abject and stringent slavery. . . . It is nonsense to talk about correcting the abuses of slavery for they will and must exist as long as the institution remains.[10]

[9] A. B. Longstreet, *A Voice from the South*, Comprising Letters from Georgia to Massachusetts (Baltimore, 1847), (Pamphlet.)
[10] Lewis W. Paine, *Six Years in a Georgia Prison* (New York, 1851), 114, 186.

Many laws were passed in Georgia against free negroes. The lot of the free negro prior to 1860 was not an easy one. With practically no civil rights, he was too often the victim of designing persons, who would take advantage of his ignorance. Then too he was usually looked upon with suspicion by his white neighbors, especially if he should own any property. Because of the attitude of many citizens toward them, the free people of color were not happy in Georgia and avoided that section. The status of a free person of color is disclosed in one of Joel Chandler Harris' stories which tells of the free person of color commonly known as Free Joe. This gives an account of a free negro in Georgia and his subsequent unhappiness.[11] Sometimes free negroes were kidnapped and sold back into slavery. Charles Ball was kidnapped in Baltimore, brought back to Georgia, and sold as a slave.[12] A law of Georgia subjected any merchant vessel with free colored persons on board to thirty days quarantine. Any person communicating with such seamen was to be whipped not exceeding thirty lashes. If any captain should refuse to carry away seamen thus detained, and pay the expenses of their imprisonment he was to be fined five hundred dollars, and also imprisoned not exceeding three months.[13]

A restriction was placed on the right of hiring houses to negroes. Any person of color, bond or free, was forbidden to occupy any tenement except a kitchen or outhouse, under penalty of from twenty to twenty-five lashes.[14] Some of these laws were applicable only to cities, towns, or counties. A law passed in 1807 provided that:

> Whereas the citizens of Savannah and Augusta, and their vicinities have heretofore, and do now experience great injury and inconvenience from the number of free negroes, mulattoes, and mustezoes, of vicious and loose habits who

---

[11] Joel Chandler Harris, *Free Joe and Other Georgian Sketches* (New York, 1887); Mims and Payne, *Southern Prose and Poetry* (New York, 1910); 139–155.
[12] Ball's *Narrative*, 374 et sequitur.
[13] Goodell, *The American Slave Code*, 363.
[14] *Ibid*, 361.

have settled and are daily settling therein . . . that from and after the first day of January next, all free negroes, mulattoes or mustezoes, who may then or any time thereafter reside within the corporate limits of the cities of Savannah and Augusta, shall be subject to the same police regulations, and restrictions as slaves are or may be by the laws of this state, and any person who shall hire or let any house or tenement to any free negro, mulatto, or mustezoe within the limits of said cities, without permission from the city council thereof, shall be subject to the same penalties as if such house or tenement had been let or hired to a slave, any law, usage or custom to the contrary notwithstanding.[15]

The commissioners of Washington, Lexington, and Milledgeville were to be vested with the same powers as to the regulation of these people.

An act of 1818 forbade the entrance into Georgia of all free persons of color, with a few specified exceptions, fixing a penalty of a fine of $100 or sale into slavery.[16] Prosecution under this act could be repeated every twenty days. The purpose of this act was to prevent the increase in the numbers of free negroes. Every free man (negro) had to have a guardian who was responsible for his behavior.[17] Colored males, between the ages of eight and twenty-one, who had no guardian were to be bound out to service by the justice of the peace with any three free holders of the district.[18] No free persons of color were allowed to be sold into slavery.[19]

A law of 1824 provided: "That all laws and parts of laws which authorize the selling of free persons of color into slavery, be and the same are hereby repealed."[20] An act of 1826, designed to prevent the illegal carrying out of the state free persons of color, provided that any person transporting, enticing, or carrying out of the state any per-

---

[15] A. S. Clayton, *Compilation of the Laws of Georgia*, 1800–1810 (Augusta, 1813), 369.
[16] Prince, *Digest*, 795.
[17] *Ibid*, (1837 ed.) 777–789.
[18] *Ibid*, 798.
[19] *Ibid*, 800.
[20] Foster, *Digest*, 310.

son of color without a certificate of registry was liable to be indicted and to pay a fine of $500 for each offense.[21]

In 1835 there was passed "An Act more effectually to protect free persons of colour, and to point out the mode of trying the right of freedom."[22] This act was designed to prevent free negroes from being fraudulently and illegally held in a state of slavery. If such a case should arise the justice of the inferior court of that county was ordered to make an investigation. If, upon investigation, it was found that the negro was justly entitled to his freedom then the court was to order such person to be set at liberty and a guardian appointed as provided by law.[23] This act of 1835 was amended in 1837 to give still further protection to the free negro and to guarantee to him his freedom.[24]

The people of Georgia were willing to give the negro his freedom provided they could remove him from the state. However they feared the presence of the free negroes among them. A bill was introduced into the House of Representatives on November 19, 1824, which provided for an increase of the tax on free persons of color and for appropriating a portion of the tax for the purpose of creating a fund to be applied towards the removal from the state of the free colored population.[25] A committee was appointed to enquire into the expediency of the matter. On December 13, 1824, this committee made the following report: "That they have given the subject due consideration, and notwithstanding your committee are of the opinion that good policy would require the removal of such free persons of color from this state, yet your committee are of the opinion, that the tax now paid by such persons is high, and would not admit of an increase, without being considered oppressive. And the tax now paid by such persons of color your committee believe to be insufficient to effect the object in

21 Dawson, *Compilation*, 411.
22 *Acts of Georgia*, 1835, 101.
23 *Ibid*, 1835, 102–103.
24 *Acts of Georgia*, 1837, 248.
25 *House Journal*, 1824, 112–113.

view."[26] The committee then submitted the resolution that it was inexpedient to legislate upon the subject in the manner proposed. The opposition was based on the inexpediency and not because the people were opposed to the emancipation and deportation of the negro. The scheme seemed too impracticable.

A law of 1859 prohibited free negroes from being brought into the state. Those who were brought in violation of the act, with seamen excepted, were to be sold into slavery.[27] Persons bringing into the state such free persons of color were subject to indictment of a fine of not less than $1,000.[28] Another law of 1859 directed that vagrant free negroes be sold for a definite period for the first offense and for life for a second offense.[29] The following table shows the proportion of free colored persons to the total population in Georgia.[30]

1790	1800	1810	1820	1830	1840	1850
.48	.63	.71	.51	.48	.40	.32

This shows an increase of free negroes in Georgia until 1810. After that year the number continually decreased. In 1850 there were even fewer free negroes in the state than in 1790.[31]

During the period before the abolition agitation the leading thinkers of Georgia, and probably the bulk of the people, considered slavery an evil.[32] They favored the abandonment of the system if a practical way could be found. It was hoped that in the future some feasible means could be provided. Professor U. B. Phillips examined the various remedies suggested or available for the situation and came to the conclusion that emancipation was the only solution.[33]

---

[26] *Ibid*, 244.
[27] *Acts of Georgia*, 1859, 68.
[28] *Ibid*, 1859, 69.
[29] *Ibid*, 1859, 69.
[30] DeBow, *Statistical View of the United States*, 65.
[31] For a discussion of Free Negroes in Georgia see, W. McDowell Rogers, "Free Negro Legislation in Georgia Before 1865," *Georgia Historical Quarterly*, XVI, 27–37.
[32] Phillips, *Georgia and State Rights*, 156–157.
[33] Phillips, *American Negro Slavery*, 399.

A great number of the most intelligent people of Georgia favored gradual emancipation. This sentiment was "slowly but surely" spreading.[34] Judge Joseph Henry Lumpkin, chief justice of the Supreme Court of Georgia, was an outspoken advocate of emancipation.[35] In a later chapter this sentiment will be shown in some of his court decisions regarding the manumission of slaves. This policy of gradual emancipation would doubtless have been adopted by Georgia, "had her people not resented what seemed like attempts to coerce them."[36] Many Georgians, not content with speeches and noble sentiments, manumitted large numbers of slaves.[37] An editorial in the Georgia Journal published as its conviction, "There is not a single editor in these States who dares advocate slavery as a principle."[38]

Nearly every Southern leader during the earlier period (before 1830) and some of those of the later were distinctly opposed to the institution of slavery *per se*, although they differed as to the best method of practical treatment.[39] The belief that the negro would be unable to care for himself if freed and the fear lest immediate emancipation would work too great a hardship upon the master led many to advocate gradual rather than immediate emancipation. In November, 1797, when the Quaker memorial, calling the attention of Congress to the oppressed condition of their African brethren, came before that body, a representative from Georgia stated in the House, without contradiction, that not a man lived in Georgia who did not wish there were no slaves, and that everybody believed they were a curse to the country.[40]

---

[34] Charles H. Smith, *History of Georgia* (Boston, 1896), 119.
[35] *Ibid.*
[36] *Ibid.*
[37] See file of the *African Repository* for numbers sent to Liberia.
[38] Georgia Journal, Jan. 9, 1821, quoted by U. B. Phillips, *Georgia and State Rights*, 158–159.
[39] Stephen B. Weeks, "Anti-Slavery Sentiment in the South," *Publications of the Southern History Association*, II, 87.
[40] John Bach McMaster, *A History of the People of the United States* (New York, 1888), II, 359; Rhodes, *History of the United States*, I, 19.

Georgia opposed the immediate abolition of slavery because of the dangers that might ensue. The very first Congress was confronted with petitions from anti-slavery societies, praying it to use its powers to further the cause of freedom. On February 11, 1790, a petition against the slave trade was presented to Congress—"The Address of the people called Quakers, in their annual assembly convened."[41] The suggestion of immediate emancipation aroused Southern members. The petitions led to ᵗhe appointment of a committee of inquiry into the scope of the powers of Congress in the matter. Jackson of Georgia said that he feared the abolition of the slave trade would "evince to the people a disposition towards a total emancipation, and they would hold their property in jeopardy."[42] He hinted at the economic objection to abolition. "I would beg to ask those, then, who are desirous of freeing the negroes, if they have funds sufficient to pay for them? If they have, they may come forward on that business with some propriety; but if they have not, they should keep themselves quiet, and not interfere with a business in which they are not interested."[43] The matter was sent to a sub committee. On February 12, Mr. Baldwin of Georgia spoke on the slave trade. He begged moderation by reciting the difficulty with which the Constitutional Convention had reached a compromise. As a member of that convention he recalled the pain and difficulty which the subject had caused that body. But, from a desire of preserving the Union, mutual concessions and compromises were finally reached, and the constitution agreed upon. "But the moment we go to jostle on that ground, I fear we shall feel it tremble under our feet."[44] On March 8, 1790, the sub committee, to whom the bill had been referred, reported the principles under which Congress acted during the next seventy years. They denied the power of Congress to interfere with slavery or the treat-

---

[41] *Annals of Congress*, 1st Congress, II, 1182.
[42] *Ibid*, II, 1187.
[43] *Ibid*, II, 1187.
[44] *Ibid*, II, 1200.

ment of slaves within the states; the legislature could not prohibit the importation of slaves prior to 1808, but it might lay a duty of ten dollars per head on such importation; It might pass laws regulating the slave trade, but it could not yet stop the importation of slaves into the United States.

Meanwhile the introduction of great numbers of slaves was considered undesirable. There was a feeling among the people that the slave-trade was an evil. Although no way of abandoning the institution of slavery seemed practicable at the time, Georgians deplored the system.

Justice James M. Wayne, mentioned in a previous chapter, severely condemned the slave trade.[45] A Georgia writer, in discussing slavery, said that there was no feature of the institution that did not work more injury to the white than to the black race. "It was the cause and the very "raison d'etre" of failure and want of enterprise in the young. It encouraged idleness by the debasement of honest manual work to the standard of slave labor. It clouded the Vision, so that only in the stronger minds were the eyes uplifted to the nobler realms of thought and action."[46] Frequently there was opposition to slavery among the skilled workmen and day laborers because of the competition with slave labor and the consequent low wages.[47]

Slavery was looked upon as a burden. The slaveholders would have rid themselves of the burden if it could have been done practically and efficiently. The most telling argument against slavery in Georgia was that it did not pay.[48] But inasmuch as it did pay some slaveowners it was hard to make the people as a whole believe that slavery was really a drain on the community. It was felt that the system of slavery was economically unprofitable.[49] Judge

---

[45] "Justice James M. Wayne's charge to the Grand Jury in 1859," *Georgia Historical Quarterly*, II, 101.

[46] C. S. Wylly, *The Seed that was Sown in the Colony of Georgia*, 14.

[47] For an interesting case of this kind see, *The Savannah Georgian*, September 14, 1850.

[48] Buckingham, *The Slave States of America*, I, 201–204.

[49] See Ralph B. Flanders, "Planters' Problems in Ante-Bellum Georgia," *Georgia Historical Quarterly*, XIV, 17–40.

A. B. Longstreet, author of "Georgia Scenes," recognized the economic evil of slavery. In 1827 he sold his slaves (whom he possessed through his wife) because they were a constant financial drain on him.[50] Throughout the entire period there were Georgians who saw the economic disadvantages of slavery. A planter of Liberty County wrote in the early twenties that the most likely circumstance to produce emancipation was the planters' realization of the disadvantages of slave-labor.[51] During the same period another planter remarked, "We are the slaves; not the blacks; we cannot make them work as men ought to work, neither can we get rid of them, nor supply their place with better subjects; they hang about us, and grow up, increasing and multiplying all our curses. They are the only people who do not care how things go on. . ."[52] One person disliked the responsibility of owning negroes, and not only refused to purchase those needed on the plantation but even considered the liberation of those he already possessed.[53] Mrs. Eliza Carter wrote her husband that slaves were a nuisance; Mr. Carter himself was inclined to sell his several hundred slaves and invest the money in Illinois lands and was with great difficulty dissuaded from doing so.[54]

Judge Jabez Bowen, of the Superior Court of the Eastern District, was an ardent opponent of slavery. He was regarded as an incendiary and provocative of trouble in the matter of the negroes. In his charge to the Grand Jury of Chatham County he spoke warmly of the evils of slavery and advocated the manumission of the slaves then owned by the people of Georgia; he predicted direful results if this were not done. Because the Grand Jury refused to have the charge published he ordered them to be sent to

---

[50] John Donald Wade, *Augustus Baldwin Longstreet* (New York, 1924), 117–118.
[51] Ralph B. Flanders, "Planters' Problems in Ante-Bellum Georgia," *Georgia Historical Quarterly*, XIV, 36.
[52] *Ibid.*
[53] *Ibid*, 37.
[54] *Ibid.*

jail. The members of the jury were later released by the justices of the county. A warrant was then sworn out against Judge Bowen; he was charged with having attempted to incite a slave insurrection and was placed in prison. He was kept there until his father could come from Rhode Island and arrange for his bond. Judge Bowen then left the state and never returned. In 1804 he was removed from office on the charge of malconduct, his malconduct consisting of his intemperate charge to the jury and his order which placed the members of that body in jail.[55]

In 1820 Congressman Reid of Georgia denounced slavery on the floor of the House of Representatives at Washington. On February 1, 1820, he declared in Congress that he was desirous of seeing the negroes set free, although he opposed the plan of bestowing American citizenship upon them. He spoke of slavery as an unnatural state, a dark cloud which obscured the lustre of free institutions.[56]

Alexander H. Stephens opposed slavery. He maintained throughout the forties that slavery was a moral evil. In a speech in Congress on January 25, 1845, in regard to the Wilmot Proviso, he said:

> I am no defender of slavery in the abstract. Liberty always had charms for me, and I would rejoice to see all the sons of Adam's family, in every land and clime, in the enjoyment of those rights which are set forth in our declaration of independence as 'natural and inalienable;' if a stern necessity, bearing the marks and impress of the hand of the Creator himself, did not, in some instance, interpose and prevent. Such is the case in the States where slavery now exists. But I have no wish to see it extended to other countries; and if the annexation of Texas were for the sole purpose of

---

[55] Warren Grice, *The Georgia Bench and Bar* (Macon, 1931), I, 82-83; Walter G. Charlton, "A Judge and a Grand Jury," *Report of the Thirty first Session of the Georgia Bar Association. 1914* (Macon, 1914), 206–215. For the content of Judge Bowen's charge to the Grand Jury of Chatham County see Appendix III.

[56] *Annals of Congress*, 16th Congress, 1st Session, 1024–1025. For the text of Congressman Reid's speech see Appendix IV.

extending slavery where it does not now, and would not otherwise exist, I should oppose it.[57]

Opposition to slavery continued in Georgia until about 1830. In the South the feeling prevailed that slavery was unprofitable but this was before the several new inventions gave an impetus to cotton planting. The Northern states had already emancipated or sold their slaves because they found it cheaper to hire labor by the day or the month than to support the slaves. It is very probable that slavery would never have become an acute problem had it not been for the sudden development of cotton growing. The anti-slavery sentiment declined after this profitable way of using the negroes was discovered. Thus, due to the extensive development of cotton planting and consequently of slavery, the South was becoming more and more reconciled to the institution. Among the many reasons given for the decline of the anti-slavery sentiment in the South after 1830 we may include the following:

1. The rapid growth of the cotton industry which resulted in an increase demand for slave labor;

2. The Nat Turner insurrection in 1831;

3. The debates in the Virginia legislature of 1831–1832, in which were offered plans for partial or total abolition of slavery;

4. The rise of the new abolition movement in the North under the leadership of Garrison;

5. And the growing opposition to the colonization plan, which many Southerners had been active in promoting. The reaction in the South following upon these events was responsible for the almost complete absence of anti-slavery sentiment after 1831.[58]

After 1830 the increased demand for cotton made the slaves economically profitable, and the prices of the negroes rose accordingly. Instead of trying to get rid of the slaves in Georgia, there was a constant demand for more.

---

[57] *The Savannah Georgian,* May 5, 1849.
[58] Lorenzo Dow Turner, *The Anti-Slavery Sentiment in American Literature Prior to 1865* (Washington, 1929), 48.

The spirit of coercion on the part of the abolitionists probably had more to do with the suppression of the emancipation sentiment existing in Georgia than all other things combined. The publication of violent abolition propoganda began to be noticed in Georgia about 1828. William Lloyd Garrison founded the Liberator in 1831, a paper devoted to immediate and unconditional abolition of slavery in the United States. He denounced the Union as a covenant with death and the constitution as an agreement with Hell. This uncompromising program adapted and pursued by him immediately aroused the opposition of the South and drove them into a defense of their position. The Abolitionists tried to arouse public opinion in the North and South, and to distribute propoganda among the slaves in order to create in them a longing for liberty. The extent to which the abolition agitation had driven the South is well illustrated by a speech made by the Honorable J. H. Lumpkin of Georgia, delivered in the House of Representatives, August 2, 1856. He concluded by saying: "If our country is still to continue to be the home of freemen and the asylum of the oppressed and the down-trodden of other climes—it will be because the gallant and patriotic national men of the non-slaveholding states shall have said: 'Thus far shalt thou go, but no farther.' "[59]

Georgians knew that the abolition agitators were a small but noisy faction and that their doctrines were condemned by all reasonable people of the North. The New York Enquirer of January 15, 1828, carried the following statement:

> "We have long been convinced that no real cause of distrust and jealousy exists between the North and South—indeed, we have reason to know, that the honest men of the North never contemplated to abridge the rights of the South. Whenever a question, therefore, is broached, and sometimes designedly broached, touching these points, and particularly

---

[59] *Speech of Hon. J. H. Lumpkin of Georgia,* delivered in the House of Representatives, August 2, 1856. 16.

about slaves, we trust, that our Southern friends will not allow every 'puny whipster' to excite their angry feelings; but relying on their own rights, and the determination of the North itself, to sustain the rights of the South, if necessary, treat with cool indifference and contempt the design of demagogues and brokendown politicians."[60]

The legislature of Georgia offered a reward of $5,000 for the apprehension and conviction in the Georgia courts of any of the editors or printers of the Liberator. On November 30, 1831, a resolution was passed:

> That the sum of five thousand dollars, be, and the same is hereby appropriated, to be paid to any person or persons who shall arrest, bring to trial and prosecute to conviction under the laws of this State; the editor or publisher of a certain paper called the Liberator, published in the town of Boston, and State of Massachusetts; or who shall arrest, bring to trial and prosecute to conviction under the laws of this State, any other person or persons who shall utter, publish or circulate within the limits of this State, said paper called the Liberator, or any other paper, circular, pamphlet, letter or address of a seditious character.[61]

Although a price was placed on Garrison's head, it was not expected to lead to his capture or trial but it showed the attitude of the State of Georgia toward the abolitionists. The Southern Recorder protested against the publication of The Liberator. It accused the editor of the Liberator of being a fanatic; he was excused on the ground of insanity.[62] Georgians opposed slavery, but they opposed Garrison even more. By the Georgia Code of 1835 publications which tended to incite insurrections were punishable by death. According to Section 5, division 3, of the penal code:

> If any person shall bring, introduce, or circulate or cause to be brought, introduced or circulated, or aid or assist, or be in any manner instrumental in bringing, introducing,

[60] *New York Enquirer*, January 15, 1828.
[61] *Acts of Georgia*, 1831, 255–256.
[62] *The Southern Recorder*, September 18, 1831.

or circulating, within this state, any printed or written paper, pamphlet or circular, for the purpose of inciting insurrection, revolt, conspiracy, or resistance, on the part of the slaves, negroes or free persons of color, in this state, against the citizens of this state, or any part of them, such person so offending, shall be guilty of a high misdemeanor, and on conviction shall be punished with DEATH.[63]

Georgia asked nothing more than to be let alone in the management of her own concerns. "The attacks of Massachusetts and the Northern States unsettled the very foundations of her government and drove her to desperation."[64] The South was extremely sensitive of criticism made by Northern writers. The Southern States recognized the evils of slavery and were making sincere attempts to handle the problem, but the South resented any interference by the North in her own personal affairs. It was a domestic problem to be handled by the States in their own way. The Southern people especially feared the circulation of seditious pamphlets among the slaves, and in 1829 the penalty of death was set for anyone found guilty of distributing them.[65] Laws against negro education were made more rigid. Any negro or white person who should engage to teach slaves to read or write were to be whipped, imprisoned, or fined.[66] At the same time the act of 1817 was reenacted which prohibited the introduction of slaves into the state.[67]

Many Georgians believed that, had the abolitionists never spoken, voluntary emancipation would have taken place. Joseph Henry Lumpkin wrote to Howell Cobb in 1848: "Had the Abolitionists let us alone we should have been guilty, I verily believe, of political and social suicide by emancipating the African race. . . . The violent assaults of these fiends have compelled us in self defense to investigate this momentous subject in all its bearings, and

[63] *Niles Register*, XLVIII, 441.
[64] Longstreet, *A Voice from the South*, 6.
[65] Dawson, *Compilation*, 413.
[66] *Ibid*, 413.
[67] *Ibid*, 414.

the result has been a firm and settled conviction that duty to the slave as well as the master forbids that the relation should be disturbed. . . ."[68] Thus it was the abolitionists themselves who prevented voluntary emancipation.

The violent agitation which abolitionists aroused placed all Southerners, even those who were opposed to slavery, on the defensive. Even though they favored emancipation, they bitterly opposed Garrisonian abolitionists. The intolerance of the agitators aroused the sensitiveness of the Southern people and drove them first into an apologetic position, and later into an open defense of slavery. Those who had formerly been opposed to slavery now began to search for reasons to defend it. An account of the persecution of the Southern slaveholders, which was copied from the New York Courier and Enquirer, appeared in the Southern Recorder on August 7, 1833. It said:

> As holders of slaves, they have been perpetually stigmatized with injustice, tyranny, and cruelty; they have been placed as it were below the other citizens of the United States; their characters have been assailed as buyers, sellers, and scourgers of their fellow creatures; their right to the possession of a large portion of their property has been questioned on abstract principles of natural law; and they have been driven into sectional combinations in defence of their rights as well as their character. They have been indirectly charged with corruption, in arguments to show the demoralizing effects of slavery, and as patriotic, as honorable, as high-minded a race as this or any other country can boast, has been held up to the world in the light of a delinquent caste, tainted with hereditary crime.[69]

William H. Crawford shows his opposition to the institution of slavery in a letter written to Governor Coles of Illinois during the struggle over slavery in that state: "Is it possible that your Convention is intended to introduce slavery into the state? I acknowledge if I were a

---

[68] U. B. Phillips, "The Correspondence of Robert Toombs, Alexander H. Stephens, and Howell Cobb," *Annual Report of the American Historical Association*, 1911, II, 94–95.
[69] *The Southern Recorder*, August 7, 1833.

citizen I should oppose it with great earnestness; where it has ever been introduced it is extremely difficult to get rid of and ought to be treated with great delicacy."[70] Thomas Clay of Georgia, condemned slavery in the following accusation: "The present economy of the slave system is, to get all you can from the slave, and give him as little as will support him in a working condition."[71] Hugh McCall, the first historian of Georgia, in alluding to the slaves, said: "This class of people, who cannot be supposed to be contented in slavery, would grasp with avidity at the most desperate attempts that promised freedom."[72]

In 1835 the legislature of Georgia reviewed the various slavery questions and declared its convictions on each. It stated:

1. That the freedom of the press and of speech were sacred and invaluable rights—rights which had been abused by those who would prostitute them for their own purposes;

2. That Georgia stood ready to protect the domestic institutions of her sister states;

3. That it was the duty of the North to crush the Abolitionists;

4. That Georgia welcomed the sentiments expressed by recent meetings at the North condemning abolitionists;

5. That Congress should regulate the postal laws to prevent the circulation of inflamatory matter;

6. And that Congress could not constitutionally interfere with slavery in the District of Columbia or in the territories.[73]

Thus we have seen that slavery was an established system in Georgia in the early years of the nineteeenth century. Most of the people of the state opposed slavery as an institution and sought for means of a gradual emancipation. Before the abolition agitation Southerners were apologetic for slavery; after the abolitionists adopted their

[70] Adams, *The Neglected Period of Anti-Slavery in America*, 22.
[71] Goodell, *The American Slave Code*, 153.
[72] Hugh McCall, *History of Georgia*.
[73] *Acts of Georgia*, 1835, 297–300.

radical program the South assumed the defensive. There had been an active opposition to slavery in Georgia from the time of the Revolution. Large numbers of individual slaves had been set free by the personal action of their masters. Many others had been sent to Liberia. The unsatisfactory condition of the free negroes deterred further emancipation. The problem of the free negro was harder to solve than the problem of the slave. The entrance of the slavery question into politics alarmed the Southern leaders who resented any interference in their local institutions. Every year the bitterness of feeling became more intense, and the people continued to grope for a solution.

CHAPTER XI

THE COLONIZATION MOVEMENT IN GEORGIA

The bulk of the people of Georgia opposed slavery as an institution and favored gradual emancipation as the most practical method of ridding the country of the slaves.[1] The idea of having the land filled with free negroes could not be tolerated. The many laws which were passed in Georgia in regard to the free negroes show that they were deemed undesirable members of society. Many of those who favored gradual abolition considered colonization the best method of attaining it.[2] The Colonization Society represented the desire to put an end to slavery.[3] The great problem confronting the anti-slavery agitators in all parts of the country was the free negro. Henry Clay well described the condition of the free negro in 1829 when he said:

> Of all the descriptions of our population, and of either portion of the African race, the free people of color are, by far, as a class, the most corrupt, depraved and abandoned . . . . They are not slaves, and yet they are not free. The laws, it is true, proclaim them free; but prejudices, more powerful than any law, deny them the privileges of freemen. They occupy a middle station between the free white population and the slaves of the United States, and the tendency of their habits is to corrupt both.[4]

Many slave-holders who recognized slavery as a great evil were convinced that emancipation without removal of the freed slaves would be yet worse, and would result in in-

---

[1] U. B. Phillips, *Georgia and State Rights*, 156–157.
[2] *Ibid*, 158.
[3] Charles Edward Merriam, *American Political Theory* (New York, 1903), 203.
[4] Speech of Henry Clay before the American Colonization Society in 1829, *African Repository*, VI, 12.

surrection, murder, and outrage in every form.[5] Friends of emancipation felt that the success of their efforts depended on the ability of the negro to reap the advantages of freedom.[6] People welcomed the colonization scheme as a solution to the problem. While it is with the history of colonization in Georgia that this chapter has to deal, it will be necessary here to notice briefly the history of the American Colonization Society with which the local Georgia societies were affiliated.

"The American Colonization Society for the Free People of Color" was founded at Washington in 1816. It was incorporated by the legislature of the state of Maryland in 1837.[7] It made an earnest effort to colonize the free negroes in Africa. The purpose of the society was to encourage emancipation and to aid the emigration of the negroes who were thus emancipated to Africa. The first two articles of the Constitution of the society state the object of the society:

Article I:

> This Society shall be called the American Society for the Colonizing the free people of colour of the United States.

Article II:

> The object to which its attention is to be exclusively directed, is to promote and execute a plan for colonizing (with their consent) the free people of color residing in our country in Africa, or such other place as Congress shall deem most expedient. And the Society shall act to effect this object in co-operation with the general government and such of the States as may adopt regulations on the subject.[8]

Georgia discountenanced the liberation of slaves within the state, but she had no objection to their liberation in the

---

[5] Asa Earl Martin, *The Anti-Slavery Movement in Kentucky Prior to 1850* (Louisville, 1918), 49.

[6] *Ibid*, 50.

[7] 25 *Ga.* 423.

[8] William Jay, *An Inquiry Into the Character and Tendency of the American Colonization and American Anti-slavery Societies*, 11–12. The charter of the American Colonization Society may be found in 25 *Ga.* 423–426.

land of their fathers, with the consent of the owners.[9] The colonization scheme was endorsed by the legislatures of Virginia, Georgia, Maryland, Tennessee and Vermont.[10] The Colonization Society drew support from many quarters. Some hoped to rid the state of free negroes. Others saw in the society an aid to eventual extinction of slavery by means of voluntary emancipation and transportation of the freedmen to Africa. Because of the fact that it promised even indirectly to advance the cause of emancipation, it could command the support of the anti-slavery element; while its program of the removal of the free negro commended itself to both the pro-slavery and the anti-slavery factions.[11]

The United States government extended its protection to Liberia, the territory on the west coast of Africa, which was selected by the society as the site for its colony. The capital of Liberia was called Monrovia in honor of President Monroe. Several thousand negroes were sent over to Liberia. Special inducements were offered to attract the free negroes and to make them contented and prosperous after their arrival there. The emigrants were to enjoy all of the advantages and privileges that they would enjoy in any of the states.[12] In 1847 Liberia became a republic with only negroes as officers. Some of the important settlements in Liberia were New Georgia, New Virginia, Kentucky, Louisiana, etc. The Colonization scheme was a noble effort on the part of the Southern statesmen and Northern philanthropists to solve the problem. Most of its supporters and friends were in the South.[13] Among the presidents of the society were Madison, Monroe, Marshall, and Henry Clay—all Southern men. William H. Crawford of Georgia was one of the first vice-presidents of the organization. The American Colonization Society,

[9] *The Missionary*, November 10, 1823.
[10] Martin, *The Anti-Slavery Movement in Kentucky*, 51.
[11] Martin, *The Anti-Slavery Movement in Kentucky*, 51–52.
[12] *The African Repository*, XXI, 283.
[13] Stephen B. Weeks, "Anti-Slavery Sentiment in the South," *Publications of the Southern History Association*, II, 90.

supported by the churches, and receiving financial support indirectly from the National government, was put forth as the real and only practicable measure for ameliorating African slavery and it had adherents and support until the Civil War.[14]

One of the new settlements in the Republic of Liberia was New Georgia, named in honor of the state of Georgia. An account of New Georgia, written in 1853 says:

> New Georgia is a small township located on the eastern side of Stockton Creek, about five miles from Monrovia. It is occupied principally by native Africans, who were formerly slaves. Upwards of two hundred of the liberated Africans who have been, or who now are, residents of New Georgia, were sent to Liberia by the United States Government, at different times. Many of these have married persons who were born in the United States; and have thereby become strongly identified with the Liberians, as citizens of the Republic. Some of them are partially educated; and, a few years ago, one of them occupied a seat in the Legislature. As most of the citizens of New Georgia have taken the oath of allegiance they are permitted to enjoy equal immunities with other citizens.[15]

The objects of the society were stated in its constitution and in numerous addresses made by the society. The annual meeting in 1826 resolved, "That its only object is, what has been at all times avowed, the removal to the coast of Africa, with their own consent, of such people of colour within the United States, as are already free, and of such others, as the humanity of the individuals, and the laws of the different states, may hereafter liberate."[16] The colonizationists believed in a gradual emancipation of slavery. They opposed immediate and unconditional emancipation as impracticable and undesirable: impracticable because (1) the federal government had no constitutional right to enact a general emancipation provision, (2) since the states

---

[14] Hart, *Slavery and Abolition*, 237.
[15] J. W. Lugenbeel, *Sketches of Liberia*, (Washington, 1853), 7.
[16] *Niles Weekly Register*, XLV, 167; *African Repository*, I, 335–336.

alone had the right to pass emancipation measures they would do so only when the public sentiment of each state became favorable to emancipation, and (3) because public sentiment in the slave states was not yet favorable; undesirable because (1) it was believed that if three millions of negro slaves were set free at one time they would be unable to care for themselves and would be more wretched than under a system of slavery, (2) the so-called free negro would not be free in the truest sense until he was taken back to his native country and there, under the supervision of sympathetic governors, was taught self-sustenance and self-government, and (3) because of the danger of a race war in the Southern States.[17]   The Emancipationists recognized that slavery was an evil.   They believed that the remedy was gradual emancipation made practicable through: (1) cooperation between the different sections of the Union, (2) the education of slaveholders, (3) and the transportation of the manumitted slaves to Africa.[18]   The Colonizationists hoped to exact a powerful moral influence in favor of emancipation, but they opposed any illegal means or means which might result in involving the sections in civil war, or in bringing about the dissolution of the union. The two direct, distinct, and primary objects of the Society were: (1) to give freedom to the American negro, to return him to his native land, and there to encourage his highest development;   (2) to exert a powerful moral pressure in favor of emancipation as rapid as practicable, and both universal and absolute.[19]

The influence of the colonization society was felt keenly in Georgia.   Robert S. Findley, one of the founders, was president of the University of Georgia for a time.   A wave of humanitarianism swept over the state of Georgia.   The sentiment in favor of the abolition of slavery found expression through these colonization societies.   In the Cleland

---

[17] Early Lee Fox, *The American Colonization Society,* 1817–1840 (Baltimore, 1919) 142–143.
[18] *Ibid,* 143.
[19] *Ibid,* 143.

versus Waters case of 1854 the following statement was made: "While public opinion has never wavered in this State, for the past fifty years, so far as domestic manumission was concerned, the same steadfastness of purpose has not been manifested, as to extra-territorial and foreign colonization. The policy of transporting our free blacks to Liberia, received at its commencement in 1816, the sanction and approbation of our greatest and best men. The Honorable William H. Crawford was, I believe, one of the Vice Presidents elected at the organization of the American Society."[20]

While the colonization idea was generally approved in Georgia, as in other sections of the country, the membership and number of auxiliary societies increased slowly. In 1832 there were four branches of the Colonization Society in Georgia. They were the Jackson County, Augusta, Augusta Female, and the Waynesboro Associations.[21] Great sums of money were subscribed for its use. One branch of the society, was established in Putnam County.[22] This branch was so strong in 1821 and 1822 that it could print its second and third reports. Another branch was established in Baldwin County.[23]

One of the earliest societies in Georgia was the above mentioned Jackson County Auxiliary Society. At a called meeting of this organization, held April 2, 1825, resolutions were drawn up stating the purposes and scope of the society.[24]

This Auxiliary Society of Jackson County, from March, 1825, to July, 1825, contributed twenty-five dollars to the movement.[25] At the annual meeting of the Jackson County Auxiliary Society on September 1, 1827, the following preamble and resolutions were offered and unanimously adopted:

---

[20] 16 *Ga.* 496.
[21] Stephen B. Weeks, "Anti-Slavery Sentiment in the South," *Publications of the Southern History Association*, II, 92.
[22] *The Missionary*, October 27, 1823.
[23] Phillips, *Georgia and State Rights*, 158. (foot-note)
[24] *The African Repository*, I, 92.
[25] *Ibid*, I, 160.

> Whereas this Society, notwithstanding the great discouragements arising out of the ill founded jealousies and fears of the South, relative to the ultimate designs of the North, and the Parent Society for Colonizing the free persons of colour, and such as may be by their respective owners from time to time emancipated; do, in the fullest confidence in the patriotism and philanthrophy of the Parent Society, again renew to each other the solemn pledge of fidelity and perseverance. Believing (as we always have,) that it is one of the greatest National and Christian enterprises, and that the jealousies and fears of our fellow citizens do not arise from the want of equal patriotism, but from the want of correct information; in order therefore, that this may be partially obtained, the following resolutions were offered and unanimously adopted.[26]

There followed two resolutions in regard to subscriptions to the African Repository and the disposal of the money in the treasury.[27] The Jackson County Auxiliary Society continued to do active work in Georgia.

The Augusta Colonization Society was a strong organization. It was organized on January 11, 1832, after an address made by the Reverend Robert S. Finley, agent of the society. Several of the citizens of Augusta had contemplated for some time, the formation of an auxiliary society. They now came forward with great decision and liberality to aid the cause of African Colonization.[28] The following were elected as officers of the Augusta society: President, Robert F. Poe; vice presidents, Samuel K. Talmadge, Robert Campbell, James Harper, and John P. King; secretary and treasurer, William Poe; managers, William I. Hobby, Benjamin Hall, Barna M'Kenney, Milton Antony, William Harper, Joseph A. Eve, and George A. B. Walker.[29] A. Campbell, member of the Augusta branch, contributed five hundred dollars.[30]

---

[26] *Ibid*, III, 370.
[27] *The African Repository*, III, 370.
[28] *Ibid*, VIII, 59, 93.
[29] *Ibid*, VIII, 59.
[30] *Ibid*, VIII, 96.

On January 13, 1832, a Female Colonization Society was organized in Augusta. The following officers were elected: President, Mrs. Barna M'Kenney; vice president, Mrs. Mary Barton; secretary and treasurer, Mrs. W. Coltin; managers, Mrs. Mary Smelt, Mrs. Elizabeth M'Kain, Mrs. Elizabeth Hand, Mrs. I. Coltin, Miss Elizabeth Kain, and Miss Eliza Tugram.[31]

The following extract of a letter from Robert S. Finley gives an account of the organization of the Augusta branches of the society:

> From Mobile I hastened to Augusta, Georgia, to meet the Methodist Conference of Georgia which commenced its session at the latter place, on the 5th inst. Upon my arrival in Augusta, I was happy to be informed that several worthy citizens of that place had for some time had it in contemplation to organize a society there.
>
> On the 9th inst. as a preparatory to holding a public meeting, I delivered an address to the Conference, and solicited their concurrence in the measure. As a testimony of their approbation, they agreed to attend the meeting themselves; and suspended the public religious services which were daily held in their church during the session of Conference, for the purpose of giving their congregation an opportunity to attend. In the evening of the 11th inst. I delivered an address to a large audience of Ladies and Gentlemen in the Masonic Hall. On the same evening a very efficient Society was organized. You will find a list of the officers in a news-paper which I directed to be forwarded to you. On the 13th, several Ladies met, moved by the mere promptings of their benevolence, without any suggestion on my part, and formed a Female Society, which from the character of the Ladies engaged in it, cannot but be efficient.
>
> I would press upon the attention of the Board, the importance of selecting emigrants for the Colony from this region of the U. States; because their constitutions are better adapted to the African climate; and with proper attention, a large number of suitable emigrants might soon be embarked from

---

[31] *Ibid,* VIII, 59.

this region. There are several in this city who wish to go.[32]

Branches of the society were also established at Waynes-boro, Eatonton, and Milledgeville. Some of the best friends of the colonization movement resided in Georgia, although there were only a few auxiliary societies there. These local societies were to some extent centers of anti-slavery thought. The African Repository was freely cir-culated in Georgia. This periodical contained many ad-dresses made before societies in other states; the institution of slavery was attacked upon moral, economic and political grounds. The many cases where Georgia masters gave up their slaves for the purpose of freeing and removing them to Liberia were repeatedly referred to as will be shown in the following pages (note the many citations to the African Repository.) There were instances of willingness on the part of masters to free their slaves for transportation, but the lack of funds greatly hampered the work. There was the case of a Georgia citizen whose fortune consisted of his slaves; upon the liberation of these he had to call on the society for aid in transporting them.[33]

A writer in the Georgia Journal in March, 1826, called attention to the existence of auxiliaries at Milledgeville, Eatonton, and in Jackson County, and expressed his desire to see auxiliaries at every county seat in the state as well as in every populous neighborhood. He also asserted that many individuals would manumit their slaves if it were practicable, but because of the existing conditions in the South it was difficult to free the slaves—hence the enact-ment of laws prohibiting it. A post-script was added stating that if Mr. Crawford, who was at that time free from the burdens of public life, were to encourage an Auxiliary Society in his county, many would join it.[34] According to the twenty-ninth annual report of the American Coloniza-tion Society, there were several local organizations in the

---

[32] *Ibid*, VIII, 123.
[33] *Ibid*, IV, 185.
[34] *Ibid*, I, 12–14.

state of Georgia but no State Society. The reason given for this was that no agent had been sent to Georgia for many years past, and that the pastors of the churches had neglected to bring the subject before the people. However, it was stated that considerable interest was manifested in Georgia and that liberal contributions had been made.[35]

A law of 1817 provided that Africans who had been illegally introduced were to be turned over to the Colonization Society, provided the society would reimburse the state for the expenses incurred and pay for the transportation.[36] The act of 1817 directed the governor of Georgia to deliver to the Society all negroes illegally imported and to "aid in promoting the benevolent views of said society in such manner as he may deem expedient."[37] The results of the efforts of the Colonization Society in Georgia are seen in the provisions of this act. It provided for the disposal of all negroes illegally imported into the state. Such slaves, if captured, were to be considered the property of the state and were to be sold at auction, provided that, in case the Colonization Society agreed to transport the negroes to such foreign colony as the Society might have established, the negroes, after payment by the Society of all expenses incurred by the state in connection with them, were to be transferred to the Society.[38]

William H. Crawford, who was presiding at a meeting of the Board of Managers of the American Colonization Society in April, 1819, called attention to an advertisement he had found in a Georgia newspaper. Thirty or forty negroes, who had been illegally imported into the state, were to be sold at auction unless, by the provision already referred to in the law of 1817, they could be taken over by the Colonization Society and transported to Africa. The Reverend William Meade, general agent of the Society, was sent to Georgia to make an effort to save the negroes from

[35] *Ibid*, XXII, 39–40.
[36] Lamar, *Compilation*, 808; Prince, *Digest*, 793–794.
[37] Prince, *Digest*, 794.
[38] Fox, *The American Colonization Society*, 53.

slavery. The governor of Georgia agreed to postpone the sale while Meade made financial arrangements for the redemption of the negroes. Liberal subscriptions were made, the arrangements were satisfactorily settled, and the negroes were turned over to the society. Meade reported that: "Some who had but little hope of our general enter-prize declared their willingness to contribute for the ransome [sic] of these; and a few who intended to have become the purchasers at this sale, expressed a pleasure at the thought of their restoration to Africa, and proved their sincerity by uniting with the Society at Milledgeville."[39] Under the direction of the most prominent citizens of the state, Meade formed three auxiliary societies in Georgia. He also re-ported a similar good feeling toward the Society at Augusta and Savannah.[40]

A conclusive and interesting proof that Colonization had a beneficial and pronounced influence upon public senti-ment in Georgia, and particularly upon slave-holders, is contained in a study of the many emancipations that were brought about by the influence of the society. Many negroes were manumitted in Georgia on condition that they be sent to Africa. The will of Zadock Simmons of Wilkin-son County, 1821, provided that his slaves should be trans-ported to the coast of Africa and there liberated.[41] In 1828 a Georgian, name not given, liberated forty-three of his slaves, the greater part of his fortune, on condition that they should go to Liberia.[42] The August number of the African Repository in that year carried an appeal to the members of the society to furnish the funds necessary for the trans-portation of the negroes.[43]

Many slaveholders offered their slaves to the society when it should be ready to take them. Many others wrote for advice as to the disposal of their slaves. An example of a

---

[39] Fox, *The American Colonization Society*, 1817–1840, 58.
[40] *Ibid*, 58.
[41] Victor Davidson, *History of Wilkinson County* (Macon, 1930), 208.
[42] *The African Repository*, IV, 185.
[43] *Ibid*, IV, 185.

letter of this nature is that of Joel Early Esquire of Greensboro, Georgia, an enthusiastic friend of the Colonization movement. Joel Early, brother of Peter Early, one of Georgia's
early governors, exhibited conscientious scruples about
owning slaves. In 1827 he wrote to R. R. Gurley, secretary
of the society, and asked his advice concerning the emancipation of the slaves of the former. Early asked for the ex-
planation of several questions which were puzzling him.
In answer Gurley explained the questions satisfactorily
and commended the work of the auxiliary societies of
Georgia.[44] Many times these letters to the officers of the
Colonization Society set forth the real sacrifice which some
of the slaveholders were willing to make in order to free
their slaves. The society was a kind of clearing house
where the views of moderate Southerners and moderate
Northerners were exchanged and where the spirit of emancipation worked "silently but mightily."[45] The opposition
to slavery in Georgia was due to economic as well as to
humanitarian reasons. The fact that slaves were liberated
in Georgia and transported to Africa is proof that the idea
of gradual emancipation was making headway in the late
twenties and early thirties. In 1831 a gentleman from
Georgia predicted the repeal of the act prohibiting emancipation, with the proviso that the slaves to be emancipated
should, within a determinate period, emigrate to Africa.[46]

A gentleman from New York wrote: "I own in Savannah
a colored man, to whom I have offered the option of going
to the American Colony in Africa. I am informed that he
consents to go, and the owner of his wife and children
is willing that they should go likewise. The man in question is a sober and industrious mechanic originally from
Africa."[47]

In 1830 the above mentioned Joel Early of Greene
County, brother of the governor of Georgia and a large

---

[44] *Ibid*, III, 289–296.
[45] Fox, *The American Colonization Society*, 207.
[46] *The African Repository*, VII, 144.
[47] *Ibid*, VI, 215.

slave owner, emancipated thirty slaves and sent them to
Liberia. They sailed on board the Brig Montgomery in
April, 1830, in company with many other emancipated
slaves of other states.[48]   Many of these negroes became
dissatisfied and asked Mr. Early to provide for their return.
This he did. Some of the negroes came back to Greene
County. Some of the descendants of the Early negroes
are still living around Greensboro, and the story of the
African venture has been told to them by their parents and
grandparents many times.

C. Bolton, Esquire, of Savannah, liberated nine of his
slaves to be sent to the colony. These sailed for Liberia
on board the Carolinian on October 20, 1830.[49]   At the
same time another Georgian, name not given, emancipated
his one slave.[50]   One Georgia writer in 1831 mentions
another Georgian, name not given, who provided in his
will for the emancipation of his fifty slaves provided that
they should go to Africa under the auspices of the Colonization Society.[51]   Dr. James Bradley of Georgia liberated
in his will his forty-six slaves. These were sent to Liberia
on board the Jupiter in 1832.[52]   In 1833 the Reverend Ripley
of Georgia manumitted fourteen slaves to be transported
to Africa.[53]   In 1834 another Georgian, name not given,
emancipated one slave.[54]   In 1835 two other Georgians,
names not given, manumitted one and eight negroes respectively.[55]   A lady from Augusta left her negro girl,
Kitty, in the custody of Bishop Andrew. According to the
provisions of the will Kitty, at the age of nineteen, was
to have her choice of going to Liberia free, or of remaining
a slave with Bishop Andrew. When the matter was explained to the girl she begged that she might remain with

---

[48] *Ibid*, V, 377; VI, 30, 62; X, 292.
[49] *Ibid*, VI, 283; X, 292.
[50] Fox, *The American Colonization Society*, 213.
[51] *The African Repository*, VII, 144.
[52] *Ibid*, VIII, 94.
[53] Fox, *The American Colonization Society*, 214.
[54] *Ibid*, 214.
[55] *Ibid*, 215.

Bishop Andrew rather than to be given her freedom in far-away Liberia.[56]

Thus we have seen that the Colonization Society did very effective work in Georgia. It succeeded in keeping alive a sentiment in favor of emancipation. Although few local societies were formed and no state society, these auxiliary branches contained many enthusiastic members. The contributions made, and the many slaves who were liberated and sent to Liberia, are evidence of this. The discussion of the work of the Colonization Society will be continued in the following chapter.

---

[56] Wade, *Augustus Baldwin Longstreet*, 274–275.

CHAPTER XII

THE COLONIZATION MOVEMENT IN GEORGIA (CONTINUED)

In the preceding chapter was discussed the organization and the work of the American Colonization Society, the influence of the society in Georgia, the organization of local auxiliary societies, and the cases where negroes were manumitted and sent to Liberia. The present chapter is only a continuation of the preceding one, showing other cases where slaves were liberated, the contributions made for the society, and the final failure of the society.

A gentleman from Decatur (DeKalb County), Georgia, in July, 1835, proposed to manumit and send to Liberia eight colored persons.[1] Among the passengers on board the Mary Caroline Stevens bound for Liberia in 1856 were London Williams, emancipated by Mrs. M. A. Williams of Savannah, and Sally Tafts, emancipated by the will of J. B. Tafts of Savannah.[2] William Rogers of Savannah donated seventy dollars for the expenses of the emigration of London Williams, and T. R. Mills of Savannah gave seventy dollars for the expenses of the emigration of Sally Tafts.[3] Richard Hoff of Elbert County, Georgia, emancipated fifty-four of his slaves in 1856. These also sailed on board the ship Mary Caroline Stevens for Liberia.[4] This liberal benefactor donated $2,000 for the expenses of the emigration of his slaves.[5]

An interesting example in Georgia is that of Richard Tubman. Although the law of Georgia did not permit the

---

[1] *The African Repository*, XI, 264.
[2] *Ibid*, XXXIII, 24.
[3] *Ibid*, XXXIII, 30.
[4] *Ibid*, XXXIII, 24–25.
[5] *Ibid*, XXXIII, 30.

emancipation of slaves within the state, Tubman tried to secure a special act of permission by making provisions for a liberal legacy to several of the literary institutions of the state if the permission to emancipate were granted. Application was made to the society to transport the slaves. Four old men begged their mistress to keep them and she consented. The remaining forty-four were under forty years of age. The legislature refused Tubman's request. The year after his death the widow of the deceased paid $1,000 to the negroes for the crop they had raised. The value of the slaves, whom Tubman attempted to free, was estimated at not less than $40,000.[6]

The will of Marshall Keith of Columbia County provided that three of his negroes should be given over to the Colonization Society and that money should be given them.[7] In 1850 Major Wood, by will, manumitted 164 negroes and left a fund of $5,000 to defray their expenses to Hayti. But "for good reasons" the negroes were transported to Liberia.[8]

By its charter the American Colonization Society was authorized to receive property by bequest or otherwise, and to use or dispose of it at its discretion for the colonizing, with their own consent, in Africa, of the free people of color residing in the United States, "and for no other uses or purposes whatsoever."[9] In 1853 Francis Gideon bequeathed, by his will, to the society all of his slaves for the purpose of sending them to Liberia. According to the interpretation of Judge Lumpkin the negroes were given as slaves, and not as free persons of color, to the Colonization Society to be sent to Africa. The testator could only give them as slaves, for if the will had changed their status to that of free people it would have been contrary to the laws of 1801 and 1818. The unconditional right to the negroes as slaves could not be vested in the society under

[6] Letters of the American Colonization Society, Quoted by, Fox, *The American Colonization Society*, 204–205.
[7] 4 *Ga.* 453.
[8] Ralph B. Flanders, "Planters' Problems in Ante-Bellum Georgia," *Georgia Historical Quarterly*, XIV, 38.
[9] 25 *Ga.* 424.

their act of incorporation. The court therefore decided that the society was incompetent to take the property under their charter.[10]

Francis J. Walker, who died in 1856, provided in his will that certain slaves therein named should be sent to Liberia at the expense of the estate. The executors were authorized to sell at public or private sale any or all of the testator's property and any or all of his slaves, except those specially directed to be colonized, in order to carry out the testator's wishes. The entire proceeds of the estate were to be invested in such manner as the executors saw fit, and transferred to the American Colonization Society, to be held by them in trust for the maintenance and support of the seven slaves specified and their descendants.[11] The Supreme Court of Georgia held that this will was legal and that the court would appoint some person to enforce it, or carry it out, because the society did not have sufficient authority under its charter to do so. It will be observed that this man freed some of his slaves by his will, and the high court of Georgia held that he acted legally, and approved his conduct and will.[12]

In 1833 many emigrants departed from Savannah on the ship Hercules.[13] Among the emigrants were 145 from Charleston, 11 from Beaufort, 24 from Georgia and Florida— in all 180. Messrs. R. and W. King from Savannah superintended the embarkation of the entire company. This expedition promised much for the moral interests of the colony; many of the emigrants were religious teachers; its departure inclined many to a favorable opinion both of the society and of Liberia. At the request of the Auxiliary Society of Augusta, Georgia, Thomas Hobby, Esquire, sailed on the Hercules in order that he might examine and, on his return, make a report of the state and prospects of

[10] 23 *Ga.* 448.
[11] 25 *Ga.* 420.
[12] 25 *Ga.* 420.
[13] *The African Repository*, VIII, 365.

the colony.[14]   The Augusta Colonization Society paid fifty dollars to the captain of the ship Hercules for Mr. Hobby's passage.[15]

Preparations were being made in November, 1833, for sending another expedition from Savannah to Liberia consisting of 83 negroes.   Of the 83 free colored persons 35 were adults and 46 were under 18 years of age.   Besides the 83 negroes from Savannah there were fourteen slaves who were liberated by the Reverend Mr. Ripley of Newton, Massachusetts.   They were to join the Savannah expedition, making the total number 97.   Thirty or forty others were under consideration and it was considered that they would be included before the expedition sailed.   According to the merchants of Savannah these emigrants were honest, industrious, sober, and respectable persons.[16]

Many philanthropists of Georgia subscribed large sums of money to the Colonization Society.   A. Campbell of Augusta contributed five hundred dollars.[17]   George Hargraves of Augusta gave two sums of five hundred dollars each and one sum of two hundred and fifty dollars.[18]   The following letters will show the liberal spirit and manner with which the friends of the society in Augusta were disposed to assist its great enterprise.

Augusta, April 30, 1832.

Sir: I enclose herein a check of the Cashier of the bank of Augusta, upon the Cashier of the Bank of America, in the city of New York, in your favour for five hundred dollars, which Be pleased to receive for the use of the Colonization Society as an evidence of my approval of the great and humane objects of the Society, and of my desire for their success.

Yours truly,

A. Campbell.[19]

---

[14] *The African Repository*, VIII, 365.
[15] *Ibid*, IX, 160.
[16] *The African Repository*, IX, 287.
[17] *Ibid*, VIII, 93.
[18] *Ibid*, VIII, 93, 96; XII, 142.
[19] *Ibid*, VIII, 93.

Augusta, May 4th, 1832.

Sir: the enclosed check of five hundred dollars, is intended as a Donation to the Colonization Society, for the removal of Free persons of Colour to Liberia—Be pleased to acknowledge the receipt by the return of mail.

I am, Sir, your humble Servant

Geo. Hargraves.[20]

This same George Hargraves of Augusta, at a later period, gave another donation of five hundred dollars to the society; then in 1836 this munificient benefactor contributed another sum of two hundred and fifty dollars.[21]   Robert Campbell of Augusta made a contribution of five hundred dollars to the society.[22]   On April 15, 1836, he gave another sum of fifty dollars.   In his letter accompanying the latter gift he says:

I continue to wish it [the American Colonization Society] prosperity, and most sincerely hope that its friends at the South will give it the support which it so richly merits from them, and as an offspring of their own benevolence.   I am very desirous to know whether there is any likelihood of a vessel being sent to Liberia, by the Society, from within this State, or South Carolina, and when vessels may be expected to sail from Norfolk, Virginia, and whether some emigrants from this State could be taken from the latter.[23]

In 1845 Robert Campbell made another contribution of $23.50.[24]   In 1857 the same Robert Campbell made two separate contributions of twenty-five dollars and of ten dollars respectively.[25]

The contributions made by Columbus, Georgia, to the American Colonization Society during the visit of the Reverend W. McLain to that city in 1841, amounted to one hundred and twenty dollars.   Of this G. Hargraves of Columbus gave $100.[26]   In 1841 an anonymous friend

---

[20] *Ibid*, VIII, 93.
[21] *The African Repository*, XII, 142.
[22] *Ibid*, XII, 142.
[23] *Ibid*, XII, 142.
[24] *Ibid*, XXI, 255.
[25] *Ibid*, XXXIII, 96, 127.
[26] *Ibid*, XVII, 206.

to colonization in Georgia remitted five hundred dollars.[27]
During this same year contributions were made by John
James Flourney of Athens, Georgia,[28] and the Reverend S.
Brag of Macon.[29] Later donations were made by Charles
F. McCoy of Athens,[30] T. Bishop and Albon Chase of
Athens,[31] Joseph Bryan of Mount Zion,[32] and Miss H. B.
Longstreet of Augusta.[33] "Two Friends" in Georgia con-
tributed five hundred dollars each.[34] Another contributor
was a Miss Cowper from Chatham County, near Savannah,
in Georgia.[35] On November 12, 1826, a gentleman from
Georgia, name unknown, who sent a contribution of five
dollars to the Colonization Society, said "I see with pain
that the funds of the society are in a depressed state, and
heartily wish, I could afford to send some efficient aid.
May the Lord bless this mite and abundantly bless the
Institution for which you are labouring."[36]

From May 20th to June 20th, 1846, eighty dollars had
been collected in Georgia by the Reverend John B. Pinney.[37]
From June 20th to July 20th, 1846, Savannah contributed
$60. The contributors were: Joseph S. Fay and Noble
A. Hardee, each $30, to constitute themselves life members.[38]
In a period of ten years, 1846–1856, Georgia gave $12,669.90
to the American Colonization Society.[39]

1846	1847	1848	1849	1850	1851	1852	1853	1854	1855
$150	142.50	662.35	305.50	5,197.50	885.25	634	3,500.25	680	512.80

Total $12,669.90

---

[27] *Ibid*, XVII, 35.
[28] *The African Repository*, XVII, 144, 266–267.
[29] *Ibid*, XVII, 272.
[30] *Ibid*, XXI, 319.
[31] *Ibid*, XXII, 359.
[32] *Ibid*, XXXIII, 63.
[33] *Ibid*, XXXIII, 127.
[34] *Ibid*, VIII, 366.
[35] *Ibid*, VIII, 30.
[36] *Ibid*, II, 284.
[37] *Ibid*, XXII, 231.
[38] *Ibid*, XXII, 263.
[39] Howell Cobb, *A Scriptural Examination of the Institution of Slavery in the United States*, (Georgia, 1856), 170.

In 1856, 141 emigrants left Georgia for Liberia.[40] From 1820 to 1856 the number of emigrants who left Georgia bound for Liberia amounted to 1,030.[41]

The following letter from a clergyman in Georgia shows the sentiment regarding the Colonization Society:

FROM A CLERGYMAN IN GEORGIA

I have delayed my reply to your favor of the 8th inst. in order to confer with some friends of the colonization cause. I am one of those who think that this question must soon engage much of the attention of the southern country and I believe the sooner it is brought permantly before us the better.   Mr. Finley's efforts have animated and united the feelings of the friends of the cause, and brought over some enemies to acknowledge the excellence of the institution he advocated.   The society here is yet small, but it is sustained by intelligent, influential, and energetic men.

The full and open debate in the Virginia Legislature has alarmed the people of the South, and I think it has for the present operated against the colonization cause here—but I believe it will in the end, greatly promote the object.   I rejoice at that event, and I feel a strong confidence, that the light which by its sudden and overpowering blaze, has dazzled many an eye, will yet prove a lamp to our path, when our sight is so far recovered as to enable us steadily to gaze at the truth which at first glance dimmed our vision, and made us turn away with sensations of pain.   The cause of colonization is sustained on the basis of truth and humanity, of wisdom and policy, through out the south.

It is the only hope, under God, for this section of the country, and I have little doubt but it will in a short time be a universal favourite among us.

A gentleman of this place, is waiting for the first favourable opportunity to liberate and send to Liberia eight slaves, and there are a number of free negroes in this place, who are willing to emigrate.[42]

---

[40] *The African Repository*, XXIII, 78.
[41] *Ibid*, XXIII, 78.
[42] *The African Repository*, VIII, 124.

Note also the following from A GENTLEMAN IN GEOR-
GIA:

> The officers of the Auxiliary Society, formed here during
> the visit of Mr. Finley, are now arranging information for
> circulation in this State, with the view of making the benev-
> olent intentions of the parent Society more generally known,
> of correcting many false impressions that exist, and of show-
> ing that the objects should be particularly fostered, by
> Planters and other slave holders.

> After this has been generally diffused, and has had sufficient
> time to be discussed and fully understood, I would be much
> pleased to see among us such an Agent as you have men-
> tioned. Before long I have no doubt Georgia will contribute
> liberally in support of your institution.[43]

Since it is rather difficult to get the opinion of the negro
on the question of colonization and emancipation, the
following extract of a letter will be of value. In this letter
a free man of color in Savannah, who was highly esteemed
for his intelligence and piety, freely expresses his opinions:

> I have always viewed the principle on which the Society
> was grounded, as one of much policy, though I saw it was
> aided by a great deal of benevolence. And when viewing
> my situation, with thousands of my colored brethren in the
> U. States, who are in a similar situation, I have often won-
> dered what prevented us from rising and with one voice,
> saying, we will accept the offer made us at the risk of sacrific-
> ing all the comforts that our present situation can afford us.
> I have often almost come to the conclusion that I would make
> the sacrifice, and have only been prevented by the unfavor-
> able accounts of the climate. I have always heretofore,
> viewed it as a matter of temporal interest, but now I view
> it spiritually. According to the accounts from Liberia, it
> wants help, and such as I trust I could give, though ever so
> little. I understand the branches of a Wheelwright, and
> Blacksmith, and Carpenter, I also have good ideas of Ma-
> chinery and other branches. I trust also, were I to go there,
> I would add one to the number of advocates for Religion.

---

[43] *Ibid*, VIII, 124–125. For other letters showing the sentiment of the people
of Georgia toward the Colonization movement see Appendix V.

I will thank you to inform me what things I should take for the comfort of myself and family. I don't expect to go at the expense of the Society, and therefore hope to be allowed to take something more than those who do not defray their own expenses.[44]

Another negro, a female emigrant to Liberia, whose transportation had been paid by people in Savannah, after she had reached Liberia wrote back to her patronesses in Savannah. She thanked them for their interest and aid, gave a favorable account of her new surroundings, commended the religious work of Mr. Hobby, "a very amiable young gentleman from Georgia," described the life and customs of the natives, and expressed her general satisfaction in her new home.[45]

Another letter from a highly intelligent and respectable colored man of Savannah showed his zeal to go to Africa but the lack of interest of some of the other negroes. The following extract from this letter, dated September 17, 1833, gives the opinion of this colored man.

. . . For my part. I am determined to go, God being my helper; for my soul yearns after poor benighted Africa; and I pity the poor unfeeling, callous-hearted men of colour— particularly those who wear the holy apellation of Christian, and do not feel it to be their duty to go over and assist in this vast field of moral usefulness, and secure for themselves and those they ought to love as themselves, a country of liberty, together with its concomitant blessings.[46]

The Georgia newspapers supported the scheme of colonization and devoted increasing attention to it. "The Missionary," edited at Mt. Zion in Hancock County, was a religious weekly which advocated colonization. It contained periodic accounts of the success and development of the African colony. The African Repository, edited at Washington by Ralph Randolph Gurley, was the official organ of the American Colonization Society. It was issued monthly

[44] *The African Repository*, VII, 216.
[45] *The African Repository*, IX, 127–128.
[46] *The African Repository*, IX, 316.

and was published by order of the managers of the society. This periodical contained all the important information in regard to the parent society, the local organizations, contributions made, the colony of Liberia, and the general progress of the movement. The National Intelligencer of May 6, 1826, gave an account of the African Colony which was copied by the Georgia Journal of June 13, 1826. This article illustrated the favorable sentiment of the people of the state in regard to the society; it showed the progress and prosperity of the colony and the optimism of the people at home; it ended with an appeal to the people as a whole to support the organization.[47]

At a special meeting of the Board of Managers of the American Colonization Society, held in the city hall of Washington on Monday, June 2, 1823, at which William H. Crawford, one of the vice-presidents of the society, was present and presided, the following resolutions were adopted: (1) that additional agents should be appointed to visit different parts of the United States to diffuse information, to collect funds, and to form auxiliary societies; (2) that a periodical publication be established; (3) that an address be prepared for general circulation to show the situation and wants of the colony; (4) and to send to the Colony three or more vessels to be fitted out from the Northern, Middle, and Southern sections of the United States.[48] The plan received the hearty support of the religious papers. "The Missionary" stated that: "The object of the Colonization Society is evidently becoming popular. We venture to predict that soon no institution in the country will receive a more liberal and extensive support. Whenever its design is understood, every good man must be its friend."[49]

In the latter part of the year, 1830, the Reverend Robert Finley of New Jersey, one of the early founders and at that

[47] *The Georgia Journal* (Milledgeville) June 13, 1826.
[48] *The Missionary,* June 30, 1823.
[49] *Ibid,* June 30, 1823.

time agent of the American Colonization Society, made an address in Brooklyn, New York, for the purpose of organizing an auxiliary society there. He described the origin, progress, and future of slavery. Remarks about his address were made in the Christian Intelligencer which were reprinted in the Southern Recorder. Mr. Finley went into the history of slavery in Georgia and defended the state's attitude toward the institution. He showed that the Colonial Assembly of Georgia had passed acts to prohibit the importation of slaves into the province eleven times, but that each time the King of England had vetoed the bill. "Hence it appears, the existence of slavery and its concomitant evils among our brethren of the South has been entailed upon them by the acts of a government, which at the time, they had not the power to resist; and that they are entitled to the sympathy and kindly feelings of their fellow citizens in other more favored sections of our country, which are exempted from the evils and dangers of slavery. Inasmuch as their situation is in a great measure the result of the cupidity and crimes of others rather than their own.[50]

Mr. Finley then asked the question why the slave states did not unite and rid themselves of the evil by providing for the immediate and entire abolition of slavery. His answer was that the remedy would be worse than the disease—that the wrong done to the masters would be equaled by the misery and wretchedness it would produce among the 2,000,000 slaves in those states. Georgia accepted the statements made by Mr. Finley as an expression of the correct view taken by the state respecting slavery and emancipation. "If from the beginning our Northern brethren had spoken of us as Mr. Finley does, no angry feelings would have sprung up in the South towards the North, and the subject of slavery would have been discussed in a friendly manner. But when our Northern Brethren wish to dictate to us our duty; when they use threatening language; defiance becomes our motto. It is hoped that the

---

[50] *The Southern Recorder,* December 11, 1830.

moderation of Mr. Finley will produce a good effect, and will henceforward be imitated."[51]

It was even proposed to colonize the negroes in Hayti. However, it was considered that Hayti was too near for the safety of the South. The numerous slave population might then become still more dangerous.[52] Mr. Loring D. Dewey, agent of the Colonization Society of New York, addressed a letter to the president of Hayti asking for the conditions on which colored emigrants might be permitted to settle there. In his answer the president of Hayti expressed a perfect willingness and a strong desire to receive the immigrants, and proffered them all the rights and immunities of citizens of Hayti. He promised government aid in defraying expenses, free land titles, and even food, tools and other necessaries. President Boyer of Hayti even dispatched an agent to New York to make arrangements on the subject with the Colonization Society.[53] The Boston Gazette encouraged emigration of free persons of color to Hayti. The National Intelligencer discouraged it. The editor of the Gazette had to admit the failure of the plan. This admission was copied by the Intelligencer.

The Colonization Society failed in its purpose. Many of the negroes sent over succumbed to the African fevers. The society failed to raise the necessary funds. Professor A. B. Hart, in commenting upon the results of the Colonization movement, says that, with the backing of the Federal Government and its auxiliary societies the society was not yet able to overcome "distance, malaria, savage neighbors, and a tropical climate."[54] On December 27, 1827, the Georgia legislature adopted resolutions which protested against the right of Congress to aid the African Colonization Society.[55] These resolutions began with a firm protest against the right of Congress to appropriate money to aid the

---

[51] *Ibid*, December 11, 1830.
[52] *The Missionary*, July 12, 1824.
[53] *Ibid*, July 12, 1824.
[54] Albert Bushnell Hart, *Slavery and Abolition*, 163.
[55] *Acts of Georgia*, 1827, 194–203.

society, and from this starting point ranged into an elaborate exposition of the constitutional limitations of the
Federal government.

> At the first establishment of the Colonization society, what-
> ever may have been intended or avowed as its object, your
> Committee believe that they can say with truth, that the
> general impression in the Southern states as to that object
> was, that it was limited to the removal beyond the U. States
> of the then free people of colour and their descendants, and
> none others. Under this impression, it at once received the
> sanction and countenance of many of the humane, the Wise,
> and the patriotic among us. Auxiliary Societies were formed
> in our own state, and the numbers, the influence and the
> resources of the society were daily increased: it is now ascer-
> tained that this impression was false, and its officers and
> your Committee believe the society itself now boldly and
> fearlessly avow, that its object is, and ever has been, to remove
> the whole coloured population of the Union to another land;
> and to effect this object, so wild, fanatical and destructive in
> itself, they ask that the general fund, to which the slave-
> holding states have so largely contributed, should be ap-
> propriated for a purpose so especially ruinous to the pros-
> perity, importance and political strength of the Southern
> states.[56]

The resolutions criticized severely the interference of the
Northern states in local concerns.

> Your committee cannot avoid reprobating the cold-blooded
> selfishness, or unthinking zeal which actuates many of our
> fellow-citizens in other states, to an interference with our
> local concerns and domestic relations, totally unwarranted
> either by humanity or constitutional right—such interfer-
> ence is becoming every day more determined and more
> alarming; it commenced with a few unthinking zealots, who
> formed themselves into abolition societies; was seized upon
> by more cunning and designing men for political purposes;
> and is now supported by more than one of the states, as is
> evident from the Amendments of the Constitution proposed
> by legislative bodies, and so frequently, and indeed insult-

---

[56] *Ibid,* 1827, 199–200.

ingly presented for our approbation—The result of such interference, if persevered in, is lawful and inevitable.[57]

In regard to the right of Congress to appropriate money to aid the society the resolutions stated:

> That the Congress of the United States have no constitutional power to appropriate monies to aid the American Colonization Society, or for objects to effect which, that Society was established; and that this Legislature, representing the feelings and will of the people, and the sovereignty of the State of Georgia, in the name and in behalf of the State of Georgia, denying the right, solemnly protest against the exercise or any attempt to exercise, such unconstitutional power by the Congress of the United States.[58]

The colonization movement was nation wide until its ineffectiveness became known. Although the colonization movement in Georgia did not accomplish much in removing the negroes or in lessening to any great extent the number of slaves, it did succeed in keeping the question of emancipation constantly before the people. A small beginning was made which it was hoped would tend toward a final solution of the problem. At the time of its establishment the society had the support of very many Southern people, but when it adopted Emancipation propoganda the Georgia leaders turned squarely against it.[59] The movement in the North progressed further than conservative Southerners were inclined to go. Opinion in the North became too radical for Georgia to follow. The work of the Northern abolition societies alienated Georgia from her sister states to the North and prevented her cooperation with them.[60] The Southerners were willing to do their duty toward the negro, but the radicalism of the abolitionists alienated the South and drove her to a defensive position. The movement for emancipation began early in Georgia but they were hindered by the intemperate and fanatical abuse of

---

[57] *Acts of Georgia*, 1827, 201.
[58] *Ibid*, 1827, 202.
[59] Phillips, *Georgia and State Rights*, 115.
[60] *Acts of Georgia*, 1829, 235–240.

slaveholders by the abolitionists, and also by the difficult problem of how to regulate the relations of the two races so radically different after emancipation. The South wanted the right to settle her own domestic affairs, free from any interference by self constituted advisers.

The South became sensitive and resentful of the inter-meddling with its institutions. The Southern states were truly perplexed. They were foiled in their plans to remove slavery from the country; they had legislated and protested in vain. A peaceful solution of the problem seemed impossible. Dissolution of the union seemed an absurdity; emancipation seemed disastrous if the negroes continued to live on the same soil with the whites; social divisions were deplored; even a return to the constitution would not solve the problem. "The South was just on the eve of abolishing slavery when the abolitionists arose and put it back within its intermost intrenchments."[61] However, during the time that the society was functioning it did effective work. In the African Repository for the year, 1842, there are notices of between five and six hundred slaves emancipated for the purpose of transporting them to Liberia,[62] and it must be remembered that many Southern slaveholders who were willing to transport their negroes to the colony refused to allow their names to appear in the public press.

---

[61] Nehemiah Adams, *A South Side View of Slavery* (Boston, 1860), 115.
[62] *The African Repository*, XVIII, passim.

CHAPTER XIII

THE SLAVERY CONTROVERSY, 1850–1860

The outstanding prosperity of the South in 1850 was to be found in Georgia, the Empire State of the South.[1] It was renowned for its railroads and manufactures as well as for its agriculture. The state held a position of unusual importance among its neighbors. Olmstead said of this state ". . . there is more life, enterprise, skill, and industry in Georgia than in any other of the old Slave Commonwealths."[2] The political preeminence of Georgia was in large part the result of economic preeminence. All phases of the crisis of 1850 in Georgia, and of the influence which Georgia exerted upon the lower South, were related to the economic, social, religious, and political conditions of the state at that time. Since the economic factors explain, to a certain extent, the social and political phases, we will turn our attention first to economic considerations.

Georgia in 1850 was divided into three main sections: the mountainous country, the Piedmont plateau, and the coastal plain.[3] These sections ran almost parallel with the coast from northeast to southwest across the state. The inland part of the state was hilly and rose into mountains where all kinds of timber grew.[4] The mountainous part of the state included about twenty counties in extreme North Georgia. These people of the hill country of the Appalachians were indifferent to the interests of slavery

---

[1] See Richard Harrison Shryock, *Georgia and the Union in 1850* (Durham, N. C., 1926).
[2] Olmstead, *A Journey in the Seaboard Slave States*, 530.
[3] Shryock, *Georgia and the Union in 1850*, 9–11.
[4] "A State of the Province of Georgia Attested upon oath in the Court of Savannah," *Georgia Historical Collections*, II, 75.

and were devotedly attached to the Union.[5]   The general
fertility of the Piedmont plateau adapted it to the cultivation of cotton, and it came to form the Georgia "Black
Belt."   This area was the most fertile.   It extended from
the mountains of the North to the Fall Line.   However,
the soil of the southwest part of this region began to be
exhausted as early as 1820 except along the river bottoms.
Here a few prosperous plantations were maintained as late
as 1850.[6]   The soil of the coastal plain was not as fertile
as the Piedmont soil except in parts of southwest Georgia.
Here were some of the most valuable lands in the state
in 1850.[7]

The Georgia planters in 1850 were a prosperous and
optimistic group because of the high prices for cotton,
the improvements in agriculture and transportation, and
the unexhausted soil.   But there was one factor, the slavery
question, which seemed to threaten most seriously that
prosperity.   The anti-slavery attack threatened to obscure
economic optimism and prosperity; it raised many delicate
problems upon which Georgians were divided in opinion.

Practically all native Georgians regarded the Northern
anti-slavery movement as an unprovoked attack upon
Southern institutions.   It seemed that the abolitionists were
determined to prevent the extension of slavery, and to
undermine it where it already existed.   Proslavery men,
and even those who had formerly been opposed to slavery,
acted on the defensive.   On the other hand the anti-slavery
Northerners viewed the Southern planters as a united and
aggressive slaveocracy.[8]   The North accused the South of
attempting to spread their institution across the country
and to control the Federal government in order to guarantee
the success of proslavery movements.   Such views were
unknown or ignored by the average Georgian.   His in-

---

[5] Shryock, *Georgia and the Union in 1850*, 7.
[6] Olmstead, *The Cotton Kingdom*, II, 385.
[7] White, *Statistics of the State of Georgia*, 37, 284.
[8] Rhodes, *History of the United States*, I, gives a good discussion of the Northern view of the united and aggressive slaveocracy.

terest was centered upon the refutation of the abolitionists' attack upon slavery.

Opinion in Georgia was divided on the chances of eventual emancipation. Many felt that slavery was an evil—but an evil that could not be abandoned. Many believed that a reverse of prosperity would lead to emancipation. A Georgian observed to Frances Kemble that there would be prompt abolition if slavery proved definitely unprofitable. He said: "I hate slavery with all my heart; I consider it an absolute curse wherever it exists; it will keep those states where it does exist fifty years behind the others in improvement and prosperity." Farther on in the conversation, he said, "As for its being an irremediable evil—a thing not to be helped or got rid of—that's all nonsense; for, as soon as people become convinced that it is their interest to get rid of it, they will soon find the means to do so, depend upon it."[9]

In Georgia before 1850 there was a distinct anti-slavery party, although unorganized, which believed that slavery should be abolished. According to Heydenfeldt, an Alabama citizen, this party included: (1) the poor whites who considered the slave as a rival in production; (2) those who were wearied with the struggle of unproductive labor; and (3) those who desired populous white communities for the purposes of trade and education.[10] Some practical men, despite the prosperity of 1848 to 1850, were uncertain as to the economic desirability of slavery. The reason that the anti-slavery element did not take a definite stand was the irritation caused by Northern criticism. They feared that, had their opinion been made known, it would have encouraged the Northern demand for immediate abolition.

All of this relates, however, to the slavery question in general. The specific phase which became most acute in this period was the question of the extension of slavery.

---

[9] Kemble, *Journal of a Residence on a Georgian Plantation*, 77.
[10] Shryock, *Georgia and the Union in 1850*, 36–37.

Opinion in Georgia on the question of slavery extension was divided. It was supported by those who feared an increase of negroes; it was opposed by those who feared a decrease of the negro population.

Fear of the race problem forced some Georgians to support slavery extension. Dire consequences were predicted in case there was no outlet for the normal increase in the slave population of the older states. If all the slaves were held in the old states where soils were exhausted, their natural increase would render their numbers superfluous. It involved the danger of the race problem and possibly race war.[11]

While some Georgians supported slavery extension to save the old states from having too many negroes, others opposed it in order that too many negroes should not leave the old states. Georgia needed a large negro population for labor, but she wanted to avoid one that was too large lest it become an economic burden.[12] The difference of opinion was occasioned by different social and economic interests.

Different social elements in the white population felt differently toward the negro. A study of the social groups, as they existed in Georgia at this time, is important in understanding the political situation. Georgia was divided into five classes, according to social and economic conditions.

The outstanding social type in Georgia was the planter aristocrat. His economic prosperity depended on the cultivation of staple crops for which negro labor was necessary. This was a small group, a wealthy group, the group which owned most of the slaves, and the group which would be chiefly affected by emancipation. The planters were generally able men, well educated, and had had opportunities of travel at home and abroad; other classes were handicapped because of lack of capital and energy. The planters domi-

---

[11] Shryock, *Georgia and the Union in 1850*, 47.
[12] *Ibid*, 48.

nated the social circle which was "no ordinary society."[13]
The planter had a high reputation in literature, philos-
ophy, and politics. Their writings ornamented the pages
of scientific works in the United States and in Europe.
Hospitality was leading characteristic.[14] The possession
of wealth and prestige enabled them to dominate the political
parties as well as the business and social life of the state.
While the planter was ready to defend his slave property
in any slave crisis, he was inclined to put aside any unnecessary excitement over the slavery question. Therefore he was less responsive to appeals featuring race prejudice than was the poor white of the same community.

The great majority of Georgians belonged to the small
farmer class. They had small holdings and owned few
slaves. The census of 1850 listed 81,364 farmers in the
state and only 1,948 planters.[15] That would leave 79,416
in the small farmer class. The members of this class were
distributed through Central and Upper Georgia, especially
in the Cherokee country. They lived as frontier farmers,
did their own work, worked in the fields with the negroes,
and made their own clothes. They were thrifty, self reliant,
provincial, and often illiterate.[16] Some of these small
farmers owned a few slaves, others of them owned no slaves
at all but belonged to the independent, non-slaveholding
class.

Besides the small farmers there was another group in
Central Georgia bordering on the Black Belt, which was
still lower in the social scale. This was the group of poor
whites who owned no slaves and had to compete with negro
labor. Those poor whites were jealous of the Southern
aristocrats, but they felt only contempt for the negro.[17]
They opposed slavery and favored emancipation, but they

---

[13] White, *Statistics of Georgia*, 284.
[14] *Ibid*, 283.
[15] *Census of 1850*, 376.
[16] For a description of the customs and amusements of this class read: Longstreet, *Georgia Scenes* (New York, 1855).
[17] For a description of this class see Olmstead, *A Journey in the Seaboard
Slave States*, 413–416.

wanted to deny the negro all social and political equality. The "poor white trash" were despised by slaves as well as by the more energetic and successful whites. This class disliked the negro most and was most race conscious. They were most responsive to appeals featuring race prejudice.

In extreme North Georgia dwelt the mountaineers who did not have to contend with the negro and were indifferent to the whole race problem. However, they were devoted to the Union and would have supported emancipation if it had been attempted.

A number of Georgia whites, who were neither planters nor farmers, lived in the towns. The merchants and professional men were associated with the planters in business and society. Smaller merchants and professional men, together with the mechanics, who were associated with the small farmers, usually held their political views. Their views upon slavery were usually those of the class into which they hoped to rise.[18]

Thus of the five social groups in Georgia we find that only one was decidedly pro-slavery. This was the smallest class—the planter aristocrats. This was the articulate class who preserved their views for posterity. The second class, the small farmers, would have defended their economic interests, but they did not have much to lose through emancipation. Small town newspapers which may have reflected the opinion of the small farmers have usually been lost. The next two groups, the poor whites and the mountaineers, were anti-slavery in sentiment. They were an inarticulate element and their views have usually been lost. The last class, the townspeople, usually held the views of those with whom they were immediately associated. So we see that there were practically four groups in Georgia which opposed slavery extension and only one group which upheld it. The protest of the non-slaveholding whites varied from statements of polite indifference to energetic objections to fighting the slaveholder's battles. The more

---

[18] Shryock, *Georgia and the Union in 1850,* 73.

conservative people of upper Georgia wanted to know why they should join a movement to protect the owners of Negroes when they owned none themselves.[19]

The several classes which have been noted were those distinguishable by social and economic conditions. There were three other groups in Georgia distinguishable by their geographical origins, each of which possessed some political significance. These were the South Carolinians, the "Yankees" and the European immigrants.[20]

The South Carolinians had moved into Georgia throughout the first half of the century. They had been of all classes: planters with their slaves, poor whites, merchants, and professional men from the towns. These immigrants tended to maintain in Georgia the same political attitude toward the slavery question and the Union as was maintained by South Carolina. As newspaper editors, lawyers, politicians and merchants they helped to lead the Southern rights movement in Georgia toward the seccessionists principles of South Carolina.[21]

Meanwhile immigrants were coming from the North during the forties. These Yankees saw in Georgia opportunities for tradespeople and professional men. Mechanics, engineers, merchants, school teachers, clerks, printers, editors, and all other types of people came. Olmstead states that the class which gave Georgia its reputation for prosperity was composed of and directed in enterprise by persons born in the free states. There were more of these in Georgia, in proportion to the white population, than in any other slave state.[22] Especially were these new immigrants needed in the new factories and railroads. These were heartily welcomed and introduced into lucrative businesses. Gradually they came to be distrusted by Southerners, even when they defended slavery.[23] Some

---

[19] Phillips, "Toombs, Stephens, and Cobb Correspondence," *American Historical Association Report*, 1911, II, 142.
[20] Shryock, *Georgia and the Union in 1850*, 78.
[21] *Ibid*, 79.
[22] Olmstead, *A Journey in the Seaboard Slave States*, 536–537.
[23] Longstreet, *A Voice from the South*, 20–21.

of these held abolitionist views; they even confided these views to slaveholders who had become their trusted friends.[24] Others were allied with the pro-slavery element for political reasons.

The last group of whites were the European immigrants. This group was small and concentrated especially in Augusta and Columbus.[25] Germans, English, and Irish were all represented. The Europeans of the laboring class joined the anti-slavery element. They were jealous of the negroes as competitors.[26] At the same time they were usually devoted to the American government which had offered them a refuge from depressing conditions in Europe.

Only a small percentage of Georgians in 1850 were slave-holders. Olmstead estimated that only twenty-seven in a hundred of the white families in Georgia possessed slaves in 1850, and that one-fifth of these owned more than one-half of all the slaves in the state.[27] A comparison of the number of slaveholders in Georgia with that of other slaveholding states may be had from the census of 1850.[28]

The total population of Georgia in 1860 was 1,057,286.[29] Of this the colored population amounted to 465,698. So then the total white population of 1860 was 591,588. Of the 465,698 colored people in Georgia, only 462,198 were slaves. The remainder were free persons of color. The tabulation of occupations of the census of 1860 gives 2,858 planters in Georgia, and 67,718 small farmers.[30] So we see that in comparison with the total white population there were very few large slaveholders in Georgia in 1860. According to the same census report it was estimated that there were 118,000 white families. Of these families 41,084 were slaveholders, leaving the overwhelming majority,

[24] Paine, *Six Years in a Georgia Prison*, 36–51.
[25] Shryock, *Georgia and the Union in 1850*, 88.
[26] Olmstead, *A Journey in the Seaboard Slave States*, 512.
[27] *Ibid*, 535.
[28] J. D. B. DeBow, *Compendium of the Seventh Census* (Washington, 1854), 190.
[29] *Census of 1860*, 73.
[30] *Census of 1860*, 77.

76,916 in the non-slaveholding class. Thus in 1860 the vast majority of Georgia families owned no slaves. The large scale planters were a small percentage of Georgia farmers. But it was these planters who controlled the politics of the period and guided public opinion.

Opposition to slavery is found among the different denominations of the state. The sect which opposed slavery earliest and most ardently was the Quakers. There were never many Quakers in Georgia, but the few who located there were unalterably opposed to slavery. Quakers were particularly favored under the Georgia charter which granted religious freedom to all except Papists. However, not many Quakers availed themselves of this opportunity. In 1758 a few Quaker families moved to Georgia and settled about seven miles North of Augusta at a place called Quaker Spring. Having been warned of an impending Indian uprising this little band abandoned the country.[31] The next immigration of Quakers into Georgia was led by Joseph Maddock and Jonathan Still to whom the General Assembly of Georgia, on July 3, 1770, granted 40,000 acres of land in St. Paul's Parish, Columbia (now McDuffie) County.[32] Here they began the town of Wrightsborough, named in honor of Sir James Wright, Governor of the colony. In 1799 the Assembly of Georgia incorporated a body of five trustees, authorized the Quakers to elect their successors, and authorized them to sell the land held there.[33] Immediately afterwards these Quakers departed from the state. What was the reason for their departure? In 1786 one of the North Carolina quarterly meetings sent a committee to the Assembly of Georgia with a petition regarding some enlargements to the enslaved negroes.[34] We do not know the results, but it probably had no visible effect. The career of the Quakers in Georgia was short. Having arrived in Georgia for the first time in 1758, by 1810 practically

[31] Jones, *History of Georgia*, I, 440.
[32] George White, *Statistics of Georgia* (Savannah, 1849), 193.
[33] Marbury and Crawford, *Digest*, 392.
[34] Stephen B. Weeks, *Southern Quakers and Slavery* (Baltimore, 1896), 219.

all of them had left the state.   The cause of the emigration was slavery.[35]   Most of the Georgia emigrants went to the free state of Ohio and settled between the Little Miami and Great Miami rivers in the counties of Miami, Warren, and Clinton.[36]   As early as 1797 the inhabitants of Wrightsborough had testified against slavery and were making efforts to keep themselves clear of it.[37]

Opposition to slavery is found among the Methodists of Georgia.   The views of John Wesley have already been stated.   His followers read and approved these views. In 1825 the Bishop of Georgia told a traveler, Stephen Grellet, that the Methodists in the state were considering the advisability of making a rule requiring all of their members to free their slaves.[38]   In 1832 the Methodist Conference of Georgia, which was to meet in Augusta, invited the Reverend R. S. Finley, agent of the American Colonization Society, to make an address before the conference.   When Mr. Finley arrived in Augusta he found the Methodists there thoroughly in sympathy with the cause of colonization.   He delivered an address to the Methodist Conference and solicited their aid in his colonization schemes.   A meeting was called in Augusta for the purpose of organizing an auxiliary Colonization Society there. The Methodists even suspended their religious services during the session of the conference, in order to give their congregation an opportunity to attend.   Mr. Finley found a great deal of his strength and support among the Methodists.[39]

Anti-slavery sentiment among the Baptists flourished and declined.   The Baptists of Georgia gained some notoriety in this respect.   In one of the early debates of Congress the Georgia Baptists are severely criticised by Mr. Jackson of Georgia because of their "interference."[40]   In

---

[35] *Ibid*, 268.
[36] *Ibid*, 269, 280, 307.
[37] *Ibid*, 123.
[38] *Ibid*, 219.
[39] *The African Repository*, VIII, 123.
[40] *Annals of Congress*, 1st Congress, II, 1416.   (2nd session).

1857 a severe indictment against the slaveholder appeared in the Christian Index. It was an address delivered by James Clark at Albany, Georgia, published also in the African Repository and in the Religious Herald. It called attention to the vast number of slaveholders who were ungodly men, who neglected their own souls and those of their slaves. It was the duty of the Church and Christians to impress these slaveholders with a sense of their grave responsibilities.

> As professed Christians, we should use our influence constantly and earnestly to induce that public sentiment and feeling amongst slaveholders which will afford a full and free access to our colored population for their religious edification, and a hearty cooperation from their masters in sustaining **and** advancing the good work. The church and ministry should be united in efforts to bring about, on the part of the owners of these people, that solemn and enlightened consideration of the subject, without which, however great the destitution, or however disastrous to the interests of immortal souls in the great day of eternity, but little can be done. If the proper efforts are used by the Christians of the land, a wide and effectual door will and must be opened for the prosecution of this sacred and holy work.[41]

The following is an extract from a letter addressed to the New York Examiner by a clergyman of the Baptist Church in the state of Georgia and quoted by the Reverend John Dixon Long in his "Pictures of Slavery in Church and State." It was clipped from a Philadelphia daily of January, 1857:

> We, Baptists of the South, have no hesitation in avowing our belief that God 'hath made of one blood all nations.' We maintain, whether against 'politicians or infidels, philosophers or fanatics,' that the negro is a man. Because we believe this, we preach the Gospel to the negro at home; and we send the missionary to Africa to preach to him there. We witness the effect of a preached Gospel in the conversation of the negro; and when converted, the negro is as gladly

[41] *The African Repository*, XXXIII, 250.

welcomed into our churches as a brother, as if he were of pure Anglo-Saxon blood. Not more than a mile from where I now write, stands an humble building erected for the worship of God. Among the people who worship there, more than a hundred negroes were baptized during last year. The church now numbers two hundred and eighty-five members, of whom two hundred and twenty-eight are colored. By invitation of the pastor, I preached there Sunday before last. Two-thirds of the congregation were negroes, and, as I proclaimed the truth, 'Ye are bought with a price,' their streaming eyes witnessed that there was a common tie of brotherhood felt and recognized between the preacher and the people, without regard to color. Not many months ago, it was my privilege, as pastor of a Baptist church, to preside in conference, when two women presented themselves as candidates for admission. They took seats on the same bench. One was a lady of wealth, intelligence, and high social position; the other a negro servant. They related their experiences. No difference could be perceived in the cordiality of the vote by which they were received. The next morning I baptized them in the same running stream. We then repaired to the church. In the beginning of the service, in the presence of an unusually large congregation, the newly baptized took a stand together in the front of the pulpit, and were addressed by the pastor in the same words of warning, exhortation, encouragement, and confidence. Then, while we sang a hymn, the members of the church, white and colored, bound and free, came forward and gave the right hand of fellowship to the new sisters. Among them, servants gave the hand to their mistress; yet was not that mistress (well though we knew her future zeal and usefulness) more sincerely welcomed as a sister in the church than the humble servant who stood by her side.[42]

Thus we see that the Baptists of Georgia recognized, in their religious services, the common humanity of the negro. In that respect, according to the author, they were far ahead of most of the churches in other states.[43]

---

[42] Rev. John Dixon Long, *Pictures of Slavery in Church and State* (Philadelphia, 1857), 162–163.
[43] *Ibid*, 163–164.

Having already considered the economic, social, and religious factors, let us now turn our attention to the politics of the period.

Texas was annexed to the Union in 1845. This brought the slavery question again to the front. War with Mexico followed, and, as a result, California and New Mexico (the Mexican Cession) were ceded to the United States. The Wilmot Proviso, designed to prevent the extension of slavery to this territory, was defeated in Congress. The discovery of gold in California and the great migration to that state made a speedy solution necessary. The admission of California as a free state would upset the balance in the Senate. There were then fifteen slave states and fifteen free states. The Southern members of Congress refused to allow California to come into the Union until the question of slavery in the rest of the Mexican cession was determined.

Georgians were inclined at first to oppose the compromise. But the great triumverate, Robert Toombs, Alexander Stephens, and Howell Cobb, returned from Washington and set about demonstrating to the people that the South had won a great victory by the Compromise.[44] Earlier in the year the governor and the legislature had provided for the meeting of a state convention which would decide upon the course which Georgia would pursue. These three Congressmen succeeded in bringing about the election of Union delegates and defeating the resistance men.[45] The convention decided to accept the compromise as the basis for the continuity of the Union. It was this same convention that drew up the celebrated Georgia Platform. The platform set forth that, "though the state was not entirely content with the Compromise just reached by Congress, still upon the ground of its provisions Georgia was willing and anxious to remain in the United States; but in case of the slightest further encroachment by the North, the attitude of Georgia

---

[44] Phillips, *Georgia and State Rights,* 164.
[45] *Ibid,* 164.

would at once be reversed and disruption would most probably ensue."[46] The platform declared for the Compromise but stated that that measure was as far as the people of Georgia would go.

When news of the Kansas Nebraska bill reached Georgia the Democrats accepted it with enthusiasm as a concession to the South by the lovers of the Union at the North. The Georgia Whigs, who held aloof at first, soon became as enthusiastic as the Democrats. We have already seen that the Georgia Legislature in 1835 declared the inability of Congress to interfere with slavery in the territories.[47] We have also seen that in 1850 the Georgia Platform was adopted as the limit of the concessions that Georgians would make. Now on February 20, 1854, the Georgia Legislature passed a resolution saying: "That opposition to the principles of the Nebuska (Nebraska?) Bill, in relation to the subject of Slavery, is regarded by the people of Georgia as hostility to the rights of the South, and that all persons who partake in such opposition are unfit to be recognized as component parts of any party organization, not hostile to the South."[48] The Legislature further stated that the commonwealth had firmly fixed itself on the principles of the compromise of 1850; that Congress could not impose on the territories any restrictions as to slavery; it stated its approval of the Kansas Nebraska bill, and instructed the Georgia Senators and Representatives to vote for it.[49]

The slavery question was finally brought before the Supreme Court of the United States in the famous Dred Scott Case. The circumstances of the case are too well known to make a review advisable here. The decision of the court was that Dred Scott was not a citizen and had no right to sue in the Federal courts. But the opinion did not rest here. It was decided that the Missouri Com-

---

[46] Phillips, *Georgia and State Rights*, 165.
[47] *Acts of Georgia*, 1835, 299–300.
[48] *Ibid*, 1853 & 1854, 589.
[49] *Acts of Georgia*, 1853 & 1854, 590.

promise was unconstitutional; that a slave was property, and that Congress had no right to exclude this particular kind of property any more than any other kind of property from the common territory of the United States. This decision was in accord with the extreme Southern view on slavery extension, but it caused deep resentment in the North. The people of Georgia readily accepted the decision.

A knowledge of the foregoing political issues is necessary in order to understand the position of Georgia at this time. At this period the whole American people expected a crisis to arrive at the end of Buchanan's administration. In Georgia there was a difference of opinion as to the best course of action for the state to pursue in case of an emergency. In 1857 Joseph E. Brown, a candidate from the non-slaveholding class, was elected governor of Georgia. He was a representative of the poorer classes of white citizens in Georgia, and was born and reared without the personal service of slaves. However, he believed that Congress had no right to abolish slavery in the territories. The election of such a man from the small farmer and non-slaveholding class was a shock to the aristocratic regime in Georgia.[50] Joseph E. Brown continued to hold the office of governor during the chaotic period of the civil war. In his inaugural address for the second time, he predicted that the great contest of 1860, which might decide the fate of the Union, would be fought between the Democratic and the Black Republican parties. He regarded the Democratic party as the last hope of the Union. Should it be broken down, the rights of the South denied, and her equality in the Union destroyed, he declared his conviction that the South would secede and organize a separate confederacy.[51]

After this time the people of Georgia began to seriously consider secession. In the opinion of many it was the only

[50] I. W. Avery, *History of Georgia*, 1850-1881 (New York, 1881), 47.
[51] *Southern Recorder*, November 8, 1859.

thing the Southern states could do in justice to themselves. In view of the hostile attitude of the Northern states against slavery, and the evident purpose to ignore the constitution in order to abolish it, the Southern states felt justified in taking the position that they were no longer bound by the Constitution and could leave the Union if they desired. The crisis came with the election of Lincoln in 1860. The other Southern states followed the lead of South Carolina and each state passed ordinances of secession. Georgia seceded from the Union on January 19, 1861. Pro-slavery advocates supported secession as a means to the more certain preservation of slavery. A plot of the vote in the secession convention shows that there was a general tendency in favor of secession among delegates from the sections where slaves were numerous. There was an opposite tendency from the districts where the whites were predominant.[52] We see then that the large slaveholders in Georgia advocated immediate secession; the non-slaveholders of the mountains and of the barren pine districts opposed immediate withdrawal.

---

[52] See map of Georgia, 1861. From Phillips, *Georgia and State Rights*, 209.

CONCLUSION

It has been our object in the preceding pages to show the opposition to slavery which existed in Georgia before 1860. Although the active opposition may have been slight, the fact that there was opposition is distinctly evident. We have seen that slavery was prohibited in Georgia from the beginning of the colony; that Georgia was the only one of the original thirteen colonies in which the system was prohibited; and that slavery was permitted in the colony only after the failure of the Trustees' plan. We have traced the reasons for the founding of the colony of Georgia; we have noticed the reasons of the Trustees for prohibiting slavery; and we have seen that the institution of slavery was incompatible with the purposes for which the colony was founded. We have shown the early attempts to import negroes into Georgia, the dissatisfaction of the colonists which led to their desire for slaves, the numerous petitions and counter-petitions for and against slavery, and the final removal of the restriction. The opinions of the early Georgia leaders have been given; the slavery regime in Georgia has been traced; the laws regarding slavery and the slave-trade have been noted, and the many attempts of Georgia (as a colony and as a state) to prevent the importation of negroes have been discussed. Not only was Georgia the only free colony, but she was one of the first states to prohibit the importation of slaves. The importation of slavery was prohibited in Georgia ten years before it was prohibited by the Federal government.

In the preceding pages and chapters numerous wills have been cited in which slaves were voluntarily emancipated. In addition to the wills various testimonials of the status of free negroes have been given. Many bills were passed by the state legislature in which slaves were manumitted;

other attempts were made to manumit slaves but the bills failed to pass. The fact that the manumission of slaves was taking place is proven by the many bills that were passed prescribing the mode of manumission and those which prohibited manumission. The Colonization movement was active in Georgia and many negroes were set free and sent to Liberia. Liberal donations were made by many Georgians for this purpose. Active interest was maintained in the American Colonization Society until the final failure of the organization. We have seen that attempts were made to manumit slaves even as late as 1859 and 1860.

It has been necessary in this work to give considerable attention to national issues, for these national issues not only over-shadowed all local issues but determined them and helped to form public sentiment in the states. Although there was much anti-slavery sentiment in Georgia before the Civil War, there was very little anti-slavery movement. These forces were unorganized. Many of those who opposed slavery belonged to the inarticulate element whose views have not been preserved. The question of slavery was hopelessly confused with the question of Southern rights. Although many of the people of Georgia were opposed to slavery, they would not countenance any outside interference with their domestic institutions.

APPENDIX I

The following pungent remarks on slavery and the slave trade are taken from Mr. Wesley's tract *Thoughts on Slavery*.

Men-buyers are exactly on a level with men-stealers. Indeed you say, 'I pay honestly for my goods; and I am not concerned to know how they are come by.' Nay, but you are; you are deeply concerned to know they are honestly come by. Otherwise you are a partaker with a thief, and are not a jot honester than him. But you know they are not honestly come by; you know they are procured by means nothing near so innocent as picking of pockets, house-breaking, or robbery upon the highway. You know they are procured by a deliberate series of more complicated villainy (of fraud, robbery, and murder) than was ever practiced either by Mohammedans or Pagans; in particular, by murders of all kinds; by the blood of the innocent poured upon the ground like water. Now, it is your money that pays the merchant, and through him the captain and the African butchers. You therefore are guilty, yea, principally guilty, of all these frauds, robberies, and murders. You are the spring that puts all the rest in motion; they would not stir a step without you; therefore the blood of all these wretches, who die before their time, whether in their country or elsewhere, lies upon your head. The blood of thy brother (for, whether thou wilt believe it or no, such he is in the sight of Him that made him) crieth against thee from the earth, from the ship, and from the waters. O whatever it costs, put a stop to its cry before it is too late: instantly, at any price, were it the half of your goods, deliver thyself from blood guiltiness! Thy hands, thy bed, thy furniture, thy house, thy lands, are at present stained with blood. Surely it is enough; accumulate no more guilt; spill no more blood of the innocent! Do not hire another to shed blood; do not pay him for doing it! Whether you are a Christian or no, show yourself a man! Be not more savage than a lion or a bear!

Perhaps you will say, 'I do not buy any negroes; I only use those left me by my father.' So far is well; but is it enough to satisfy your own conscience? Had your father, have you, has any man living, a right to use another as a slave? It cannot be, even setting Revelation aside. It cannot be, that either war, or contract, can give any man such a property in another as he has in his sheep and oxen. Much less is it possible that any child of man should ever be born a slave. Liberty is the right of every human creature, as soon as he breathes the vital air; and no human law can deprive him of that right which he derives from the law of nature.

If, therefore, you have any regard to justice, (to say nothing of mercy, nor the revealed law of God), render unto all their due. Give liberty to whom liberty is due, that is, to every child of man, to every partaker of human nature. Let none serve you but by his own act and deed, by his own voluntary choice. Away with all whips, all chains, all compulsion! Be gentle toward all men: and see that you invariably do unto every one as you would he should do unto you.[1]

---

[1] John Wesley, *Thoughts on Slavery* (Pamphlet, 1774), 22–23.

APPENDIX II

PROCLAMATION OF GOVERNOR JAMES JACKSON

Georgia

By His Excellency James Jackson Governor; and Commander in Chief of the Army and Navy of this State, and of the Militia thereof.

A PROCLAMATION

WHEREAS I have received information from the mayor of the City of Savannah, that certain negroes or people of colour, are Shipped off from Port au Prince, in the West Indies, for the ports of South Carolina and Georgia, and many of them are on Board vessels bound directly to Savannah:—

AND WHEREAS policy dictates that persons of colour, used to the horrid scenes of massacre, which of late years have been so barbarously practised in the West Indies, without respect to age or sex, Should be prevented from coming within the limits of this State, to diffuse their seditious and cruel tenents; and the Act entitled, "An Act to organize the Militia in the Several new counties of this State" makes it the duty of the Officers of Militia, in the first Brigade of the first Division in their respective districts to apprehend any negro, mustee, mulatto freeman or freemen, slave or slaves, who shall hereafter arrive in any part of this State, from the West India or Bahama Islands, and to keep such persons in safe custody, until they be examined before the Corporation of Savannah, or any three justices of the peace for any County, in the said Division, who are authorized to cause such persons to be exported, at the expence of the importer, or owner, who are also made liable for the expence of apprehending them:—

Taking the same, therefore, and the situation of the present state of public affairs, and our local concerns, into my most serious deliberation, I Have Thought Fit, to issue this my Proclamation, hereby charging and requiring all Officers, civil and military, to be active and vigilant within their respective districts, in preventing and opposing any of the people of colour, described by the aforesaid law, passed the twenty-second day of February, one thousand seven hundred and ninety-six, from landing within any port or place within this State: And in case of such landing, that the militia of the district where such landing may be, and those of any other districts into which such persons may come, do immediately pursue and apprehend them, and all of them, in order that they may be exported agreeably to law:—

And I further charge and require the different magistrates of districts and captains of companies, to be vigilant and active in having the patrole law fully enforced without any excuse whatever, as they will answer the contrary at their peril: And I call on all classes of citizens to come forward with cheerfulness, and to perform those duties, which the Situation of public, and domestic affairs, requires of them:—

And I also further charge and require all Officers, civil and military, to be vigilant in apprehending and exporting all and every other negro, mustee, mulatto freeman or freemen; Slave or Slaves, who has or may have come within the limits of this State, under the description aforesaid, Since the passing of the aforementioned law of the twenty Second of February, one thousand Seven hundred and ninety Six, in any manner or way whatever; and to keep a watchful eye over all and every Suspicious Slave or Slaves, free negroes, or mulattoes, although not within the description of the Said law.—

> Given under My Hand, and the Great Seal of the said State, at the State-House, in Louisville, this eleventh day of June, in the year one thousand seven hundred and ninety-eight, and in the twenty-second year of the Independence of the United States of America.

By the Governor   Jas. Jackson[2]
Jno. Milton, Secy.

---

[2] *Proclamations,* 1782–1823, 162–164 (Manuscript found in the State Department of Archives and History, Atlanta.)

APPENDIX III

THE CHARGE OF JUDGE JABEZ BOWEN TO THE GRAND JURY OF CHATHAM COUNTY, APRIL 23, 1804.

Gentlemen of the Grand Jury, the period has at length arrived when the citizens of Georgia shall hear from the Bench sentiments which ought long since to have emanated from our Legislature. Why is it that the silence of the grave has hitherto pervaded every discussion of men on a subject so highly important as that on which I am about to address you? . . . Why is it that on our legislative floor, amongst those who are annually elected to guard our safety and secure our repose the most important avenue by which danger may assail us has neither been anticipated or guarded! Is it that cold blooded fear has paralysed [sic] the minds and the nerves of our legislators? Is it that the apprehension of drawing down the vengeance of the wealthy and the powerful has silenced the cries of oppression and the voice of truth, or is it that alike interested in one and the same species of criminality each individual is willing that his own mal-conduct should operate as an apology for that of his neighbor and then, with a view of benefitting, expose to future ruin all those whom he most loves upon earth! . . . Hear then, my fellow-citizens, listen to what experience and wisdom suggest as the only means of rescuing you from the abyss which yawns beneath your feet and now, even now, opens its destructive and capacious jaws to ensnare and devour you! . . . Impious wretches, cease your calumnies on that God whose decrees are just and immutable and who will confound your misinterpretations of his ordinances! How then does slavery exist not from the fiat of heaven, but from the municipal institution of base, degenerate man! . . . What then have we eventually to expect! What but blood, massacre and devastation! . . . There is yet a method by which these horrors may be averted. I entreat you to adopt it whilst in your power. Believe that you hear the voice of inspiration when I solemnly assure you that an immediate and implicit obedience to the dictates of justice will be an obedience to the dictates of sound policy and can alone avert those miseries to which we are exposed.[3]

Judge Bowen then lays down a remedy to avert what he declares is an impending slave insurrection. His plan is to emancipate every female slave at the age of ten, and every male slave at the age of twenty-one; the master to bring them up in the practice of religious and moral duties and teach them the common rudiments of education; to lay up for each slave annually a certain quantity of meat and fish in addition to what he terms "their usual allowance of rice or corn;" and their punishment was to be restricted to twenty lashes unless an attending magistrate authorized a greater number. The Judge then continued:

Let these observations, gentlemen, occupy your attention—be assured your minds cannot be more advantageously directed. For my own part I possess as great a stake in this country as the most wealthy for my little all is here and no man's heart beats higher with a love of country than mine. But although I love my country much, very much, yet I love, I adore the principles of liberty, of justice, and of humanity, and I will no longer acknowledge this my country, when these sound principles are thus prostrated by such accursed avarice, such infamous conduct—but I will seek in other climes for that tranquillity and repose which is here every moment liable to be interrupted, the instant I am convinced there is not virtue and understanding enough in Georgia to listen to and pursue the paths I have pointed out to you. I have delivered these sentiments after the most mature and deliberate reflection, and I solemnly swear in the presence of that God who enacted and who knows the inmost secrets of my heart, that if stretched upon the bed of death, I should be called upon to advise the most proper means to secure the safety and tranquillity of this country I should dictate what I have now expressed to you. You will know, or you ought ere this to have known, that I am far above the im-

---

[3] Walter G. Charlton, "A Judge And a Grand Jury," *Report of the Thirty First Annual Session of the Georgia Bar Association, 1914* (Macon, 1914), 209–211.

pulse of fear, or of hope in regard to anything the people of this country can achieve for or against me: Within myself, the bosom of my family and the approbation of my God alone. So I look for happenings. I despise from my soul the threats of the haughty and the vindictive and the applause of the unreflecting multitude, and have dared to avow sentiments which while life mantles in my veins *I will support;* because I am convinced the pursuance of them will be only an act of partial yet prudent justice, and can alone secure my country from all the horrors of civil warfare. Careless of the approbation or disapprobation of the public in this respect, when I lay my head on my pillow it will be with the reflection that I have discharged my duty to God, my country and the poor miserables who claim your compassion, and I hope, gentlemen, that you will so conduct yourselves in this particular as to merit the same heart consoling pleasure.[4]

---

[4] *Ibid,* 211–212.

APPENDIX IV

SPEECH OF CONGRESSMAN REID OF GEORGIA, 1820.

In 1820 Congressman Reid of Georgia denounced slavery on the floor of the House of Representatives at Washington. On February 1, 1820, he declared in Congress that he was desirous of seeing the negroes set free, although he opposed the plan of bestowing American citizenship upon them. He spoke of slavery as an unnatural state, a *dark cloud* which obscured the lustre of free institutions.

I am not the panegyrist of slavery. It is an unnatural state; a dark cloud which obscures half the lustre of our free institutions! It is a fixed evil, which we can only alleviate. Are we called upon to emancipate our slaves? I answer, their welfare—the safety of our citizens, forbid it. Can we incorporate them with us, and make them and us one poeple? The prejudices of the North and of the South rise up in equal strength against such a measure; and even those, who clamor most loudly for the sublime doctrines of your Declaration of Independence, who shout in your ears, "All men are by nature equal!" Would turn with abhorence and disgust from a party-colored progeny! Shall we then be blamed for a state of things to which we are obliged to submit? Would it be fair; would it be manly; would it be generous; would it be just; to offer contumely and contempt to the unfortunate man who wears a cancer in his bosom, because he will not submit to cantery at the hazard of his existence? For my own part, surrounded by slavery from my cradle to the present moment, I yet

> "Hate the touch of servile hands;
> I loathe the slaves who cringe around:"

and I would hail that day as the most glorious in its dawning, which should behold, with safety to themselves and our citizens, the black population of the United States placed upon the high imminence of equal rights and clothed in the privileges and immunities of American citizens. But this is a dream of philanthropy which can never be fulfilled; and whoever shall act in this country on such wild theories, shall cease to be a benefactor, and become a destroyer of the human family.[5]

Later, in the same speech, in regard to the slave trade, Congressman Reid said:

Certainly, the framers of the Constitution desired to destroy a traffic, of all others the most cruel and iniquitous; a trade stained by the blood, and drenched in the tears of humanity! By inhibiting "the importation after 1808 of such persons as any of the States then existing thought proper to admit," it was intended to convey a power to prevent the introduction of Africans into the United States. By inhibiting the "migration" after 1808, of such persons—for the Constitution, it appears to me, still refers to Africans, and I express this opinion with deference and humility—may it not have been intended the more effectually to provide against evasions of the laws interdicting the importation of slaves? The object was to prevent the accumulation of this species of property.[6]

---

[5] *Annals of Congress,* 16th Congress, 1st Session, 1024–1025.
[6] *Ibid,* 1026.

APPENDIX V

LETTERS IN REGARD TO THE COLONIZATION SOCIETY

The following letters from Georgians will show the sentiment of the people of the state in regard to the American Colonization Society and the movement to colonize the negroes in Africa.

A gentleman from Georgia wrote March 13, 1841:

I regard your Society as among the most important benevolent institutions of the day, and richly deserving the well directed and persevering efforts, the liberal contributions, and the fervent prayers, of all who care for the temporal and spiritual interests of the colored race.[7]

Another from Georgia wrote March 12, 1841:

Your kind epistle inquiring whether any thing can be done by myself or in my region for Colonization, is at hand. The period of time is a most unpropitious one for collections or donations. I am myself suffering from the pressure of the times. I will, nevertheless, as far as lies in my individual power, do something, if possible by pittance, for a cause so sacredly just, and so worthy of our special regard. I therefore enclose a five dollar bill.

I had promised one day to devote one thousand dollars to the Society, but my means have since contracted, and I find myself involved; yet, when I shall emerge from the present poverty of resources, I shall not forget the Colonization Society.

Notwithstanding the faint encouragement which I am thus obliged to give from my own region, yet if you had an agent here, or would dispatch one, something cheering might be done in Georgia for the Society.

---

[7] *The African Repository*, XVII, 123.

Wishing your Society a vastness of success commensurate with the truly laudable nature of the enterprise, of removing the colored population and civilizing Africa, I am, &.[8]

Another letter from Georgia dated March 30, 1841:

I beg to inquire where and how I may send an African slave back to his country. He is about forty years of age, remarkable intelligent for one of his opportunities—was imported in 1817 to this port, in a prize to some cruiser, with many others. He states that he is from Guelo, and not above fifteen or twenty miles from the seashore that his country was thickly inhabited, and a trading establishment of Frenchmen (he thinks) near it.

He is, I believe, a sincere Christian, and has given evidence of it, by good conduct for eight or ten years past. He is in good health, strong and likely, fully six feet high, is anxious to return, though he will leave a wife behind, by whom he has no child, however, and some children by a previous one who are in Alabama.

If you can advise me how to send him, and where and when, and whether from the scanty materials given above, his country can be truly indicated, and be put safely into it, I will provide him clothes, &., and pay his passage, and give him his freedom to go; and you will much oblige yours, &.[9]

An extract from a letter received from John James Flournoy of Athens, Georgia, a devoted friend of and contributor to the colonization movement, gives information as to the state of feeling in that section of the state. He states the chief aims of the society: (1) to provide an asylum for the free colored population of the United States, and (2) to provide for the comfortable reception and maintenance of such slaves as may gradually and ultimately become free. He showed that the colony of Liberia had been successfully tested as an experiment and had realized the views of its founders. He called attention to the prejudices and obstacles against which the colony had had to struggle and how these were overcome by the steady movement of benevolence.

---

[8] *The African Repository*, XVII, 123.
[9] *Ibid*, XVII, 123.

The hand of mercy cannot be stayed, and the fruitions of charity are ever forthcoming. A new country with a population imbued with Christian feelings and sympathies, began to open upon a heathen religion, and gives omen of the regeneration of benighted Africa from that worst of bondage—the slavery of Paganism. Our hopes are all well set to realize the certainty of the christian civilization—the work is well laid, and the foundation sure. African capacity may now be tested and left to itself. But should they fail to keep among themselves the purity of the church and of liberty—should the star of Liberia be set in darkness, and her people return to idolatry, or assimilate in habit and natural feeling with the native hordes, the last hope of the pious and the good for African amelioration, will be utterly extinguished.

I confidently look on Liberia as the only beacon in the wide world, of African hope. Nor is this anticipation erroneous; for no where else are trains laid for the decided improvement of the negro as a man. In other places on the earth amalgamation may change the nature and constitution of the race, but there is no glory in this for the black; his offspring become superior to him from mingling with another race, and his own pure Ethiopian blood is thus inferred to be of itself unimprovable. The contempt of the whites for the genuine African remains unaltered, while he respects the quadroon or the mulatto! But this is incidentally a respect for the white blood that is mixed in the negro—and none for the negro himself. Hence fix it how it can be fixed, amalgamation will not advance the dignity of the African, but change his form, and make his race entirely to banish, or become extinct from the face of the earth. The plan of Liberia is to elevate the race as they are—to place them amid privileges and opportunities similar to those enjoyed by the Anglo-Saxon race, whereby availing of the resources of their latent intelligence, they may so advantage themselves and progress on a higher scale of improvement, step by step, with time.

We should not precipitantly or harshly judge the progress of things at Liberia, but give the assembled populations time and opportunity to ameliorate themselves in their new situation, even though it be ever so slowly. Make them all an educated people and let them have stated ministers of the Gospel from our own shores, until their religious ideas on the christian basis, be made into a system. Then only can they fairly and without hazard, be left to their own free volition—and then will be tested the ability and moral rectitude of their nature. Thus will facts be mathematically evidenced, and theories be adopted or rejected concerning the Ethiopians, according to the experience that must come before us.

By experience and by constant intercourses throughout Georgia, I find her people, though violently disinclined to, and hostile with, emancipation, so far as to leaving the slaves free here, are far less reluctant to colonize them so soon as they can find the plan of Liberia feasible and never-failing. In time, I predict, Colonization will become the favorite maxim of my State.[10]

---

[10] *The African Repository,* XVII, 266–267.

BIBLIOGRAPHY

Acts of the General Assembly of the State of Georgia. 1778–to the present (except 1777–1799 and 1805–1810).

ADAMS, ALICE DANA, *The Neglected Period of Anti-Slavery in America,* (1808–1831). Radcliffe College Monographs, XIV. Boston and London, 1908.

ADAMS, NEHEMIAH, *A South Side View of Slavery, or Three Months at the South, in 1854.* Boston, 1860.

African Repository, and Colonial Journal. Ralph Randolph Gurley, Editor. Published by order of the Managers of the American Colonization Society. Washington, 1826–

American Historical Association Report for 1903, 1911.

American Historical Review.

Annals of Congress, 16th Congress, 1806–1807. (Washington.)

Atlanta Journal, March 30, 1928.

AVERY, I. W., *History of Georgia,* 1850–1881. New York, 1881.

BALL, CHARLES, *Slavery in the United States:* A Narrative of the Life and Adventures of Charles Ball, A Black Man. (He lived forty years in Maryland, South Carolina, and Georgia as a slave, twice escaped, finally attained freedom.) Lewistown, Pennsylvania, 1836.

BANCROFT, GEORGE, *History of the United States of America,* II. New York, 1888.

BENEZET, ANTHONY, and WESLEY, JOHN, *Views of American Slavery taken A Century Ago.* Philadelphia, 1858.

Bonds, Bills of Sale, Deeds of Gift, Powers of Attorney, 1755–1762; 1761–1765; 1765–1772; 1779–1780; 1783–1792. Manuscripts in the department of Archives and History of the State of Georgia.

BRUCE, HENRY, *Life of General Oglethorpe.* New York, 1890.

BUCKINGHAM, J. S., *The Slave States of America, 1.* (2 volumes). (An Englishman's journey through North America.) London and Paris, 1842.

BURKE, EMILY P., *Reminiscences of Georgia.* (No place, 1850.)

CATTERALL, HELEN TUNNICLIFF, *Judicial Cases Concerning American Slavery and the Negro.* (2 volumes). Washington, 1926, 1929.

Census Reports, 1850 and 1860. Compiled by direction of the United States Government.

CHAMEROVZOW, L. A., *Slave Life in Georgia.* London, 1855.

CHANNING, EDWARD, *A History of the United States,* VI. New York, 1925.

CHARLTON, WALTER G., "A Judge and a Grand Jury," *Report of the Thirty-First Annual Session of the Georgia Bar Association,* 1914, 206–215. Macon, 1914.

CLAYTON, A. S., *Compilation of the Laws of Georgia,* 1800–1810. Augusta, 1813.

COBB, HOWELL, *A Scriptural Examination of the Institution of Slavery in the United States.* Georgia: Printed for the Author, 1856.

COBB, THOMAS R. R., *A Digest of the Statute Laws of the State of Georgia to 1851.* Athens, Georgia, 1851.

COBB, THOMAS R. R., *An Historical Sketch of Slavery from the Earliest Periods,* Philadelphia, 1858.

COLLINS, WINFIELD H., *The Domestic Slave Trade of the Southern States,* New York, 1904.

Colonial Acts of Georgia, Wormsloe Print, 1755–1774. Wormsloe, 1881. Savannah.

Colonial Records of the State of Georgia, Edited by Allen D. Candler. Compiled and published by order of the legislature of Georgia. Atlanta, 1904–1916. 26 volumes. *1.* Official Journal of the Trustees, kept by the secretary, 1904. *2.* Minutes of the Common Council of the Board of Trustees, 1904. *3.* Accounts Monies and Effects, 1732–1751, 1905. *4.* Stephens' Journal, 1737–1740, 1906. *5.* Private Journal kept by the Earl of Egmont, First President of the Board of Trustees. *13.* Journal of the Commons House of Assembly, 1755–1762, 1907. *18.* Statutes enacted by the Royal Legislature of Georgia from its First Session in 1754–1768. *19.* Statutes, Colonial and Revolutionary, 1768–1773; 1774–1805. *22.* Original Papers: Correspondence: Trustees, General Oglethorpe, and Others, 1737–1739; 1737–1740. *23.* Same, 1741–1742. *25.* Same, 1742–1745. *26.* Original Papers, Trustees, President and Assistants and Others.

Colonial Wills of Georgia, Book A; Book AA. Manuscripts in the Georgia State Department of Archives and History, Atlanta.

COOK, MRS. ANNA MARIA GREEN, *History of Baldwin County.* Anderson, South Carolina, 1925.

COOPER, HARRIET C., *James Oglethorpe—The Founder of Georgia.* New York, 1904.

COULTER, E. MERTON, "A Century of A Georgia Plantation," *Mississippi Valley Historical Review,* XVI, 334–346.

DAVIDSON, VICTOR, *History of Wilkinson County.* Macon, 1930.

DAWSON, W. C., *Compilation of the Laws of Georgia,* 1819–1829. Milledgeville, 1831.

DEBOW, J. D. B., *The Industrial Resources, etc., of the Southern and Western States,* (3 volumes), New Orleans, 1852–1853.

DEBOW'S REVIEW. New Orleans, 1846–1871.

DEBOW, J. D. B., *Statistical View of the United States.* (A Compendium of the Seventh Census.) Washington, 1854.

DE BRAHM, JOHN GERAR WILLIAM, *History of the Province of Georgia.* Wormsloe, 1849.

Deeds on file at various counties visited.

DODD, WILLIAM E., *The Cotton Kingdom.* (Chronicles of America, XXVII.) Yale University Press, New Haven, 1921.

DU BOIS, W. E. BURGHARDT, *The Supression of the African Slave Trade to the United States of America, 1638–1870.* Harvard University Studies, *1.* Harvard University Press, Cambridge, 1896.

EGMONT, *Manuscripts of the Earl of Egmont.* III, London, 1923.

ELLIOT, JONATHAN, *Debates on the Adoption of the Federal Constitution.* 5 volumes. Philadelphia, 1888.

Executive Minutes, 1789–1797. Manuscript in Georgia Department of Archives and History.

FANT, H. B., "The Labor Policy of the Trustees," *Georgia Historical Quarterly,* XVI, 1–16.

FLANDERS, RALPH B., "Planters' Problems in Ante-Bellum Georgia," *Georgia Historical Quarterly,* XIV, 17–40.

FORCE, PETER, *American Archives,* in six series. Edited by Peter Force. Prepared and published under authority of an Act of Congress.

FORD, WORTHINGTON CHAUNCEY, *Journals of the Continental Congress,* 1774–1789. Edited from the original records in the Library of Congress by Worthington Chauncey Ford, Chief, Division of Manuscripts. Washington. Government Printing Office, 1904.

FOSTER, ARTHUR, *A Digest of the Laws of Georgia, 1820–1829.* Philadelphia, 1831.

FOX, EARLY LEE, *The American Colonization Society, 1817-1840,* Johns Hopkins University Studies, Series *XXXVII,* No. 3. Johns Hopkins Press, Baltimore, 1919.

Georgia Historical Collections (Collections of the Georgia Historical Society.)
    I. New and Accurate Account of the Provinces of Georgia and South Carolina.
        Impartial Inquiry into the State and Utility of the Province of Georgia.
        Reasons for Establishing the Colony of Georgia.
    II. A State of the Province of Georgia.
        A Brief Account of the Causes that have Retarded the Progress of the Colony of Georgia.
        A True and Historical Narrative of the Colony of Georgia, by Pat. Tailfer, H. Anderson, Dr. Douglas and Others.
        Account Showing the Progress of the Colony of Georgia.
    III. Letters of General Oglethorpe to Trustees of the Colony of Georgia, 1735–1744.

Georgia Journal, from 1817. Published at Milledgeville, Georgia.

GILMER, GEORGE R., *Sketches of Some of the First Settlers of Upper Georgia.* New York, 1854.

GOODELL, WILLIAM, *The American Slave Code In Theory and Practice: Its Distinctive Features Shown by Its Statutes, Judicial Decisions, and Illustrative Facts.* New York, 1853.

GOODLOE, DANIEL R., *The Southern Platform: or Manual of Southern Sentiment on the Subject of Slavery.* Boston, 1858.

GREENE, EVERTS BOUTELL, *The Foundations of American Nationality.* New York, 1922.

GRICE, WARREN, *The Georgia Bench and Bar, 1.* Macon, 1931.

HARRIS, JOEL CHANDLER, *Free Joe and Other Georgian Sketches.* New York, 1887.

HART, ALBERT BUSHNELL, *Slavery and Abolition, 1831–1841.* New York, 1906.

HELPER, HINTON ROWAN, *The Impending Crisis of the South: How to Meet It.* New York, 1857.

House Executive Documents, 36th Congress, 2nd Session, 4.

HULL, AUGUSTUS LONGSTREET, *Annals of Athens, Georgia, 1801–1901.* Athens, Georgia, 1906.

HURD, JOHN CODMAN, *The Law of Freedom and Bondage.* (2 volumes) Boston, New York, 1858.

JACKSON, THE HONORABLE HENRY R., *The Wanderer Case.* The Speech of Honorable Henry R. Jackson of Savannah, Georgia. Introduction by Bill Arp. Atlanta. No date.

JAY, WILLIAM, *An Inquiry into the Character and Tendency of the American Colonization, and American Anti-Slavery Societies.* 2nd edition, New York, 1835.

JONES, CHARLES C. JR. and DUTCHER, SALEM, *Memorial History of Augusta, Georgia.* Syracuse, 1890.

JONES, CHARLES C., JR., *History of Georgia.* (2 volumes). Boston, 1883.

JONES, CHARLES C., JR., *History of Savannah, Georgia.* Syracuse, 1890.

Journals of the House of Representatives, 1817–1859.

Journals of the Senate, 1817–1859.

KEMBLE, FRANCES ANNE, *A Journal of a Residence on a Georgian Plantation in 1838–1839.* New York, 1863.

KNIGHT, LUCIEN LAMAR, *A Standard History of Georgia and Georgians.* (6 volumes). New York, 1917.

LAMAR, L. Q. C., *Compilation of the Laws of Georgia, 1810–1819.* Augusta, 1821.

LOCKE, MARY STOUGHTON, *Anti-Slavery in America from the Introduction of African Slaves to the Prohibition of the Slave Trade, 1619–1808.* Radcliffe College Monographs, XI. Boston, 1901.

LONG, REV. JOHN DIXON, *Pictures of Slavery in Church and State.* Philadelphia, 1857.

LONGSTREET, A. B., *A Voice from the South.* (Comprising letters from Georgia to Massachusetts). Baltimore, 1847.

LONGSTREET, A. B., *Georgia Scenes.* New York, 1855.

LUGENBEEL, J. W., *Sketches of Liberia: Comprising A Brief Account of the Geography, Climate, Productions, and Diseases, of the Republic of Liberia.* 2nd edition. Pamphlet. Washington, 1853.

LUMPKIN, HONORABLE J. H., *Speech delivered in the House of Representatives, August 2, 1856.* (pamphlet).

McCALL, HUGH, *History of Georgia.* (2 volumes). Savannah, 1811 and 1816. New edition, Atlanta, 1909.

McHENRY, GEORGE, *The Cotton Trade: Its Bearing Upon the Prosperity of Great Britain and Commerce of the American Republics Considered in connection with the system of Negro Slavery in the Confederate States.* London, 1863.

McMASTER, JOHN BACH, *A History of the People of the United States, 2.* New York, 1888.

MACY, JESSE, *The Anti-Slavery Crusade. Chronicles of America,* XXVIII. Yale University Press. New Haven, 1919.

MARBURY, HORATIO, and CRAWFORD, WILLIAM H., *A Compilation of the Laws of Georgia from 1755–1800.* Contains also the constitutions of Georgia of 1777, 1789, and 1798. Savannah, 1802.

MARTIN, ASA EARL, *The Anti-Slavery Movement in Kentucky Prior to 1850.* Filson Club Publication, 29. Louisville, 1918.

MERRIAM, CHARLES EDWARD, *American Political Theory.* New York, 1903.

MIMS, EDWIN, and PAYNE, BRUCE R., *Southern Prose and Poetry,* New York, 1910.

Missionary, The, from 1825. Published at Mount Zion, (Hancock County), Georgia.

New York Enquirer, January 15, 1828.

Niles' Weekly Register. Baltimore. (Weekly Newspaper).

OLMSTEAD, FREDEICK LAW, *A Journey In the Seaboard Slave States.* New York, 1856.

PAINE, L. W., *Six Years In A Georgia Prison.* New York, 1851.

PHILLIPS, ULRICH BONNELL, *American Negro Slavery.* New York, 1918.

PHILLIPS, ULRICH BONNELL, *Georgia and State Rights.* Washington, 1902.

PHILLIPS, ULRICH BONNELL, *Plantation and Frontier Documents, 1649–1863.* (2 volumes). Cleveland, Ohio, 1909.

POOLE, WILLIAM FREDERICK, *Anti-Slavery Opinions before the Year 1800.* Cincinnati, 1873.

PRINCE, O. H., *Digest of the Laws of Georgia to 1820.* Milledgeville, 1822.

PRINCE, O. H., *Digest of the Laws of Georgia to 1837.* Athens, Georgia, 1837.

Proclamations, 1782–1823. (Contains proclamations of the governors during this period). Manuscript in Georgia State Department of Archives and History, Atlanta.

RANDOLPH, THOMAS JEFFERSON, *Memoir, Correspondence, and Miscellanies* from the papers of Thomas Jefferson, 1. Charlottesville, 1829.

Reports of the Supreme Court of Georgia, Volumes 4, 6, 10, 16, 18, 19, 20, 25, 26, 34, 38, 40, 42, 50.

RHODES, JAMES FORD, *A History of the United States from the Compromise o f 1850 to The McKinley–Bryan Campaign of 1896.* 1, 1850–1854. New Yor 1892. Reprinted, 1920.

Savannah Georgian (Savannah, Georgia Daily).

SCOMP, H. A., "Georgia—The Only Free Colony," *Magazine of American History.* October, 1889, 280–306.

SHRYOCK, RICHARD HARRISON, *Georgia and The Union In 1850.* Durham, North Carolina, 1926.

SMITH, CHARLES H., *A School History of Georgia.* Boston, 1896.

Southern Recorder, from 1830. Published at Milledgeville, Georgia.

STEPHENS, ALEXANDER HAMILTON, *History of the United States.* New York, 1872.

STEVENS, WILLIAM BACON, *History of Georgia.* (2 volumes). New York, 1847, 1858.

STROBEL, P. A., *The Salzburgers.* Baltimore, 1855.

STROUD, GEORGE M., *A Sketch of the Laws Relating to Slavery in the Several States of the United States of America.* Philadelphia, 1856.

TURNER, LORENZO DOW, *Anti-Slavery Sentiment in American Literature Prior to 1865.* Washington, 1929.

WADE, JOHN DONALD, *Augustus Baldwin Longstreet.* A Study of the Development of Culture in the South. New York, 1924.

WADE, JOHN DONALD, *John Wesley*, New York, 1930.

WATKINS, ROBERT and GEORGE, *Digest of the Laws of Georgia to 1800.* Philadelphia, 1802.

WAYNE, JAMES M., "Charge to the Grand Jury in 1859," *Georgia Historical Quarterly, 2.*

WEATHERFORD, W. D., *The Negro from Africa to America.* New York, 1924.

WEEKS, STEPHEN B., "Anti-Slavery Sentiment in the South; with Unpublished Letters from John Stuart Mill and Mrs. Stowe." *Publications of the Southern History Association, 2*, 87–130. Washington, 1898.

WEEKS, STEPHEN B., *Southern Quakers and Slavery*, Johns Hopkins University Studies, *15*. Johns Hopkins Press. Baltimore, 1896.

WENDER, HERBERT, "The Southern Commercial Convention at Savannah, 1856," *Georgia Historical Quarterly, 15.*

WESLEY, JOHN, *The Journal of the Reverend John Wesley.* London, 1788. Everyman's Library. Edited by Ernest Rhys.

WESLEY, JOHN, *Thoughts on Slavery.* (Pamphlet). London, 1774.

WHITE, GEORGE, *Statistics of Georgia*, Savannah, 1849.

Wills on file at various counties visited.

WYLLY, CHARLES SPAULDING, *The Seed That was Sown in the Colony of Georgia —The Harvest and the Aftermath, 1740–1870*   New York 1910.